FAVORITE BRAND NAME
Country Christmas

Publications International, I

Favorite Brand Name Recipes at www.fbnr.c

Microwave Cooking: Microwave ovens vary in wattage. Use the cooking times as guidelines and check for doneness before adding more time.

Preparation/Cooking Times: Preparation times are based on the approximate amount of time required to assemble the recipe before cooking, baking, chilling or serving. These times include preparation steps such as measuring, chopping and mixing. The fact that some preparations and cooking can be done simultaneously is taken into account. Preparation of optional ingredients and serving suggestions is not included.

Contents

Pleasing Poultry

Chicken with Tomato-Basil Cream Sauce

4 boneless, skinless chicken breast halves (about 1¼ pounds), pounded, if desired

3 tablespoons I CAN'T BELIEVE IT'S NOT BUTTER!® Spread, divided

2 plum tomatoes, chopped

1 small onion, chopped

¼ teaspoon salt

¼ cup dry white wine or chicken broth

½ cup whipping or heavy cream

2 tablespoons loosely packed fresh basil leaves, cut in thin strips

Season chicken, if desired, with salt and ground black pepper.

In 12-inch nonstick skillet, melt 2 tablespoons I Can't Believe It's Not Butter! Spread over medium-high heat and cook chicken 8 minutes or until chicken is no longer pink, turning once. Remove chicken and set aside.

In same skillet, melt remaining 1 tablespoon I Can't Believe It's Not Butter! Spread and cook tomatoes, onion and salt, stirring occasionally, 3 minutes or until tomatoes are tender. Stir in wine and cook, stirring occasionally, 2 minutes or until wine evaporates. Stir in cream. Reduce heat to low and return chicken to skillet. Simmer uncovered 4 minutes or until sauce is thickened and chicken is heated through. Garnish with basil.

Makes 4 servings

Chicken with Tomato-Basil Cream Sauce

Classic Chicken Puffs

1 box UNCLE BEN'S® Long Grain & Wild Rice Original Recipe

2 cups cubed cooked TYSON® Fresh Chicken

$\frac{1}{2}$ can ($10\frac{3}{4}$ ounces) condensed cream of mushroom soup

$\frac{1}{3}$ cup chopped green onions

$\frac{1}{3}$ cup diced pimientos or diced red bell pepper

$\frac{1}{3}$ cup diced celery

$\frac{1}{3}$ cup chopped fresh parsley

$\frac{1}{3}$ cup chopped slivered almonds

$\frac{1}{4}$ cup milk

1 box frozen prepared puff pastry shells, thawed

COOK: CLEAN: Wash hands. Prepare rice according to package directions. When rice is done, add remaining ingredients (except pastry shells). Mix well. Reheat 1 minute. Fill pastry shells with rice mixture.

SERVE: Serve with a mixed green salad and balsamic vinaigrette, if desired.

CHILL: Refrigerate leftovers immediately.

Makes 6 servings

Tip: This recipe is a great way to use leftover chicken.

Prep Time: none
Cook Time: 20 minutes

Chicken Vegetable Skillet

8 chicken thighs, skinned, fat trimmed

$\frac{3}{4}$ teaspoon salt, divided

1 tablespoon vegetable oil

3 medium red-skinned potatoes, scrubbed, cut in $\frac{1}{4}$-inch slices

1 medium onion, sliced

$\frac{1}{2}$ pound mushrooms, quartered

1 large tomato, coarsely chopped

$\frac{1}{4}$ cup chicken broth

$\frac{1}{4}$ cup dry white wine

$\frac{1}{2}$ teaspoon dried oregano leaves

$\frac{1}{4}$ teaspoon black pepper

1 tablespoon chopped fresh parsley

Sprinkle chicken with $\frac{1}{4}$ teaspoon salt. In large nonstick skillet, heat oil over medium-high heat until hot. Add chicken and cook about 8 minutes, turning once, until brown on both sides. Remove chicken; set aside. In same pan, layer potatoes, onion, chicken, mushrooms and tomato. In 1-cup measure, mix broth and wine. Pour over chicken and vegetables. Sprinkle with oregano, remaining $\frac{1}{2}$ teaspoon salt and pepper. Heat to boiling; cover and reduce heat to medium-low. Cook about 20 minutes or until chicken and vegetables are fork-tender. Sprinkle with parsley before serving.

Makes 4 servings

*Favorite recipe from **Delmarva Poultry Industry, Inc.***

Classic Chicken Puff

New England Roast Turkey

¼ cup butter

1 large onion, coarsely chopped

4 ribs celery, sliced

1 Granny Smith apple, coarsely chopped

1 package (about 11 ounces) diced dried fruit mix

¾ cup slivered almonds

⅓ cup chopped fresh parsley

⅛ teaspoon ground cloves

Salt and black pepper

1 whole turkey (12 to 14 pounds)

6 medium sweet potatoes, peeled and cut into 1-inch pieces

8 large carrots, thickly sliced

5 large shallot cloves, peeled

½ cup dry white wine

Preheat oven to 325°F. Melt butter in large saucepan over medium-low heat. Add onion; cook and stir 8 minutes or until tender. Remove from heat; stir in celery, apple, dried fruit, almonds, parsley and cloves. Add salt and pepper to taste.

Place fruit mixture in turkey cavity. Tie turkey legs together with kitchen string. Place turkey, breast side down, on rack in large oiled roasting pan. Season with salt and pepper, if desired. Add ½ cup water to pan. Bake, uncovered, 1½ hours.

Remove turkey from roasting pan; remove rack. Place turkey breast side up in roasting pan. Arrange sweet potatoes, carrots and shallots around turkey; season with salt and pepper, if desired. Baste turkey with pan juices. Add wine to roasting pan. Bake 2 to 2½ hours or until turkey is tender and thermometer inserted in thickest part of thigh registers 180°F, basting with pan juices every 30 minutes.

Transfer turkey to cutting board; tent with foil. Let stand 10 minutes before carving. Drain vegetables and place in food processor; process until smooth. Place fruit stuffing from turkey cavity in serving bowl. Serve turkey with vegetable purée and fruit stuffing. *Makes 12 servings*

Holiday Hint:

Shallots are a member of the onion family. They have a mild onion-garlic flavor. Each shallot head is made up of two or three cloves, and each clove is covered with a papery skin.

New England Roast Turkey

Crispy Duck

1 whole duck (about 5 pounds)
1 tablespoon dried rubbed sage
1 teaspoon salt
¼ teaspoon black pepper
3 cups vegetable oil
1 tablespoon butter or margarine
2 large Granny Smith or Rome Beauty
   apples, cored and cut into thin wedges
½ cup clover honey
   Fresh sage sprigs and crab apples for
   garnish

1. Remove neck and giblets from duck. Cut wing tips and second wing sections off duck; wrap and freeze for another use. Trim excess fat and excess skin from duck; discard. Rinse duck and cavity under cold running water; pat dry with paper towels. Cut duck into quarters, removing backbone and breast bone.

2. Place duck in 13×9-inch baking pan. Combine sage, salt and black pepper. Rub duck with sage mixture. Cover; refrigerate 1 hour.

3. To steam duck, place wire rack in wok. Add water to 1 inch below rack. (Water should not touch rack.) Cover wok; bring water to a boil over medium-high heat. Arrange duck, skin sides up, on wire rack. Cover; steam 40 minutes or until fork-tender. (Add boiling water to wok to keep water at same level.)

4. Transfer cooked duck to plate. Carefully remove rack from wok; discard water. Rinse wok and dry. Heat oil in wok over medium-high heat until oil registers 375°F on deep-fry thermometer. Add ½ of duck, skin sides down. Fry 5 to 10 minutes or until crisp and golden brown, turning once. Drain duck on paper towels. Repeat with remaining duck, reheating oil.

5. Pour off oil. Melt butter in wok over medium heat. Add apples; cook and stir 5 minutes or until wilted. Stir in honey and bring to a boil. Transfer apples with slotted spoon to warm serving platter. Arrange duck on apples. Drizzle honey mixture over duck. Garnish, if desired.

Makes 4 servings

Holiday Hint:

Ducks available in supermarkets are almost always farm raised; they are fattier than wild birds. Be sure to remove any excess fat and skin before cooking.

Holiday Turkey with Herbed Corn Bread Dressing

    1 pound bulk pork sausage
1½ cups chopped onions
    1 cup chopped celery
    6 cups coarsely crumbled corn bread
      (two 8-inch squares)
   ⅓ cup light cream
   ¼ cup sherry
    1 teaspoon dried thyme leaves
    1 teaspoon dried basil leaves
    1 teaspoon dried oregano leaves
   ½ teaspoon LAWRY'S® Garlic Powder with
      Parsley
    1 (14- to 16-pound) turkey, thawed
      LAWRY'S® Seasoned Salt

In large skillet, cook sausage until brown and crumbly. Add onions and celery and cook over medium heat 5 minutes or until tender. Add corn bread, cream, sherry, thyme, basil, oregano and Garlic Powder with Parsley. Rub cavities and outside of turkey with Seasoned Salt, using about ¼ teaspoon Seasoned Salt per pound of turkey. Pack dressing loosely into turkey cavity. Skewer opening closed. Insert meat thermometer in thickest part of breast away from bones. Place turkey, breast side up, on rack in roasting pan. Roast, uncovered, in 325°F oven 4 to 5 hours, basting frequently with melted butter or cover with foil and place on hot grill 16 to 18 minutes per pound.

When internal temperature reaches 185°F, remove and let stand 20 minutes before carving. (Tent loosely with aluminum foil if turkey becomes too brown, being careful not to touch meat thermometer.) *Makes 10 servings*

Serving Suggestion: Garnish with lemon leaves and whole fresh cranberries.

Holiday Hint:

To carve perfect turkey breast slices, make a horizontal cut across the base of the breast meat to the bone with a carving knife. Cut the slices with straight even strokes down to the horizontal cut. Carving breast slices is easier if the leg is removed first.

Coq au Vin

½ cup all-purpose flour
1¼ teaspoons salt
¾ teaspoon black pepper
3½ pounds chicken pieces
2 tablespoons margarine or butter
8 ounces mushrooms, cut in half if large
4 cloves garlic, minced
¾ cup chicken broth
¾ cup dry red wine
2 teaspoons dried thyme leaves
1½ pounds red potatoes, quartered
2 cups frozen pearl onions (about 8 ounces)
Chopped fresh parsley (optional)

Preheat oven to 350°F.

Combine flour, salt and pepper in large resealable plastic food storage bag or paper bag. Add chicken, two pieces at a time, and seal bag. Shake to coat chicken; remove chicken and set aside. Repeat with remaining pieces. Reserve remaining flour mixture.

Melt margarine in ovenproof Dutch oven over medium-high heat. Arrange chicken in single layer in Dutch oven and cook 3 minutes per side or until browned. Transfer to plate; set aside. Repeat with remaining pieces.

Add mushrooms and garlic to Dutch oven; cook and stir 2 minutes. Sprinkle reserved flour mixture over mushroom mixture; cook and stir 1 minute. Add broth, wine and thyme; bring to a boil over high heat, stirring to scrape up browned bits on bottom of Dutch oven. Add potatoes and onions; return to a boil. Remove from heat and place chicken in Dutch oven, partially covering chicken with broth mixture.

Bake chicken, covered, about 45 minutes or until juices run clear, potatoes are tender and sauce is slightly thickened. Transfer chicken and vegetables to shallow bowls. Spoon sauce over chicken and vegetables. Sprinkle with parsley, if desired.

Makes 4 to 6 servings

Coq au Vin

Crab-Stuffed Chicken Breasts

1 package (8 ounces) cream cheese, softened
6 ounces frozen crabmeat or imitation crabmeat, thawed and drained
1 envelope LIPTON® RECIPE SECRETS® Savory Herb with Garlic Soup Mix
6 boneless skinless chicken breast halves (about 1½ pounds)
¼ cup all-purpose flour
2 eggs, beaten
¾ cup plain dry bread crumbs
2 tablespoons olive or vegetable oil
1 tablespoon margarine or butter

Preheat oven to 350°F. Combine cream cheese, crabmeat and savory herb with garlic soup mix; set aside. With knife parallel to cutting board, slice horizontally through each chicken breast, stopping 1 inch from opposite edge; open breasts. Evenly spread each breast with cream cheese mixture. Close each chicken breast, securing open edge with wooden toothpicks.

Dip chicken in flour, then eggs, then bread crumbs, coating well. In 12-inch skillet, heat oil and butter over medium-high heat and cook chicken 10 minutes or until golden, turning once. Transfer chicken to 13×9-inch baking dish and bake uncovered 15 minutes or until chicken is done. Remove toothpicks before serving.

Makes about 6 servings

Menu Suggestion: Serve with a mixed green salad and warm garlic bread.

Bistro Turkey Sandwiches

¼ cup reduced-calorie mayonnaise
2 tablespoons finely chopped fresh basil
2 tablespoons chopped drained sun-dried tomatoes in oil
2 tablespoons finely chopped pitted kalamata olives
⅛ teaspoon red pepper flakes
1 loaf focaccia bread, quartered and split *or* 8 slices sourdough bread
1 jar (7 ounces) roasted red bell peppers, rinsed and drained
4 romaine or red leaf lettuce leaves
2 packages (4 ounces each) HEBREW NATIONAL® Sliced Oven Roasted or Smoked Turkey Breast

Combine mayonnaise, basil, sun-dried tomatoes, olives and red pepper in small bowl; mix well. Spread evenly over cut sides of bread. Remove excess liquid from roasted red bell peppers with paper towels. Layer roasted peppers, lettuce and turkey breast between bread slices.

Makes 4 servings

Crab-Stuffed Chicken Breast

Old-Fashioned Chicken with Dumplings

3 to 3½ pounds chicken pieces

3 tablespoons butter or margarine

2 cans (about 14 ounces each) ready-to-serve chicken broth

3½ cups water

1 teaspoon salt

¼ teaspoon white pepper

2 large carrots, cut into 1-inch slices

2 ribs celery, cut into 1-inch slices

8 to 10 small boiling onions

¼ pound small mushrooms, cut into halves

Parsley Dumplings (recipe follows)

½ cup frozen peas, thawed, drained

Brown chicken in melted butter in 6- to 8-quart saucepan over medium-high heat. Add broth, water, salt and pepper. Bring to a boil over high heat. Reduce heat to low. Cover; simmer 15 minutes. Add carrots, celery, onions and mushrooms. Simmer, covered, 40 minutes or until chicken and vegetables are tender.

Prepare Parsley Dumplings. When chicken is tender, skim fat from broth. Stir in peas. Drop dumpling mixture into broth, making 6 large or 12 small dumplings. Cover; simmer 15 to 20 minutes or until dumplings are firm to the touch and wooden pick inserted in center comes out clean. *Makes 6 servings*

Parsley Dumplings: Sift 2 cups all-purpose flour, 4 teaspoons baking powder and ½ teaspoon salt into medium bowl. Cut in 5 tablespoons cold butter until mixture resembles coarse meal. Make a well in center; pour in 1 cup milk, all at once. Add 2 tablespoons chopped parsley; stir with fork until mixture forms a ball.

Holiday Hint:

Boiling onions are about 1 inch in diameter and slightly larger than pearl onions; they have a mild flavor. If boiling onions are unavailable, pearl onions can be substituted.

Apricot-Glazed Hens with Wild Rice Stuffing

¼ cup butter or margarine

½ cup chopped onion

¾ cup diced celery

1 (6-ounce) package long-grain and wild rice mix

2½ cups water

1 cup (12-ounce jar) SMUCKER'S® Apricot Preserves, divided

2 tablespoons chopped parsley

⅓ cup chopped toasted pecans

4 Cornish game hens (about 22 ounces each)

Salt and pepper

Lemon slices and celery leaves

Melt butter in large saucepan; remove 2 tablespoons melted butter and reserve. Add onion and celery to saucepan. Sauté over medium heat, stirring frequently, until onion begins to turn golden. Add rice mix and water; cover and cook according to package directions. Add ¼ cup of the apricot preserves, parsley and pecans.

Fill hens with stuffing; secure cavities with poultry pins or toothpicks or, heat stuffing in 3- to 4-cup casserole dish. Brush hens with reserved butter; sprinkle lightly with salt and pepper.

Roast at 350°F for 70 to 75 minutes or until legs of hens can be moved easily and juices run clear. Baste hens with remaining apricot preserves during last 15 minutes of roasting.

To serve, remove poultry pins from hens; place hens on large serving platter. Garnish with lemon slices and celery leaves. Serve apricot drippings from hens as sauce in small dish; thin with water and heat, if necessary. *Makes 4 servings*

Holiday Hint:

Toasting gives nuts a richer, fuller flavor. To toast nuts, spread them in a single layer on a baking sheet and toast them in a preheated 350°F oven for 8 to 10 minutes. Watch them carefully and stir them once or twice for even browning.

Roasted Chicken and Vegetables over Wild Rice

3½ pounds chicken pieces

¾ cup olive oil vinaigrette dressing, divided

1 tablespoon margarine or butter, melted

1 package (6 ounces) long-grain and wild rice mix

1 can (about 14 ounces) chicken broth

1 small eggplant, cut into 1-inch pieces

2 red potatoes, cut into 1-inch pieces

1 yellow summer squash, cut into 1-inch pieces

1 medium zucchini, cut into 1-inch pieces

1 medium red onion, cut into wedges

1 package (4 ounces) crumbled feta cheese with basil

Chopped fresh cilantro (optional)

Fresh thyme sprig (optional)

Remove skin from chicken; discard. Combine chicken and ½ cup dressing in large resealable plastic food storage bag. Seal bag and turn to coat. Refrigerate 30 minutes or overnight.

Preheat oven to 375°F. Coat bottom of 13×9-inch baking dish with margarine. Add rice and seasoning packet; stir in broth. Combine vegetables in large bowl. Place on top of rice mixture.

Remove chicken from bag and place on top of vegetables; discard marinade. Pour remaining ¼ cup dressing over chicken.

Bake, uncovered, 45 minutes. Sprinkle with cheese. Bake 5 to 10 minutes or until juices run clear and cheese is melted. Sprinkle with cilantro, if desired. Garnish with thyme, if desired.

Makes 4 to 6 servings

Brandy-Orange Barbecued Hens

2 PERDUE® Fresh Cornish Hens (1½ pounds each)

1 tablespoon vegetable oil

2 tablespoons lemon juice, divided

½ teaspoon ground ginger, divided

Salt and pepper

¼ cup orange marmalade

1 tablespoon brandy

Prepare coals for grilling. Rinse hens and pat dry. With kitchen string, tie drumsticks together. Rub outside of hens with oil and 1 tablespoon lemon juice; sprinkle with ¼ teaspoon ginger. Season with salt and pepper.

Combine marmalade, brandy, remaining 1 tablespoon lemon juice and remaining ¼ teaspoon ginger in small bowl; set aside. Place hens, breast side up, on grill. Grill, covered, 5 to 6 inches over medium-hot coals 50 to 60 minutes. Brush outside of hens with brandy-orange sauce after 40 minutes of grilling. Cook until juices run clear when thigh is pierced, basting additional 3 to 4 times. *Makes 2 to 4 servings*

Roasted Chicken and Vegetables over Wild Rice

Italian Vegetable Farfalle

8 ounces BARILLA® Farfalle

1 tablespoon olive oil

1 pound boneless skinless chicken breasts, cubed

Salt and pepper

1 medium zucchini, coarsely chopped

1 medium yellow squash, coarsely chopped

1 jar (26 ounces) BARILLA® Tomato and Basil Pasta Sauce

Grated Parmesan cheese

1. Cook farfalle according to package directions; drain.

2. Meanwhile, heat olive oil in large skillet. Add chicken; cook and stir over medium-high heat until cooked through. Add salt and pepper to taste. Add zucchini and yellow squash to skillet; cook and stir 5 minutes.

3. Reduce heat; stir in pasta sauce. Cook 5 minutes. Pour sauce over hot drained farfalle. Sprinkle with cheese.   *Makes 6 to 8 servings*

Note: Nonstick cooking spray can be used as an alternative to olive oil.

Tip: When purchasing zucchini and yellow squash, look for firm squash that are brightly colored and are free of spots or bruises. Store them in a plastic bag in the refrigerator for up to five days.

Chicken with Stuffing and Peaches

1 can (16 ounces) sliced peaches in heavy syrup, undrained

2 tablespoons oil

4 boneless skinless chicken breast halves

1 tablespoon brown sugar

1 tablespoon cider vinegar

⅛ teaspoon ground allspice

2 cups STOVE TOP® Chicken Flavor Stuffing Mix in the Canister

DRAIN peaches, reserving syrup. Add water to syrup to measure 1 cup; set aside.

HEAT oil in large skillet on medium-high heat. Add chicken; brown on both sides.

STIR in measured liquid, sugar, vinegar and allspice. Bring to boil. Reduce heat to low; cover and simmer 8 minutes or until chicken is no longer pink in center. Move chicken to side of skillet.

STIR in stuffing mix and peaches; cover. Remove from heat. Let stand 5 minutes.

Makes 4 servings

Prep Time: 5 minutes
Cook Time: 20 minutes

Buffet Cranberry Biscuits with Smoked Turkey

1 BUTTERBALL® Fully Cooked Smoked
    Young Turkey, thawed, sliced thin
3½ cups packaged biscuit mix
2 tablespoons butter or margarine
¾ cup dried cranberries
1 cup milk

CRANBERRY BUTTER
½ cup butter
¼ cup honey
¼ cup dried cranberries

Place biscuit mix in large bowl. Cut in butter with pastry blender until mixture resembles coarse crumbs. Stir in cranberries; add milk. Stir until soft dough forms. Turn dough onto lightly floured surface; knead gently 10 times. Roll to ½-inch thickness. Cut 20 biscuits with 2½-inch round cutter. Place on *ungreased* baking sheet. Bake in preheated 400°F oven 10 minutes or until golden brown.

To prepare Cranberry Butter, combine butter, honey and cranberries in food processor; process just until blended.

To assemble sandwiches, split each biscuit in half. Spread each biscuit half generously with cranberry butter. Stack turkey on bottom of each biscuit. Place top half of biscuit on turkey.

Makes 20 buffet sandwiches

Preparation Time: 30 minutes

Holiday Hint:

Biscuits and Cranberry Butter can each be made several hours prior to serving. Store cooled biscuits loosely covered at room temperature. Store Cranberry Butter, covered, in the refrigerator until 20 or 30 minutes before assembling sandwiches.

Buffet Cranberry Biscuits with Smoked Turkey

Roast Turkey with Cranberry Stuffing

1 loaf (12 ounces) Italian or French bread, cut into ½-inch cubes

2 tablespoons margarine

1½ cups chopped onions

1½ cups chopped celery

2 teaspoons poultry seasoning

1 teaspoon dried thyme leaves

½ teaspoon dried rosemary, crushed

¼ teaspoon salt

¼ teaspoon black pepper

1 cup coarsely chopped fresh cranberries

1 tablespoon sugar

¾ cup fat-free reduced-sodium chicken broth

1 turkey (8 to 10 pounds)

1. Preheat oven to 375°F. Arrange bread on two 15×10-inch jelly roll pans. Bake 12 minutes or until lightly toasted. *Reduce oven temperature to 350°F.*

2. Melt margarine in large saucepan over medium heat. Add onions and celery; cook and stir 8 minutes or until vegetables are tender; remove from heat. Add bread cubes, poultry seasoning, thyme, rosemary, salt and pepper; mix well. Combine cranberries and sugar in small bowl; mix well. Add to bread mixture; toss well. Drizzle chicken broth evenly over mixture; toss well.

3. Remove giblets from turkey. Rinse turkey and cavity in cold water; pat dry with paper towels. Fill turkey cavity loosely with stuffing. Place remaining stuffing in casserole sprayed with nonstick cooking spray. Cover casserole; refrigerate until baking time.

4. Spray roasting pan with nonstick cooking spray. Place turkey, breast side up, on rack in roasting pan. Bake 3 hours or until thermometer inserted in thickest part of thigh registers 180°F and juices run clear.

5. Transfer turkey to serving platter. Cover loosely with foil; let stand 20 minutes. Place covered casserole of stuffing in oven; increase temperature to 375°F. Bake 25 to 30 minutes or until hot.

6. Slice turkey and serve with cranberry stuffing. Garnish with fresh rosemary sprigs, if desired.

Makes 20 servings

Holiday Hint:

Do not stuff poultry until just before cooking it. Harmful bacteria can multiply during storage. If you wish to make stuffing ahead of time, be sure to refrigerate it in a covered container until you are ready to use it.

Basic Turkey Gravy

Reserved neck, heart, gizzard from Turkey giblets package
1 medium carrot, thickly sliced
1 medium onion, thickly sliced
1 medium rib celery, thickly sliced
1 teaspoon salt, divided
1 turkey liver
3 tablespoons fat from poultry drippings
3 tablespoons all-purpose flour

1. In 3-quart saucepan, over high heat, place neck, heart, gizzard, vegetables and ½ teaspoon salt in enough water to cover. Heat to boiling. Reduce heat to low; cover and simmer 45 minutes.

2. Add liver and simmer 15 minutes. Strain broth into large bowl; cover and reserve broth in refrigerator.

3. To make gravy, remove cooked turkey and roasting rack from roasting pan. Strain poultry drippings into 4-cup measuring cup.

4. Add 1 cup giblet broth to roasting pan and stir until crusty brown bits are loosened; pour liquid into cup with drippings. Let mixture stand until fat rises to top.

5. Over medium heat, spoon 3 tablespoons fat from poultry drippings into 2-quart saucepan. Whisk flour and remaining ½ teaspoon salt into fat; cook and stir until flour turns golden.

6. Meanwhile, skim and discard any fat remaining on top of poultry drippings. Add remaining broth and enough water to poultry drippings to equal 3½ cups.

7. Gradually whisk in warm poultry drippings-broth mixture. Cook and stir until gravy boils and thickens slightly. *Makes about 4 cups*

Giblet Gravy: Pull cooked meat from the neck and discard bones. Coarsely chop neck meat and cooked giblets. Cover and reserve in refrigerator. Stir reserved giblets and neck meat into prepared Basic Turkey Gravy. Season with salt and black pepper. Heat to a simmer.

Sherry Gravy: Add ⅓ cup sherry to prepared Basic Turkey Gravy. Season with salt and black pepper. Heat to a simmer.

Mushroom Gravy: Melt 1½ tablespoons butter in large skillet over high heat. Add ½ pound mushrooms and sauté until mushrooms are tender and all liquid has evaporated, about 3 to 4 minutes. Cover and reserve. Add mushrooms to prepared Basic Turkey Gravy and heat to a simmer. Season with salt and black pepper.

Favorite recipe from **National Turkey Federation**

Savory Crust Chicken Breasts

4 TYSON® Individually Fresh Frozen® Chicken Half Breasts

1 cup fine dry bread crumbs

¼ cup grated Parmesan cheese

1 tablespoon dried minced onion

¾ teaspoon salt

¼ teaspoon garlic powder

¼ teaspoon crushed dried oregano leaves

¼ cup Dijon mustard

3 tablespoons butter, melted

PREP: Preheat oven to 400°F. Line 13×9-inch baking pan with foil; spray with nonstick cooking spray. CLEAN: Wash hands. Remove protective ice glaze from frozen chicken by holding under cool running water 1 to 2 minutes. Arrange chicken in single layer, meaty side up, in prepared pan. CLEAN: Wash hands.

COOK: Bake 20 minutes; drain and discard juices. In large shallow dish, combine bread crumbs, cheese, onion, salt, garlic powder and oregano. Baste chicken with mustard. Divide crumb mixture evenly over chicken; pat firmly in place. Drizzle melted butter over chicken. Bake 35 to 40 minutes or until internal juices of chicken run clear. (Or insert instant-read meat thermometer in thickest part of chicken. Temperature should read 170°F.)

SERVE: Remove chicken from pan and serve hot.

CHILL: Refrigerate leftovers immediately.

Makes 4 servings

Prep Time: 10 minutes
Cook Time: 1 hour

Holiday Hint:

Always wash all utensils and surfaces, including your hands, that come in contact with raw poultry, with hot, soapy water. This will prevent any bacteria found in raw poultry from contaminating other foods.

Savory Crust Chicken Breast

Holiday Hens with Sherry Sauce

4 teaspoons butter or margarine

2 teaspoons lemon juice

1 teaspoon Worcestershire sauce

3 packages (3 pounds each) PERDUE® Fresh Cornish Game Hens (6 hens)

Salt and ground black pepper to taste

Scallion greens (optional)

6 sprigs fresh rosemary (optional)

3 tablespoons all-purpose flour

1 can (about 14 ounces) chicken broth

½ cup dry sherry

Preheat oven to 350°F. In large skillet over low heat, melt butter. Stir in lemon juice and Worcestershire sauce. Brush hens with butter mixture; sprinkle with salt and pepper, and tie legs together with kitchen string.

Place hens in shallow roasting pan. Roast 1 to 1¼ hours until skin is crisp and golden, juices run clear and no hint of pink remains when thigh is pierced. Remove hens to serving platter; discard string. Tie legs with scallion greens; garnish with rosemary.

To prepare sauce, stir flour into pan drippings. Cook over medium-low heat, 4 to 5 minutes until flour is brown, stirring constantly. Gradually whisk in chicken broth and sherry; cook 3 to 4 minutes longer, until gravy is smooth and thickened, stirring often. Strain gravy into a sauce dish and serve with hens. *Makes 8 to 12 servings*

One-Pot Chicken Couscous

2 pounds boneless, skinless chicken breasts, cut into 1-inch chunks

¼ cup olive oil

4 large carrots, peeled and sliced

2 medium onions, diced

2 large cloves garlic, minced

2 cans (13¾ ounces each) chicken broth

2 cups uncooked couscous

2 teaspoons TABASCO® brand Pepper Sauce

½ teaspoon salt

1 cup raisins or currants

1 cup slivered almonds, toasted

¼ cup chopped fresh parsley or mint

Cook chicken in hot oil in 12-inch skillet over medium-high heat until well browned on all sides. With slotted spoon, remove chicken to plate. Reduce heat to medium. In remaining drippings, cook carrots and onions 5 minutes. Add garlic; cook 2 minutes longer, stirring frequently.

Add chicken broth, couscous, TABASCO® Sauce, salt and chicken. Heat to boiling, then reduce heat to low. Cover and simmer 5 minutes. Stir in raisins, almonds and parsley. *Makes 8 servings*

Holiday Hens with Sherry Sauce

Home-Style
Chicken 'n Biscuits

5 slices bacon, fried crisp and crumbled

1½ cups (7 ounces) cubed cooked chicken

1 package (10 ounces) frozen mixed vegetables, thawed and drained

1½ cups (6 ounces) shredded Cheddar cheese

2 medium tomatoes, chopped (about 1 cup)

1 can (10¾ ounces) condensed cream of chicken soup

¾ cup milk

1½ cups biscuit baking mix

⅔ cup milk

1⅓ cups *French's® Taste Toppers*™ French Fried Onions, divided

Preheat oven to 400°F. In large bowl, combine bacon, chicken, mixed vegetables, *1 cup* cheese, tomatoes, soup and ¾ cup milk. Pour chicken mixture into greased 12×8-inch baking dish. Bake, covered, for 15 minutes. Meanwhile, in medium bowl, combine baking mix, ⅔ cup milk and *⅔ cup Taste Toppers* to form soft dough. Spoon biscuit dough in 6 mounds around edges of casserole. Bake, uncovered, 15 to 20 minutes or until biscuits are golden brown. Top biscuits with remaining cheese and ⅔ cup *Taste Toppers;* bake 1 to 3 minutes or until *Taste Toppers* are golden brown.

Makes 6 servings

Microwave Directions: Prepare chicken mixture as directed, except reduce ¾ cup milk to ½ cup; pour into 12×8-inch microwave-safe dish.

Cook, covered, on HIGH 10 minutes or until heated through. Stir chicken mixture halfway through cooking time. Prepare biscuit dough as directed. Stir casserole and spoon biscuit dough over hot chicken mixture as directed. Cook, uncovered, 7 to 8 minutes or until biscuits are done. Rotate dish halfway through cooking time. Top biscuits with remaining cheese and ⅔ cup *Taste Toppers;* cook, uncovered, 1 minute or until cheese melts. Let stand 5 minutes.

Stuffed Chicken with Apple Glaze

1 (3½- to 4-pound) frying chicken

½ teaspoon salt

¼ teaspoon black pepper

2 tablespoons vegetable oil

1 package (6 ounces) chicken-flavored stuffing mix plus ingredients to prepare mix

1 large apple, chopped

½ teaspoon grated lemon peel

¼ cup chopped walnuts

¼ cup raisins

¼ cup thinly sliced celery

½ cup apple jelly

1 tablespoon lemon juice

½ teaspoon ground cinnamon

Celery leaves and lemon peel twists

1. Preheat oven to 350°F.

2. Sprinkle inside of chicken with salt and pepper; rub outside with oil.

3. Prepare stuffing mix according to package directions in large bowl.

4. Add apple, lemon peel, walnuts, raisins and celery to prepared stuffing; mix thoroughly.

5. Stuff body cavity loosely with stuffing.

6. Place chicken in shallow baking pan. Cover loosely with foil; roast chicken 1 hour.

7. Combine jelly, lemon juice and cinnamon in small saucepan. Simmer over low heat 3 minutes, stirring often, until jelly dissolves and mixture is well blended. Remove foil from chicken; brush with jelly glaze.

8. Roast chicken, uncovered, brushing frequently with jelly glaze, 30 minutes or until meat thermometer inserted into thickest part of thigh, not touching bone, registers 180°F. Let chicken stand 15 minutes before carving. Garnish, if desired, with celery leaves and lemon peel twists.

Makes 4 servings

Grilled Chicken Breast and Peperonata Sandwiches

1 tablespoon olive oil or vegetable oil

1 medium red bell pepper, cut into strips

1 medium green bell pepper, cut into strips

¾ cup onion slices (about 1 medium onion)

2 cloves garlic, minced

¼ teaspoon salt

¼ teaspoon black pepper

4 boneless skinless chicken breast halves (about 1 pound)

4 small French rolls, split and toasted

1. Heat oil in large nonstick skillet over medium heat until hot. Add bell peppers, onion and garlic; cook and stir 5 minutes. Reduce heat to low; cook and stir about 20 minutes or until vegetables are very soft. Sprinkle with salt and black pepper.

2. Grill chicken on covered grill over medium-hot coals 10 minutes on each side or until chicken is no longer pink in center. Or, broil chicken, 6 inches from heat source, 7 to 8 minutes on each side or until chicken is no longer pink in center.

3. Place chicken in rolls. Divide bell pepper mixture evenly; spoon over chicken.

Makes 4 servings

Hot & Spicy Arroz con Pollo

2 tablespoons vegetable oil

1 medium onion, chopped

1 can (14½ ounces) whole tomatoes

1 can (13¾ ounces) chicken broth

1¼ cups long-grain rice

1 teaspoon salt

Pinch saffron threads (optional)

1 jar (4 ounces) chopped pimientos, drained

½ cup sliced pitted ripe olives

1 package (10 ounces) frozen peas, thawed

1 package (16 ounces) PERDUE® Hot & Spicy Wings

Water (optional)

In large deep skillet or Dutch oven over medium-high heat, heat oil. Add onion; cook 3 to 5 minutes or until tender. Stir in tomatoes with their liquid, broth, rice, salt and saffron; bring to a boil. Reduce heat to low; cover and simmer 10 minutes. Stir in pimientos, olives and peas; gently stir in chicken wings. Cover and cook 10 to 15 minutes longer or until all liquid is absorbed, rice is tender and wings are heated through; add ¼ to ½ cup water if mixture becomes too dry. Serve hot.

Makes 4 servings

Note: For a larger crowd, recipe may be doubled using PERDUE® Hot & Spicy Wings Party Pak (24 ounces). Double other ingredients and cook in large Dutch oven.

Grilled Chicken Breast and Peperonata Sandwich

Cranberry Orange Game Hens with Vegetable Stuffing

GAME HENS

4 small Cornish game hens (16 ounces each)

2 cups bread stuffing mix

1 carrot, finely diced

1 stalk celery, finely diced

1 teaspoon poultry seasoning

1 cup chicken stock or broth

Salt and pepper

SAUCE

1 cup fresh or frozen cranberries, chopped

1 cup (12-ounce jar) SMUCKER'S® Sweet Orange Marmalade

$\frac{1}{4}$ cup water

1 teaspoon lemon juice

Lemon wedges for garnish (optional)

Remove as much fat as possible from game hens. Combine stuffing mix, carrot, celery, poultry seasoning and chicken stock. Season with salt and pepper. Fill cavity of each hen with stuffing; place on roasting pan. Bake at 400°F for 45 minutes.

Meanwhile, prepare sauce. In medium saucepan, combine all sauce ingredients except lemon wedges. Cook over medium-high heat for 5 to 8 minutes until cranberries have released their juice. Set aside.

Remove game hens from oven. Spread sauce over top and sides of hens. Reserve any extra sauce to serve later with hens. Return hens to oven and continue baking 10 to 15 minutes.

To serve, place game hens on 4 serving plates. Spoon some stuffing onto each plate. Spoon additional sauce over hens. Garnish with lemon wedges, if desired. *Makes 4 servings*

Cranberry Orange Game Hen with Vegetable Stuffing

A Feast of Meats

Crown Roast of Pork with <u>Peach Stuffing</u>

   1 (7- to 8-pound) crown roast of pork (12 to 16 ribs)

1½ cups water

   1 cup FLEISCHMANN'S® Original Margarine, divided

   1 (15-ounce) package seasoned bread cubes

   1 cup chopped celery

   2 medium onions, chopped

   1 (16-ounce) can sliced peaches, drained and chopped, liquid reserved

   ½ cup seedless raisins

1. Place crown roast, bone tips up, on rack in shallow roasting pan. Make a ball of foil and press into cavity to hold open. Wrap bone tips in foil. Roast at 325°F, uncovered, for 2 hours; baste with pan drippings occasionally.

2. Heat water and ¾ cup margarine to a boil in large heavy pot; remove from heat. Add bread cubes, tossing lightly with a fork; set aside.

3. Cook and stir celery and onions in remaining margarine in large skillet over medium-high heat until tender, about 5 minutes. Add celery mixture, peaches with liquid and raisins to bread cube mixture, tossing to mix well.

4. Remove foil from center of roast. Spoon stuffing lightly into cavity. Roast 30 to 45 minutes more or until meat thermometer registers 155°F (internal temperature will rise to 160°F upon standing). Cover stuffing with foil, if necessary, to prevent overbrowning. Bake any remaining stuffing in greased, covered casserole during last 30 minutes of roasting. *Makes 12 to 16 servings*

Preparation Time: 45 minutes
Cook Time: 2 hours and 30 minutes
Total Time: 3 hours and 15 minutes

Crown Roast of Pork with Peach Stuffing

Roast Leg of Lamb

3 tablespoons coarse-grained mustard
2 cloves garlic, minced*
1½ teaspoons dried rosemary, crushed
½ teaspoon black pepper
1 leg of lamb, well trimmed, boned, rolled and tied (about 4 pounds)
Mint jelly (optional)

*For more intense garlic flavor inside the meat, cut garlic into slivers. Cut small pockets at random intervals throughout roast with tip of sharp knife; insert garlic slivers.

Preheat oven to 400°F. Combine mustard, garlic, rosemary and pepper. Rub mustard mixture over lamb.** Place roast on meat rack in shallow, foil-lined roasting pan. Roast 15 minutes. *Reduce oven temperature to 325°F;* roast about 20 minutes per pound for medium or until internal temperature reaches 145°F when tested with meat thermometer inserted into thickest part of roast.

Transfer roast to cutting board; cover with foil. Let stand 10 to 15 minutes before carving. Internal temperature will continue to rise 5° to 10°F during stand time.

Cut strings; discard. Carve roast into thin slices; serve with mint jelly, if desired.

Makes 10 to 12 servings

**At this point lamb may be covered and refrigerated up to 24 hours before roasting.

Sweet & Sour Cocktail Meatballs

1 pound ground turkey
¾ cup plain dry bread crumbs
½ cup GREY POUPON® Dijon Mustard, divided
½ cup chopped green onions, divided
1 egg, beaten
½ teaspoon ground ginger
½ teaspoon ground black pepper
1 (8-ounce) can pineapple chunks, undrained
⅓ cup firmly packed light brown sugar
¼ cup apple cider vinegar
¼ cup diced red bell pepper
1 teaspoon cornstarch

Combine turkey, bread crumbs, ¼ cup mustard, ¼ cup green onions, egg, ginger and black pepper in large bowl. Shape into 32 (1-inch) balls. Place in greased 13×9×2-inch baking pan. Bake at 350°F for 20 minutes.

Combine pineapple chunks with juice, sugar, vinegar, red bell pepper, cornstarch and remaining mustard and green onions in medium saucepan. Cook over medium heat until sauce thickens and begins to boil. Spoon pineapple sauce over meatballs. Bake 5 to 7 minutes more or until meatballs are done. Spoon into serving dish and serve with toothpicks. *Makes 32 appetizers*

Roast Leg of Lamb

Baked Ham with Sweet and Spicy Glaze

1 (8-pound) bone-in smoked half ham
Sweet and Spicy Glaze (recipe follows)

Preheat oven to 325°F. Place ham, fat side up, on rack in roasting pan. Insert meat thermometer into thickest part of ham away from fat or bone. Roast ham in oven about 3 hours.

Prepare Sweet and Spicy Glaze. Remove ham from oven. Brush half of glaze over ham; return to oven 30 minutes or until meat thermometer registers 160°F. Remove from oven; brush with remaining glaze. Let ham stand about 20 minutes before slicing. *Makes 8 to 10 servings*

Sweet and Spicy Glaze

¾ cup packed brown sugar
⅓ cup cider vinegar
¼ cup golden raisins
1 can (8¾ ounces) sliced peaches in heavy syrup, drained, chopped and syrup reserved
1 tablespoon cornstarch
¼ cup orange juice
1 can (8¼ ounces) crushed pineapple in syrup, undrained
1 tablespoon grated orange peel
1 clove garlic, crushed
½ teaspoon red pepper flakes
½ teaspoon grated fresh ginger

Combine brown sugar, vinegar, raisins and peach syrup in medium saucepan. Bring to a boil over high heat; reduce to low and simmer 8 to 10 minutes. In small bowl, dissolve cornstarch in orange juice; add to brown sugar mixture. Add remaining ingredients; mix well. Cook over medium heat, stirring constantly, until mixture boils and thickens. Remove from heat.

Makes about 2 cups

Beef with Dry Spice Rub

3 tablespoons firmly packed brown sugar
1 tablespoon black peppercorns
1 tablespoon yellow mustard seeds
1 tablespoon whole coriander seeds
4 cloves garlic
1½ to 2 pounds beef top round steak or London broil, about ½ inch thick
Vegetable or olive oil
Salt

Place sugar, peppercorns, mustard seeds, coriander seeds and garlic in blender or food processor; process until seeds and garlic are crushed. Rub beef with oil; pat on spice mixture. Season generously with salt.

Lightly oil hot grid to prevent sticking. Grill beef on covered grill over medium-low KINGSFORD® Briquets 16 to 20 minutes for medium or until desired doneness, turning once. Let stand 5 minutes before cutting across the grain into thin diagonal slices. *Makes 6 servings*

Baked Ham with Sweet and Spicy Glaze

40

Prime Rib with Yorkshire Pudding and Horseradish Cream Sauce

3 cloves garlic, minced

1 teaspoon black pepper

3 rib standing beef roast, trimmed* (about 6 to 7 pounds)

    Yorkshire Pudding (recipe follows)

    Horseradish Cream Sauce (recipe page 44)

*Ask meat retailer to remove the chine bone for easier carving. Fat should be trimmed to ¼-inch thickness.

Preheat oven to 450°F. Combine garlic and pepper; rub over surfaces of roast.

Place roast, bone side down (the bones take the place of a meat rack), in shallow roasting pan. Roast 15 minutes.

Reduce oven temperature to 325°F. Roast 20 minutes per pound for medium or until internal temperature reaches 145°F, when tested with meat thermometer inserted into the thickest part of roast, not touching bone.

Meanwhile, prepare Yorkshire Pudding batter and Horseradish Cream Sauce.

When roast has reached desired temperature, transfer to cutting board; cover with foil. Let stand 10 to 15 minutes before carving. Internal temperature will continue to rise 5°F to 10°F during stand time.

Reserve ¼ cup drippings from roasting pan for Yorkshire Pudding. Immediately after roast has been removed from oven, *increase oven temperature to 450°F.*

While pudding is baking, carve roast. Serve with Yorkshire Pudding and Horseradish Cream Sauce.

Makes 6 to 8 servings

Yorkshire Pudding

1 cup milk

2 eggs

½ teaspoon salt

1 cup all-purpose flour

¼ cup reserved drippings from roast or unsalted butter

Process milk, eggs and salt in food processor or blender 15 seconds. Add flour; process 2 minutes. Let batter stand in blender at room temperature 30 minutes to 1 hour.

Place reserved meat drippings in 9-inch square baking pan. Place in 450°F oven 5 minutes.

Process batter another 10 seconds; pour into hot drippings. Do not stir.

Immediately return pan to oven. Bake 20 minutes. *Reduce oven temperature to 350°F;* bake 10 minutes until pudding is golden brown and puffed. Cut into squares.

Makes 6 to 8 servings

continued on page 44

Prime Rib with Yorkshire Pudding and Horseradish Cream Sauce

Horseradish Cream Sauce

1 cup cold whipping cream

⅓ cup prepared horseradish, undrained

2 teaspoons balsamic or red wine vinegar

1 teaspoon dry mustard

¼ teaspoon sugar

⅛ teaspoon salt

Beat cream until soft peaks form. *Do not overbeat.* Combine remaining ingredients in medium bowl. Fold whipped cream into horseradish mixture. Cover and refrigerate at least 1 hour or up to 8 hours. *Makes 1½ cups*

Special Occasion Meat Loaf

1 pound ground beef

1 pound Italian sausage, removed from casings and crumbled

1½ cups seasoned bread crumbs

2 eggs, lightly beaten

2 tablespoons chopped fresh parsley

2 cloves garlic, minced

1 teaspoon salt

½ teaspoon black pepper

2 cups water

1 tablespoon butter

1 package (about 4 ounces) Spanish rice mix

2 packages (10 ounces each) frozen chopped spinach, thawed and well drained

Combine ground beef, sausage, bread crumbs, eggs, parsley, garlic, salt and pepper in large bowl; mix well. Place on 12×12-inch sheet of foil moistened with water. Cover with 12×14-inch sheet of waxed paper moistened with water. Press meat mixture into 12×12-inch rectangle with hands or rolling pin. Refrigerate 2 hours or until well chilled.

Bring water, butter and rice mix to a boil in medium saucepan. Continue boiling over medium heat 10 minutes or until rice is tender, stirring occasionally. Refrigerate 2 hours or until well chilled.

Preheat oven to 350°F. Remove waxed paper from ground beef mixture. Spread spinach over ground beef mixture, leaving 1-inch border. Spread rice evenly over spinach. Starting at long end, roll up jelly-roll style, using foil as a guide and removing foil after rolling. Seal edges tightly. Place meat loaf seam side down in 13×9-inch baking pan. Bake, uncovered, about 1 hour. Let stand 15 minutes before serving. Cut into 1-inch slices.

Makes about 8 servings

London Broil with Marinated Vegetables

¾ cup olive oil

¾ cup red wine

 2 tablespoons red wine vinegar

 2 tablespoons finely chopped shallots

 2 teaspoons bottled minced garlic

½ teaspoon dried marjoram leaves

½ teaspoon dried oregano leaves

½ teaspoon dried basil leaves

½ teaspoon black pepper

 2 pounds top round London broil
    (1½ inches thick)

 1 medium red onion, cut into ¼-inch-thick
    slices

 1 package (8 ounces) sliced mushrooms

 1 medium red bell pepper, cut into strips

 1 medium zucchini, cut into ¼-inch-thick
    slices

1. Combine olive oil, wine, vinegar, shallots, garlic, marjoram, oregano, basil and pepper in medium bowl; whisk to combine.

2. Combine London broil and ¾ cup marinade in large resealable food storage bag. Seal bag and turn to coat. Marinate up to 24 hours in refrigerator, turning once or twice.

3. Combine onion, mushrooms, bell pepper, zucchini and remaining marinade in separate large food storage bag. Seal bag and turn to coat. Refrigerate up to 24 hours, turning once or twice.

4. Preheat broiler. Remove meat from marinade and place on broiler pan; discard marinade. Broil 4 to 5 inches from heat about 9 minutes per side or until desired doneness. Let stand 10 minutes before slicing. Cut meat into thin slices.

5. While meat is standing, drain marinade from vegetables and arrange on broiler pan. Broil 4 to 5 inches from heat about 9 minutes or until edges of vegetables just begin to brown. Serve meat and vegetables immediately on platter.

Makes 6 servings

Make-Ahead Time: up to 1 day before serving
Final Prep and Cook Time: 24 minutes

Pork Tenderloin with Sherry-Mushroom Sauce

1 pork tenderloin (1 to 1½ pounds)

1½ cups chopped button mushrooms or shiitake mushroom caps

2 tablespoons sliced green onion

1 clove garlic, minced

1 tablespoon reduced-fat margarine

1 tablespoon cornstarch

1 tablespoon chopped fresh parsley

½ teaspoon dried thyme leaves

Dash black pepper

⅓ cup water

1 tablespoon dry sherry

½ teaspoon beef bouillon granules

Preheat oven to 375°F. Place pork on rack in shallow baking pan. Insert meat thermometer into thickest part of tenderloin. Roast, uncovered, 25 to 35 minutes or until thermometer registers 165°F. Let stand, covered, 5 to 10 minutes while preparing sauce.

Cook and stir mushrooms, green onion and garlic in margarine in small saucepan over medium heat until vegetables are tender. Stir in cornstarch, parsley, thyme and pepper. Stir in water, sherry and bouillon granules. Cook and stir until sauce boils and thickens. Cook and stir 2 minutes more. Slice pork; serve with sauce.   *Makes 4 servings*

Barbecue Beef Ribettes

1 clove garlic, minced

1 tablespoon vegetable oil

½ cup ketchup

⅓ cup A.1.® Original or A.1.® BOLD & SPICY Steak Sauce

¼ cup chili sauce

2 tablespoons packed light brown sugar

2 thin slices fresh lemon

½ teaspoon liquid hot pepper seasoning

2½ pounds beef ribs, cut into 2-inch pieces

In medium saucepan, over low heat, cook garlic in oil until tender. Stir in ketchup, steak sauce, chili sauce, sugar, lemon and hot pepper seasoning; cook 1 to 2 minutes or until heated through. Reserve ⅔ cup for serving with cooked ribs. Set aside remaining sauce for basting ribs.

Arrange ribs on rack in large roasting pan. Bake at 400°F for 30 minutes.

Brush ribs generously with ¼ cup basting sauce. Grill ribs over medium heat or broil 6 inches from heat source 20 to 25 minutes or until ribs are tender, turning and basting often with remaining basting sauce. Serve with reserved ⅔ cup sauce. Garnish as desired.   *Makes 8 appetizer servings*

Pork Tenderloin with Sherry-Mushroom Sauce

Veal Chops with Brandied Apricots and Pecans

8 dried apricot halves

¼ cup water

¼ cup honey

4 (¾-inch-thick) boneless veal chops (about 5 ounces each)*

¼ teaspoon salt

¼ teaspoon black pepper

3 tablespoons all-purpose flour

2 tablespoons butter or margarine

16 pecan halves

2 tablespoons brandy

Celery or mint leaves for garnish

*If boneless chops are unavailable, chops with bones may be substituted.

1. Cut apricot halves into ¼-inch slivers.

2. Combine water and honey in 2-cup glass measuring cup; microwave at HIGH (100% power) 2 minutes or until mixture begins to boil. Stir in slivered apricots; cover with plastic wrap, turning back 1 corner to vent. Microwave 30 seconds more; let stand, covered, 1 hour.

3. Sprinkle veal chops with salt and pepper. Place flour in shallow bowl; dredge veal chops, 1 at a time, in flour, shaking off excess.

4. Melt butter in large skillet over medium heat; arrange veal chops and pecan halves in single layer in skillet. Cook veal chops and pecans 5 minutes per side or until browned.

5. Add apricot mixture and brandy; bring to a boil. Reduce heat to low; cover and simmer 10 minutes or until veal chops are tender.

6. Transfer veal chops and pecans to 4 warm serving plates with slotted spatula. Bring apricot mixture in skillet to a boil over high heat; cook 1 minute or until slightly thickened. To serve, spoon apricot mixture over veal chops. Garnish, if desired. *Makes 4 servings*

Tenderloins with Roasted Garlic Sauce

2 whole garlic bulbs, separated but not peeled (about 5 ounces)

⅔ cup A.1.® Steak Sauce, divided

¼ cup dry red wine

¼ cup finely chopped onion

4 (4- to 6-ounce) beef tenderloin steaks, about 1 inch thick

Place unpeeled garlic cloves on baking sheet. Bake at 500°F for 15 to 20 minutes or until garlic is soft; cool. Squeeze garlic pulp from skins; chop pulp slightly. In small saucepan, combine garlic pulp, ½ cup steak sauce, wine and onion. Heat to a boil; reduce heat and simmer for 5 minutes. Keep warm.

Grill steaks over medium heat for 5 minutes on each side or until done, brushing occasionally with remaining steak sauce. Serve steak with warm garlic sauce. *Makes 4 servings*

Veal Chop with Brandied Apricots and Pecans

Beef Tenderloin with Dijon-Cream Sauce

2 tablespoons olive oil

3 tablespoons balsamic vinegar*

1 beef tenderloin roast (about 1½ to 2 pounds)

Salt

1½ tablespoons white peppercorns

1½ tablespoons black peppercorns

3 tablespoons mustard seeds

Dijon-Cream Sauce (recipe follows)

*Substitute 2 tablespoons red wine vinegar plus 1½ teaspoons sugar for the balsamic vinegar.

Combine oil and vinegar in a cup; rub onto beef. Season generously with salt. Let stand 15 minutes. Meanwhile, coarsely crush peppercorns and mustard seeds in a blender or food processor or by hand with a mortar and pestle. Roll beef in crushed mixture, pressing it into the surface to coat.

Oil hot grid to help prevent sticking. Grill beef, on a covered grill, over medium KINGSFORD® Briquets, 16 to 24 minutes (depending on size and thickness) until a meat thermometer inserted in the center almost registers 150°F for medium-rare. (Cook until 160°F for medium or 170°F well-done; add another 5 minutes for every 10°F.) Turn halfway through cooking. Let stand 5 to 10 minutes before slicing. Slice and serve with a few spoonfuls of sauce. *Makes 6 servings*

Note: When choosing a beef tenderloin roast, purchase a center-cut piece or a piece cut from the thicker end, as it will grill more evenly. Test doneness with a thermometer and remove beef from the grill just before it reaches the desired temperature (the internal temperature can rise 5°F as the roast stands).

Dijon-Cream Sauce

1 can (14½ ounces) beef broth

1 cup whipping cream

2 tablespoons butter, softened

1½ to 2 tablespoons Dijon mustard

1 to 1½ tablespoons balsamic vinegar*

Coarsely crushed black peppercorns and mustard seeds for garnish

*Substitute 2 teaspoons red wine vinegar plus 1 teaspoon sugar for the balsamic vinegar.

Bring beef broth and whipping cream to a boil in a saucepan. Boil gently until reduced to about 1 cup; sauce will be thick enough to coat a spoon. Remove from heat; stir in butter, a little at a time, until all the butter is melted. Stir in mustard and vinegar, adjusting amounts to taste. Sprinkle with peppercorns and mustard seeds.

Makes about 1 cup

Beef Tenderloin with Dijon-Cream Sauce

Pork Schnitzel

4 boneless pork chops, ¼ inch thick,
trimmed (3 ounces each)
½ cup corn flake crumbs or cracker crumbs
1 egg, lightly beaten
2 to 4 teaspoons olive oil, divided
⅓ cup lemon juice
¼ cup chicken broth

1. Preheat oven to 200°F. Place baking sheet or ovenproof platter in oven. Place pork chops between layers of waxed paper; pound with smooth side of mallet to ⅛ to ¼ inch thick. Place crumbs in medium bowl. Dip 1 pork chop at a time in egg; gently shake off excess. Dip in crumbs to coat both sides. Place breaded pork chops in single layer on plate. Sprinkle with pepper.

2. Heat 2 teaspoons oil in large skillet over medium-high heat until hot. Working in batches, add chops in single layer. Cook 1 minute or until golden brown. Turn and cook ½ to 1 minute or until golden brown and pork is no longer pink in center. (Add oil as needed to prevent meat from sticking.) Transfer to platter in oven.

3. Remove pan from heat. Add lemon juice and broth. Stir to scrape cooked bits from pan bottom. Return to heat; bring to a boil, stirring constantly, until liquid is reduced to 3 to 4 tablespoons. Remove platter from oven. Pour over meat.

Makes 4 servings

Prep and Cook Time: 20 minutes

Heartland Shepherd's Pie

¾ pound ground beef
1 medium onion, chopped
1 can (14½ ounces) DEL MONTE® Original
Recipe Stewed Tomatoes
1 can (8 ounces) DEL MONTE® Tomato
Sauce
1 can (14½ ounces) DEL MONTE® Mixed
Vegetables, drained
Instant mashed potato flakes plus
ingredients to prepare (enough for
6 servings)
3 cloves garlic, minced (optional)

1. Preheat oven to 375°F. In large skillet, brown meat and onion over medium-high heat; drain.

2. Add tomatoes and tomato sauce; cook over high heat until thickened, stirring frequently. Stir in mixed vegetables. Season with salt and pepper, if desired.

3. Spoon into 2-quart baking dish; set aside. Prepare 6 servings mashed potatoes according to package directions, first cooking garlic in specified amount of butter.

4. Top meat mixture with potatoes. Bake 20 minutes or until heated through. Garnish with chopped parsley, if desired.

Makes 4 to 6 servings

Prep Time: 5 minutes
Cook Time: 30 minutes

Pork Schnitzel

Beef Wellington

6 center cut beef tenderloin steaks, cut
  1 inch thick (about 2½ pounds)
¾ teaspoon salt, divided
½ teaspoon black pepper, divided
2 tablespoons butter or margarine
8 ounces crimini or button mushrooms,
  finely chopped
¼ cup finely chopped shallots or sweet onion
2 tablespoons ruby port or sweet Madeira
  wine
1 package (17¼ ounces) frozen puff pastry,
  thawed
1 egg, separated
½ cup (4 ounces) purchased liver pâté or
  chicken liver mousse*
2 teaspoons water
  Baby pattypan squash (optional)
  Fresh currant and pineapple sage leaves

*You can find pâté in the gourmet or deli section of most
supermarkets or in specialty food stores.

1. Sprinkle steaks with ½ teaspoon salt and
¼ teaspoon pepper. Heat large nonstick skillet over
medium-high heat until hot. Cook steaks in
batches about 3 minutes per side or until well
browned and instant-read thermometer inserted
into steaks registers 110°F. Transfer to clean plate;
set aside. (If meat is tied, remove string; discard.)

2. Melt butter in same skillet over medium heat;
add mushrooms and shallots. Cook and stir
5 minutes or until mushrooms are tender. Add

port, remaining ¼ teaspoon salt and ¼ teaspoon
pepper. Bring to a boil. Reduce heat; simmer
10 minutes or until liquid evaporates, stirring
often. Remove from heat; cool completely.

3. Roll out each pastry sheet to 18×10-inch
rectangle on lightly floured surface with lightly
floured rolling pin. Cut each sheet into 3 (10×6-
inch) rectangles. Cut small amount of pastry from
corners to use as decoration, if desired.

4. Beat egg white in small bowl with whisk until
foamy; brush over each pastry rectangle with pastry
brush. Place 1 cooled steak on each pastry
rectangle. Spread pâté over steaks, dividing evenly;
top with mushroom mixture, pressing lightly so
mushrooms adhere to pâté.

5. Carefully turn each steak over, mushroom side
down. Fold pastry over steak. Fold edge of bottom
dough over top; press edges to seal. Place on
ungreased baking sheet. Repeat with remaining
steaks and pastries.

6. Beat egg yolk and water in small bowl; brush
over pastry. Cut pastry scraps into decorative shapes
and decorate pastry, if desired. Brush decorations
with egg yolk mixture. Cover loosely with plastic
wrap; refrigerate 1 to 4 hours until cold.

7. Preheat oven to 400°F. Bake 20 to 25 minutes
until pastry is puffed and golden brown and steaks
are medium or when internal temperature reaches
145°F when tested with a meat thermometer. Let
stand 10 minutes before serving. Serve with squash.
Garnish, if desired.   *Makes 6 servings*

Beef Wellington

Roast Beef with Red Wine Gravy

2 tablespoons oil
1 sirloin tip roast (3 to 4 pounds)
   Salt and black pepper
2 tablespoons all-purpose flour
1 jar (7 ounces) cocktail onions, drained
1 can (14½ ounces) beef broth
2 tablespoons HOLLAND HOUSE® Red
   Cooking Wine

Heat oven to 350°F. Heat oil in Dutch oven. Season roast to taste with salt and pepper; brown on all sides. Remove from Dutch oven. Drain excess fat, reserving ¼ cup drippings in Dutch oven. Sprinkle flour over reserved drippings. Cook over medium heat until lightly browned, stirring constantly. Add roast and onions to Dutch oven. Roast for 1¾ to 2¼ hours or until desired doneness. Remove roast to cutting board. Let stand 5 to 10 minutes before slicing. Gradually stir in beef broth and cooking wine. Bring to a boil; reduce heat. Cook until gravy thickens. Slice roast and arrange with onions on serving platter. Serve with gravy.   *Makes 6 servings*

Fruited Pork Loin

1 cup dried apricot halves
½ cup dry sherry
1 (3- to 5-pound) center cut pork rib or loin
   roast, backbone cracked
1 cup KARO® Light or Dark Corn Syrup
½ cup orange juice
¼ cup soy sauce
1 tablespoon grated orange peel

1. In small saucepan, combine apricots and sherry. Cover and cook over medium heat, stirring occasionally, until liquid is absorbed.

2. Trim excess fat from surface of roast. Cut deep slits in meat directly over rib bones; insert 3 or 4 apricots in each slit. Place roast, bone-side down, on rack in roasting pan.

3. Roast in 325°F oven 1 to 2 hours* or until meat thermometer registers 160°F.

4. Meanwhile, prepare glaze. In small saucepan, stir corn syrup, orange juice, soy sauce and orange peel. Bring to boil; reduce heat and simmer 5 minutes. Set aside half of glaze to serve with pork loin.

5. Brush pork loin frequently with remaining glaze during last 30 minutes of roasting. Serve with reserved glaze.   *Makes 6 to 10 servings*

*Roast pork loin at 325°F for 20 to 25 minutes per pound.

Prep Time: 20 minutes
Bake Time: 1 to 2 hours

Roast Beef with Red Wine Gravy

Supreme Seafood

Angel Hair Pasta with Seafood Sauce

½ pound firm fish, such as sea bass, monkfish or grouper

2 teaspoons olive oil

½ cup chopped onion

2 cloves garlic, minced

3 pounds fresh plum tomatoes, seeded and chopped

¼ cup chopped fresh basil

2 tablespoons chopped fresh oregano

1 teaspoon crushed red pepper

½ teaspoon sugar

2 bay leaves

½ pound fresh bay scallops or shucked oysters

8 ounces uncooked angel hair pasta

2 tablespoons chopped fresh parsley

1. Cut fish into ¾-inch pieces. Set aside.

2. Heat oil in large nonstick skillet over medium heat; add onion and garlic. Cook and stir 3 minutes or until onion is tender. Reduce heat to low; add tomatoes, basil, oregano, crushed red pepper, sugar and bay leaves. Cook, uncovered, 15 minutes, stirring occasionally.

3. Add fish and scallops. Cook, uncovered, 3 to 4 minutes or until fish flakes easily when tested with fork and scallops are opaque. Remove bay leaves; discard. Set seafood sauce aside.

4. Cook pasta according to package directions, omitting salt. Drain well.

5. Combine pasta with seafood sauce in large serving bowl. Mix well. Sprinkle with parsley. Serve immediately. *Makes 6 servings*

Angel Hair Pasta with Seafood Sauce

Stir-Fried Scallops with Vegetables

1 pound sea scallops

¼ teaspoon salt

⅛ teaspoon black pepper

½ cup vegetable broth

1 tablespoon cornstarch

3 tablespoons butter or margarine, divided

1 package (6 ounces) red radishes, quartered

¼ cup dry white wine

1 package (6 ounces) frozen snow peas, partially thawed

½ cup sliced bamboo shoots

Hot cooked couscous

1. Rinse scallops and pat dry with paper towels. Sprinkle with salt and black pepper.

2. Stir broth into cornstarch in cup until smooth; set aside.

3. Heat wok over high heat about 1 minute or until hot. Add 1½ tablespoons butter; swirl to coat bottom and heat 30 seconds. Arrange half the scallops in single layer in wok, leaving ½ inch between. (Scallops should not touch.) Cook scallops until browned on both sides. Remove scallops to large bowl. Repeat with remaining 1½ tablespoons butter and scallops. Reduce heat to medium-high.

4. Add radishes to wok; stir-fry about 1 minute or until crisp-tender. Remove radishes to bowl with scallops.

5. Add wine to wok. Stir broth mixture; add to wok. Add snow peas and bamboo shoots; cook and stir until heated through.

6. Return scallops and radishes to wok; cook and stir until heated through. Serve over couscous. Garnish, if desired.   *Makes 4 servings*

Broiled Orange Roughy with Green Peppercorn Sauce

1 cup loosely packed cilantro leaves

2 tablespoons dry white wine

2 tablespoons Dijon mustard

½ teaspoon green peppercorns, rinsed, drained

4 orange roughy fillets (about 6 ounces each)

1. Preheat broiler. Position oven rack about 4 inches from heat source.

2. Combine all ingredients except fish in food processor or blender; process until well blended. Set aside.

3. Place fish in shallow baking pan; top with sauce.

4. Broil 10 minutes or until fish flakes easily when tested with fork.   *Makes 4 servings*

Stir-Fried Scallops with Vegetables

Chesapeake Crab Strata

4 tablespoons butter or margarine

4 cups unseasoned croutons

2 cups shredded Cheddar cheese

2 cups milk

8 eggs, beaten

½ teaspoon dry mustard

½ teaspoon seafood seasoning

   Salt and black pepper to taste

1 pound crabmeat

Preheat oven to 325°F. Place butter in 11×7-inch baking dish. Heat in oven until melted, tilting to coat dish. Remove dish from oven; spread croutons over melted butter. Top with cheese; set aside.

Combine milk, eggs, dry mustard, seafood seasoning, salt and black pepper; mix well. Pour egg mixture over cheese in dish; sprinkle with crabmeat. Bake 50 minutes or until mixture is set. Remove from oven and let stand about 10 minutes. Garnish, if desired. *Makes 6 to 8 servings*

Holiday Hint:

Crabmeat may contain bits of cartilage and shell. Using your fingers, carefully pick over crabmeat and remove and discard any pieces of cartilage or shell.

Soleful Roulettes

1 package (6 ounces) long-grain and wild rice mix

1 package (3 ounces) cream cheese, softened

2 tablespoons milk

32 medium fresh spinach leaves, washed

4 sole fillets (about 1 pound)

   Salt and black pepper

½ cup water

¼ cup dry white wine

Cook rice mix according to package directions. Place 2 cups cooked rice in large bowl. (Refrigerate remaining rice for another use.) Combine cream cheese and milk in medium bowl. Stir into rice; set aside.

Place spinach in heatproof bowl. Pour very hot water (not boiling) over spinach to wilt leaves slightly. Rinse sole and pat dry with paper towels. Sprinkle both sides of each fillet with salt and pepper. Cover each fillet with spinach leaves. Divide rice mixture evenly and spread over top of each spinach-lined fillet. To roll fillets, begin with thin end of fillet, roll up and secure with wooden toothpicks.

Combine water and wine in large, heavy saucepan. Stand fillets upright on rolled edges in saucepan; cover. Simmer over low heat 10 minutes or until fish flakes easily when tested with fork. (Do not boil. This will cause fish to break apart.)

Makes 4 servings

Chesapeake Crab Strata

Nutty Pan-Fried Trout

2 tablespoons oil
4 trout fillets (about 6 ounces each)
½ cup seasoned bread crumbs
½ cup pine nuts

1. Heat oil in large skillet over medium heat. Lightly coat fish with crumbs. Add to skillet.

2. Cook 8 minutes or until fish flakes easily when tested with fork, turning after 5 minutes. Remove fish from skillet to serving platter; keep warm.

3. Add nuts to drippings in skillet. Cook and stir 3 minutes or until nuts are lightly toasted. Sprinkle over fish.
Makes 4 servings

Herb-Baked Fish & Rice

1½ cups hot chicken bouillon
½ cup uncooked regular rice
¼ teaspoon Italian seasoning
¼ teaspoon garlic powder
1 package (10 ounces) frozen chopped broccoli, thawed and drained
1⅓ cups *French's® Taste Toppers™* French Fried Onions, divided
1 tablespoon grated Parmesan cheese
1 pound unbreaded fish fillets, thawed if frozen
Paprika (optional)
½ cup (2 ounces) shredded Cheddar cheese

Preheat oven to 375°F. In 12×8-inch baking dish, combine hot bouillon, uncooked rice and seasonings. Bake, covered, at 375°F for 10 minutes. Top with broccoli, ⅔ cup *Taste Toppers* and the Parmesan cheese. Place fish fillets diagonally down center of dish; sprinkle fish lightly with paprika. Bake, covered, at 375°F for 20 to 25 minutes or until fish flakes easily with fork. Stir rice. Top fish with Cheddar cheese and remaining ⅔ cup *Taste Toppers;* bake, uncovered, 3 minutes or until *Taste Toppers* are golden brown.
Makes 3 to 4 servings

Microwave Directions: In 12×8-inch microwave-safe dish, prepare rice mixture as above, except reduce bouillon to 1¼ cups. Cook, covered, on HIGH 5 minutes, stirring halfway through cooking time. Stir in broccoli, ⅔ cup *Taste Toppers* and the Parmesan cheese. Arrange fish fillets in single layer on top of rice mixture; sprinkle fish lightly with paprika. Cook, covered, on MEDIUM (50-60%) 18 to 20 minutes or until fish flakes easily with fork and rice is done. Rotate dish halfway through cooking time. Top fish with Cheddar cheese and remaining ⅔ cup *Taste Toppers;* cook, uncovered, on HIGH 1 minute or until cheese melts. Let stand 5 minutes.

Nutty Pan-Fried Trout

Shrimp Louis Muffins

1 cup HELLMANN'S® or BEST FOODS®
    Real or Light Mayonnaise or Low Fat
    Mayonnaise Dressing
½ cup chili sauce
1 teaspoon lemon juice
1 teaspoon prepared horseradish
½ teaspoon grated onion
⅛ teaspoon salt
⅛ teaspoon freshly ground pepper
4 Thomas' original flavor English muffins,
    split, toasted and buttered
    Lettuce leaves
4 hard-cooked eggs, sliced
¾ pound medium shrimp, shelled, deveined
    and cooked

1. In small bowl, stir mayonnaise, chili sauce, lemon juice, horseradish, onion, salt and pepper until blended. Cover; chill.

2. Top each muffin half with lettuce, egg slices, shrimp and dressing. *Makes 4 servings*

Grilled Swordfish Steaks

1 cup uncooked UNCLE BEN'S®
    ORIGINAL CONVERTED® Brand Rice
4 (1-inch-thick) swordfish steaks (about
    4 ounces each)
3 tablespoons Caribbean jerk seasoning
1 can (8 ounces) crushed pineapple in juice,
    drained
⅓ cup chopped macadamia nuts
1 tablespoon honey

1. Cook rice according to package directions.

2. During the last 10 minutes of cooking, coat both sides of swordfish steaks with jerk seasoning. Lightly spray grid of preheated grill with nonstick cooking spray. Grill swordfish over medium coals 10 to 12 minutes or until fish flakes easily when tested with fork, turning after 5 minutes.

3. Stir pineapple, nuts and honey into hot cooked rice; serve with fish. *Makes 4 servings*

Holiday Hint:

For a nuttier flavor, macadamia nuts can be toasted. Place nuts in small nonstick skillet and heat over medium-high heat until lightly browned about 5 minutes, stirring occasionally.

Shrimp Louis Muffins

Trout with Apples and Toasted Hazelnuts

1/3 cup whole hazelnuts

5 tablespoons butter or margarine, divided

1 large Red Delicious apple, cored and cut
    into 16 wedges

2 butterflied rainbow trout fillets (about
    8 ounces each)

    Salt and black pepper

3 tablespoons all-purpose flour

1 tablespoon snipped fresh chives

1 tablespoon lemon juice

    Lemon slices and fresh chives for garnish

Preheat oven to 350°F. To toast hazelnuts, spread in single layer on baking sheet. Bake 8 to 10 minutes or until skins split.

Wrap hazelnuts in kitchen towel; set aside 5 minutes to cool slightly. Rub nuts with towel to remove as much of the papery skins as possible. Process hazelnuts in food processor until coarsely chopped; set aside.

Melt 3 tablespoons butter in medium skillet over medium-high heat. Add apple; cook 4 to 5 minutes or until crisp-tender, stirring frequently. Remove from skillet with slotted spoon; set aside.

Rinse trout and pat dry with paper towels. Sprinkle fish with salt and pepper, then coat with flour. Place fish in skillet. Cook 4 minutes or until golden and fish flakes easily when tested with fork, turning halfway through cooking time. Return apple to skillet. Reduce heat to low and keep warm.

Melt remaining 2 tablespoons butter in small saucepan over low heat. Stir in chives, lemon juice and hazelnuts. Sprinkle fish and apple with hazelnut mixture. Garnish, if desired.

Makes 2 servings

A.1.® Grilled Fish Steaks

1 pound salmon steaks or other fish steaks,
    about 1 inch thick

1/4 cup A.1.® Steak Sauce

1 tablespoon margarine or butter, melted

1/2 teaspoon garlic powder

Coat large sheet of aluminum foil with nonstick cooking spray; place fish steaks on foil. In small bowl, combine steak sauce, margarine and garlic powder; spoon over fish. Fold edges of foil together to seal; place seam side up on grill. Grill for about 10 minutes or until fish flakes easily when tested with fork. Carefully remove from grill. Serve immediately. *Makes 4 servings*

Holiday Hint:

Grilling fish in a foil package prevents it from drying out and reduces the chance that tender fillets and steaks will break apart. Be sure to seal foil well to prevent sauces from draining off.

*Trout with Apples and
Toasted Hazelnuts*

Chesapeake Crab Cakes

1 pound backfin crabmeat

½ cup soft bread crumbs

1 tablespoon minced onion

1 tablespoon finely chopped green bell
  pepper

1 tablespoon chopped fresh parsley

¼ cup mayonnaise

1 egg

2 teaspoons white wine Worcestershire sauce

2 teaspoons lemon juice

1 teaspoon prepared mustard

½ teaspoon salt

¼ teaspoon white pepper

  Vegetable oil for frying (optional)

  Tartar sauce

Pick out and discard any shell or cartilage from crabmeat. Flake with fork. Place crabmeat in medium bowl. Add bread crumbs, onion, bell pepper and parsley; set aside.

Mix remaining ingredients except oil and tartar sauce in small bowl. Stir well to combine. Pour mayonnaise mixture over crabmeat mixture. Gently mix so large lumps will not be broken. Shape mixture into 6 large (¾-inch-thick) cakes or 36 bite-sized cakes.

To pan-fry crab cakes, pour enough oil into 12-inch skillet to cover bottom. Heat oil over medium-high heat until hot. Add crab cakes; fry 10 minutes for large cakes and 6 minutes for bite-sized cakes or until cakes are lightly browned on bottom. Using spatula, carefully turn halfway through cooking without breaking cakes.

To broil crab cakes, preheat broiler. Place crab cakes on broiler pan. Broil 4 to 6 inches below heat 10 minutes for large cakes and 6 minutes for bite-sized cakes or until cakes are lightly browned on surface, turning halfway through cooking.

Makes 6 servings

Serving Suggestion: Serve large crab cakes on plates or as sandwiches with round buns. Serve bite-sized cakes on plates or with toothpicks as appetizers. Accompany with tartar sauce.

Grilled Fresh Fish

3 to 3½ pounds fresh tuna or catfish

¾ cup prepared HIDDEN VALLEY® Original
  Ranch® Salad Dressing

  Chopped fresh dill

  Lemon wedges (optional)

Place fish on heavy-duty foil. Cover with salad dressing. Grill over medium-hot coals until fish turns opaque and flakes easily when tested with fork, 20 to 30 minutes. Or, broil fish 15 to 20 minutes. Sprinkle with dill; garnish with lemon wedges, if desired. *Makes 6 servings*

Chesapeake Crab Cake

Pasta with Tuna Sauce

3 cups bow tie pasta, uncooked
1 box (9 ounces) BIRDS EYE® frozen Italian Green Beans
1 jar (15 ounces) prepared spaghetti sauce
1 can (6 ounces) tuna packed in water, drained
Chopped Italian parsley (optional)

• Cook pasta according to package directions; drain.

• Cook vegetables according to package directions; drain.

• Combine pasta, beans, spaghetti sauce, tuna and parsley. Cook and stir over medium-high heat 5 minutes or until heated through.

Makes about 2 servings

Prep Time: 5 minutes
Cook Time: 20 minutes

Holiday Hint:

Choose solid white tuna or chunk tuna for this recipe. Solid white tuna is firm and mild in flavor; break up large pieces with a fork. Chunk tuna is not as firm and pieces are generally smaller than those of solid white tuna.

Salmon on a Bed of Leeks

3 to 4 leeks
2 teaspoons butter or margarine
½ cup dry white wine or vermouth
2 salmon fillets (6 to 8 ounces)
Salt and black pepper to taste
2 tablespoons grated Gruyère cheese

Trim green tops and root ends from leeks; cut lengthwise into quarters, leaving ½ inch together at root end. Separate sections. Rinse under cold running water; drain well. Trim off root end.

In 10-inch skillet, melt butter over medium heat. Add leeks; cook 2 to 3 minutes, stirring often, until leeks are wilted. Stir in wine; arrange salmon on leeks. Sprinkle with salt and pepper. Reduce heat to low. Cover; cook 5 minutes. Sprinkle cheese over salmon. Cover; cook another 3 to 5 minutes or until salmon is firm and opaque around edges and cheese is melted. Transfer to warm dinner plate with broad spatula; serve immediately.

Makes 2 servings

Favorite recipe from **National Fisheries Institute**

Rainbow Stir-Fried Fish

SAUCE
- ½ **cup chicken broth**
- 2 **tablespoons LA CHOY® Soy Sauce**
- 1 **tablespoon cornstarch**
- 1 **teaspoon sugar**
- ¼ **teaspoon crushed red pepper (optional)**

FISH AND VEGETABLES
- 1 **pound orange roughy filets*, cut into 1-inch chunks**
- 1 **tablespoon LA CHOY® Soy Sauce**
- 3 **tablespoons WESSON® Oil**
- ½ **cup julienne-cut carrots**
- 1 **teaspoon minced fresh garlic**
- 1 **teaspoon minced fresh ginger**
- 2 **cups fresh broccoli flowerettes**
- 1 **can (8 ounces) LA CHOY® Sliced Water Chestnuts, drained**
- 1 **package (6 ounces) frozen pea pods, thawed and drained**
- ½ **cup diagonally sliced green onions**

*Any firm-fleshed white fish may be substituted.

In small bowl, combine sauce ingredients; set aside. In medium bowl, combine fish and soy sauce; toss lightly to coat. In large nonstick skillet or wok, heat oil. Add fish mixture; stir-fry 2 to 3 minutes or until fish flakes easily with fork. Remove fish from skillet; drain. Set aside. Add carrots, garlic and ginger to same skillet; stir-fry 30 seconds. Add broccoli; stir-fry 1 minute. Add water chestnuts and pea pods; heat thoroughly, stirring occasionally. Return fish to skillet. Stir sauce; add to skillet. Heat, stirring gently, until sauce is thick and bubbly. Sprinkle with green onions. Garnish, if desired. *Makes 4 servings*

Fish Broccoli Casserole

- 1 **package (10 ounces) frozen broccoli spears, thawed, drained**
- 1 **cup cooked flaked Florida whitefish**
- 1 **can (10¾ ounces) condensed cream of mushroom soup**
- ½ **cup milk**
- ¼ **teaspoon salt**
- ⅛ **teaspoon freshly ground black pepper**
- ½ **cup crushed potato chips**

Preheat oven to 425°F. Grease 1½-quart casserole. Layer broccoli in prepared casserole. Combine fish, soup, milk, salt and pepper in large bowl.

Spread fish mixture over broccoli. Sprinkle with potato chips. Bake 12 to 15 minutes or until golden brown. *Makes 4 servings*

Favorite recipe from **Florida Department of Agriculture and Consumer Services, Bureau of Seafood and Aquaculture**

Baked Stuffed Snapper

1 red snapper (1½ pounds)

2 cups hot cooked rice

1 can (4 ounces) sliced mushrooms, drained

½ cup diced water chestnuts

¼ cup thinly sliced green onions

¼ cup diced pimiento

2 tablespoons chopped parsley

1 tablespoon finely shredded lemon peel

½ teaspoon salt

⅛ teaspoon black pepper

1 tablespoon margarine, melted

Preheat oven to 400°F. Clean and butterfly fish. Combine rice, mushrooms, water chestnuts, onions, pimiento, parsley, lemon peel, salt and pepper; toss lightly. Fill cavity of fish with rice mixture; close with wooden toothpicks soaked in water. Place fish in 13×9-inch baking dish coated with nonstick cooking spray; brush fish with margarine. Bake 18 to 20 minutes or until fish flakes easily when tested with fork. Wrap any remaining rice in foil and bake in oven with fish.

Makes 4 servings

Favorite recipe from **USA Rice Federation**

Flounder Fillets with Carrots

1 pound carrots, julienned (about 4 large)

2 tablespoons minced parsley

1 teaspoon olive oil

⅛ teaspoon salt

⅛ teaspoon pepper

4 (4- to 5-ounce) flounder fillets*

2 teaspoons coarse-grain Dijon mustard

1 teaspoon honey

*Or, substitute other fish fillets, such as tilapia, sole, cod, catfish, halibut, ocean perch, trout, orange roughy or pollock.

Combine carrots, parsley, oil, salt and pepper in 11×7-inch microwavable baking dish. Cover with waxed paper. Microwave at HIGH 5 minutes, stirring once.

Fold thin fillets in half to give all fillets even thickness. Place fillets over carrots with thick parts toward corners of dish. Combine mustard and honey; spread over fillets.

Cover with waxed paper. Microwave at HIGH 2 minutes. Rotate fillets, placing cooked parts toward center; continue to cook 1 to 3 minutes longer or just until fish flakes easily when tested with a fork. Let stand, covered, 2 minutes. Arrange fish and carrots on warm plates.

Makes 4 servings

Favorite recipe from **National Fisheries Institute**

Baked Stuffed Snapper

Wild Rice Shrimp Paella

1½ cups canned chicken broth

2 tablespoons butter or margarine

1/16 teaspoon saffron or 1/8 teaspoon turmeric

2 boxes UNCLE BEN'S® Butter & Herb Fast Cook Recipe Long Grain & Wild Rice

1 pound medium shrimp, peeled and deveined

1 can (14½ ounces) diced tomatoes, undrained

1 cup frozen green peas, thawed

2 jars (6 ounces each) marinated artichoke hearts, drained

1. Combine broth, butter, saffron and contents of seasoning packets, reserving rice, in large saucepan. Bring to a boil.

2. Add shrimp; cook over medium-high heat 2 minutes or until shrimp turn pink. Remove shrimp with slotted spoon and set aside.

3. Add tomatoes and reserved rice. Bring to a boil. Cover; reduce heat and simmer 15 minutes.

4. Stir in peas; cover and cook 5 minutes. Add artichoke hearts and shrimp; cover and cook 5 minutes or until hot and rice is tender. Let stand 3 minutes before serving.   *Makes 6 servings*

Surfin' Tuna Casserole

3 eggs

¾ cup milk

2 cups STOVE TOP® Chicken Flavor Stuffing Mix in the Canister

1½ cups (6 ounces) KRAFT® Natural Shredded Colby/Monterey Jack Cheese, divided

1 cup frozen green peas, thawed

1 can (6 ounces) tuna, drained, flaked

½ cup condensed cream of mushroom soup

¼ cup chopped green onions

2 tablespoons chopped pimiento

BEAT eggs in large bowl; stir in milk. Stir in stuffing mix, 1 cup of the cheese, peas, tuna, soup, onions and pimiento until well mixed. Spoon into greased 9-inch microwavable pie plate. Cover loosely with wax paper.

MICROWAVE on HIGH 5 minutes. Stir thoroughly to completely mix center and outside edges; smooth top. Cover.

MICROWAVE 5 minutes or until center is no longer wet. Sprinkle with remaining ½ cup cheese; cover. Let stand 5 minutes.   *Makes 6 servings*

Prep Time: 10 minutes
Cook Time: 15 minutes

Wild Rice Shrimp Paella

Red Snapper with Lime-Ginger Butter

5 tablespoons butter, cut into small pieces

1 tablespoon bottled lime juice

3 cloves garlic

2 teaspoons ground ginger

½ teaspoon hot pepper sauce

   Salt

   Black pepper

6 red snapper fillets (about 1½ pounds)

1. Preheat broiler.

2. Combine butter, lime juice, garlic, ginger, pepper sauce, and salt and pepper to taste in food processor; process until smooth paste forms.

3. Broil red snapper 4 to 5 inches from heat 5 minutes. Turn fillets over and broil 4 minutes.

4. Place about 1 tablespoon butter mixture on top of each fillet; broil 45 seconds. Serve immediately.

Makes 6 servings

Serving Suggestion: For a special touch, serve fish with rice and garnish with fresh lime slices and chives.

Tip: Halibut or swordfish can be substituted for the red snapper.

Prep and Cook Time: 18 minutes

Trout Stuffed with Fresh Mint and Oranges

2 pan-dressed* trout (1 to 1¼ pounds each)

½ teaspoon coarse salt, such as Kosher salt

1 orange, sliced

1 cup fresh mint leaves

1 sweet onion, sliced

*A pan-dressed trout has been gutted and scaled with head and tail removed.

1. Rinse trout under cold running water; pat dry with paper towels.

2. Sprinkle cavities of trout with salt; fill each with orange slices and mint. Cover each fish with onion slices.

3. Spray 2 large sheets of foil with nonstick cooking spray. Place 1 fish on each sheet and seal using Drugstore Wrap technique.**

4. Place foil packets seam-side down directly on medium-hot coals; grill on covered grill 20 to 25 minutes or until trout flakes easily when tested with fork, turning once.

5. Carefully open foil packets, avoiding hot steam; remove and discard orange-mint stuffing and trout skin. Serve immediately. *Makes 6 servings*

**Place food in the center of an oblong piece of heavy-duty foil, leaving at least a two-inch border around the food. Bring the two long sides together above the food; fold down in a series of locked folds, allowing for heat circulation and expansion. Fold short ends up and over again. Press folds firmly to seal the foil packet.

Red Snapper with Lime-Ginger Butter

Soup & Salad Time

Chicken Gumbo

4 TYSON® Fresh Skinless Chicken Thighs

4 TYSON® Fresh Skinless Chicken
   Drumsticks

¼ cup all-purpose flour

2 teaspoons Cajun or Creole seasoning blend

2 tablespoons vegetable oil

1 large onion, chopped

1 cup thinly sliced celery

3 cloves garlic, minced

1 can (14½ ounces) stewed tomatoes,
   undrained

1 can (14½ ounces) chicken broth

1 large green bell pepper, cut into ½-inch
   pieces

½ to 1 teaspoon hot pepper sauce or to taste

PREP: CLEAN: Wash hands. Combine flour and Cajun seasonings in reclosable plastic bag. Add chicken, 2 pieces at a time; shake to coat. Reserve excess flour mixture. CLEAN: Wash hands.

COOK: In large saucepan, heat oil over medium heat. Add chicken and brown on all sides; remove and set aside. Sauté onion, celery and garlic 5 minutes. Add reserved flour mixture; cook 1 minute, stirring frequently. Add tomatoes, chicken broth, bell pepper and hot sauce. Bring to a boil. Return chicken to saucepan, cover and simmer over low heat, stirring occasionally, 30 minutes or until internal juices of chicken run clear. (Or instant-read meat thermometer inserted in thickest part of chicken reads 180°F.)

SERVE: Serve in shallow bowls, topped with hot cooked rice, if desired.

CHILL: Refrigerate leftovers immediately.

Makes 6 to 8 servings

Prep Time: 10 minutes
Cook Time: 1 hour

Chicken Gumbo

Quick Beef Soup

1½ pounds lean ground beef

1 cup chopped onion

2 cloves garlic, finely chopped

1 can (28 ounces) tomatoes, undrained

6 cups water

6 beef bouillon cubes

¼ teaspoon black pepper

1½ cups frozen peas, carrots and corn
   vegetable blend

½ cup uncooked orzo

French bread (optional)

Cook beef, onion and garlic in large saucepan over medium-high heat until beef is brown, stirring to separate meat; drain fat.

Purée tomatoes with juice in covered blender or food processor. Add tomatoes with juices, water, bouillon cubes and pepper to meat mixture. Bring to a boil; reduce heat to low. Simmer, uncovered, 20 minutes. Add vegetables and orzo. Simmer 15 minutes more. Serve with French bread.

Makes 6 servings

Favorite recipe from **North Dakota Beef Commission**

Italian Tomato Soup

½ pound lean ground beef

½ cup chopped onion

1 clove garlic, minced

1 can (28 ounces) tomatoes, undrained, cut
   into pieces

1 can (15 ounces) white kidney beans,
   drained, rinsed

½ cup thinly sliced carrots

¾ cup HEINZ® Tomato Ketchup

1 teaspoon dried basil leaves

¼ teaspoon salt

In medium saucepan, brown beef, onion and garlic; drain excess fat. Add tomatoes with juices and remaining ingredients. Cover; simmer 15 minutes.

Makes 4 to 6 servings (about 6 cups)

Holiday Hint:

White kidney beans are also referred to as cannellini beans. These beans are the traditional beans for the Italian soup pasta e fagioli. Look for them in the canned vegetable section of the supermarket.

Sausage Minestrone Soup

2 tablespoons olive oil

1 large onion, chopped

3 cloves garlic, minced

3 cups water

1 can (14½ ounces) stewed tomatoes, undrained

1 can (10½ ounces) kosher condensed beef or chicken broth

1 teaspoon dried basil leaves

1 teaspoon dried oregano leaves

¼ teaspoon crushed red pepper

1 package (12 ounces) HEBREW NATIONAL® Beef Polish Sausage

½ cup small pasta such as ditalini or small bow ties

1 can (16 ounces) cannellini beans, drained

Heat oil in large saucepan over medium heat. Add onion and garlic; cook 8 minutes, stirring occasionally. Add water, tomatoes with liquid, broth, basil, oregano and red pepper; bring to a boil.

Meanwhile, cut sausage crosswise into ½-inch slices. Cut each slice into quarters. Stir sausage and pasta into soup; simmer 15 minutes or until pasta is tender. Add beans; cook until heated through.

Makes 6 servings

Turkey Chowder

2 tablespoons butter or margarine

½ cup chopped carrot

½ cup chopped celery

½ cup chopped onion

⅓ cup uncooked long-grain white rice

⅓ cup barley

2 cans (14½ ounces each) chicken broth

½ teaspoon dried thyme leaves

2 cups chopped cooked turkey

1 package (10 ounces) frozen corn, thawed

½ cup half-and-half

Salt and pepper

1. Melt butter in large saucepan. Add carrot, celery and onion; cook and stir until tender. Stir in rice and barley; cook 2 minutes. Add broth and thyme; bring to a boil. Reduce heat to low; simmer 20 to 25 minutes or until rice and barley are tender.

2. Add turkey and corn to broth mixture; cook 5 minutes or until heated through. Add half-and-half; heat briefly, but do not boil. Season with salt and pepper to taste. *Makes 5 servings*

Sausage Minestrone Soup

Oniony Mushroom Soup

2 cans (10¾ ounces each) condensed golden mushroom soup

1 can (13¾ ounces) reduced-sodium beef broth

1⅓ cups *French's® Taste Toppers™* French Fried Onions, divided

½ cup water

⅓ cup dry sherry wine

4 slices French bread, cut ½ inch thick

1 tablespoon olive oil

1 clove garlic, finely minced

1 cup (4 ounces) shredded Swiss cheese

Combine mushroom soup, beef broth, *1 cup **Taste Toppers***, water and sherry in large saucepan. Bring to a boil over medium-high heat, stirring often. Reduce heat to low. Simmer 15 minutes, stirring occasionally.

Preheat broiler. Place bread on baking sheet. Combine oil and garlic in small bowl. Brush oil over both sides of bread slices. Broil bread until toasted and crisp, turning once.

Ladle soup into 4 broiler-safe bowls. Place 1 slice of bread in each bowl. Sprinkle evenly with cheese and remaining *⅓ cup **Taste Toppers***. Place bowls on baking sheet. Place under broiler about 1 minute or until cheese is melted and ***Taste Toppers*** are golden.

Makes 4 servings

Classic French Onion Soup

¼ cup butter

3 large yellow onions, sliced

1 cup dry white wine

3 cans (about 14 ounces each) beef or chicken broth

1 teaspoon Worcestershire sauce

½ teaspoon salt

½ teaspoon dried thyme

1 loaf French bread, sliced and toasted

1 cup (4 ounces) shredded Swiss cheese

Fresh thyme for garnish

SLOW COOKER DIRECTIONS

Melt butter in large skillet over high heat. Add onions, cook and stir 15 minutes or until onions are soft and lightly browned. Stir in wine.

Combine onion mixture, beef broth, Worcestershire, salt and thyme in slow cooker. Cover and cook on LOW 4 to 4½ hours. Ladle soup into 4 individual bowls; top with bread slice and cheese. Garnish with fresh thyme, if desired.

Makes 4 servings

Oniony Mushroom Soup

Golden Apple Mulligatawny

2 tablespoons vegetable oil

1 broiler-fryer chicken, cut into serving pieces (2½ pounds)

6 cups water

1 teaspoon salt, divided

2 tablespoons butter or margarine

2 Washington Golden Delicious apples, cored and chopped

1 small onion, chopped

1 small red bell pepper, chopped

½ cup chopped carrots

½ cup chopped celery

1½ teaspoons curry powder

1 tablespoon all-purpose flour

¼ teaspoon ground black pepper

⅛ teaspoon ground cloves

⅛ teaspoon ground red pepper

2 cups hot cooked rice

¼ cup chopped fresh parsley leaves

1. Heat oil in Dutch oven over medium-high heat. Add chicken; cook until brown on all sides. Drain excess fat. Add water and ½ teaspoon salt. Reduce heat to low. Cover and simmer 1 hour.

2. Remove chicken from liquid; set aside to cool slightly. Reserve liquid in separate container. Cool chicken; remove skin and bones and discard. Cut remaining chicken into bite-size pieces; set aside.

3. Melt butter in same Dutch oven; add apples, onion, bell pepper, carrots and celery. Cook and stir over medium-high heat until apples are just tender. Add curry powder; cook and stir 2 minutes. Blend in flour, black pepper, cloves and ground red pepper. Stir reserved liquid into apple mixture. Reduce heat to low. Cover and simmer 15 minutes.

4. Just before serving, add reserved chicken and remaining ½ teaspoon salt; heat through. To serve, place ⅓ cup rice in each soup bowl; ladle soup over rice. Sprinkle with parsley and serve.

Makes 6 servings

Favorite recipe from **Washington Apple Commission**

Holiday Hint:

Mulligatawny is a traditional soup from southeastern India. It is a spicy soup made with chicken and rice and flavored with pepper and curry. Some versions include egg, cream or coconut.

Chunky Garden Stew

Spicy Hot Sauce (recipe follows)

1 tablespoon olive or canola oil

3 medium Colorado Sangre red potatoes, cut into chunks

1 large carrot, sliced diagonally

1 medium onion, quartered

1 large yellow squash or zucchini, sliced

1 Japanese eggplant *or* ½ regular eggplant, cut into cubes

2 stalks celery, sliced

1 small red or green bell pepper, cut into chunks

1 teaspoon ground cinnamon

1 teaspoon coriander

1 teaspoon turmeric

½ teaspoon ground cumin

½ teaspoon ground cardamom

½ teaspoon salt

2 cans (14½ ounces each) vegetable broth *or* 1½ cups water

1 can (15 ounces) chick-peas, drained

⅔ cup raisins

6 cups hot cooked rice

Prepare Spicy Hot Sauce; set aside. Heat oil in Dutch oven over medium-high heat. Add potatoes and carrot; cook and stir 5 minutes. Add onion, squash, eggplant, celery, bell pepper, spices and salt; cook and stir 3 to 5 minutes. Add broth, chick-peas and raisins; bring to a simmer. Simmer, covered, about 15 minutes or until potatoes are tender. Serve vegetable stew over rice. Serve with Spicy Hot Sauce. *Makes 5 to 6 servings*

Spicy Hot Sauce

⅓ cup coarsely chopped cilantro

¼ cup water

1 tablespoon olive or canola oil

2 cloves garlic

½ teaspoon salt

½ teaspoon turmeric

¼ to ½ teaspoon ground red pepper

¼ teaspoon sugar

¼ teaspoon ground cumin

¼ teaspoon ground cardamom

¼ teaspoon ground coriander

Combine all ingredients in blender; process until smooth. Adjust flavors to taste.

Favorite recipe from **Colorado Potato Administrative Committee**

Chicken and Homemade Noodle Soup

¾ cup all-purpose flour

2 teaspoons finely chopped fresh thyme *or* ½ teaspoon dried thyme, divided

¼ teaspoon salt

1 egg yolk, beaten

2 cups plus 3 tablespoons cold water, divided

1 pound boneless skinless chicken thighs, cut into ½- to ¾-inch pieces

5 cups chicken broth

1 medium onion, chopped

1 medium carrot, thinly sliced

¾ cup frozen peas

Chopped fresh parsley for garnish

1. To prepare noodles, stir together flour, 1 teaspoon thyme and salt in small bowl. Add egg yolk and 3 tablespoons water. Stir together until mixed. Shape into small ball. Place dough on lightly floured surface; flatten slightly. Knead 5 minutes or until dough is smooth and elastic, adding more flour to prevent sticking if necessary. Cover with plastic wrap. Let stand 15 minutes.

2. Roll out dough to ⅛-inch thickness or thinner on lightly floured surface with lightly floured rolling pin. If dough is too elastic, let rest a few minutes. Let rolled out dough stand about 30 minutes to dry slightly. Cut into ¼-inch-wide strips. Cut pieces 1½ to 2 inches long.

3. Combine chicken and 2 cups water in medium saucepan. Bring to a boil over high heat. Reduce heat to medium-low; cover and simmer 5 minutes. Drain and rinse chicken; set aside. Combine chicken broth, onion, carrot and remaining 1 teaspoon thyme in 5-quart Dutch oven or large saucepan. Bring to a boil over high heat. Add noodles. Reduce heat to medium-low; simmer, uncovered, 8 minutes or until noodles are done. Stir in chicken and peas. Bring soup just to a boil. Sprinkle parsley over each serving.

Makes 4 servings

Holiday Hint:

To prevent noodles from sticking together when cooked, dry them for 5 to 10 minutes before cooking by arranging them on a clean kitchen towel or hanging them on a wooden pasta rack.

Chicken and Homemade Noodle Soup

Wild Rice Soup

½ cup lentils

1 package (6 ounces) long grain and wild
    rice blend

1 can (about 14 ounces) vegetable broth

1 package (10 ounces) frozen mixed
    vegetables

1 cup fat-free (skim) milk

½ cup (2 ounces) reduced-fat processed
    American cheese, cut into pieces

1. Rinse and sort lentils, discarding any debris or
blemished lentils. Place lentils in small saucepan;
cover with about 3 cups water. Bring to a boil;
reduce heat to low. Simmer, covered, 5 minutes.
Let stand, covered, 1 hour. Drain and rinse lentils.

2. Cook rice according to package directions in
medium saucepan. Add lentils and remaining
ingredients. Bring to a boil; reduce heat to low.
Simmer, uncovered, 20 minutes. Garnish as
desired.   *Makes 6 servings*

Holiday Hint:

Wild Rice Soup makes a filling meal
on a cold winter day—and it is
surprisingly easy to prepare. Round out
the meal with warm sour dough bread
and a green salad.

Dijon Roasted Vegetable Soup

2 plum tomatoes, halved

1 medium zucchini, split lengthwise and
    halved

1 large onion, quartered

1 red bell pepper, sliced

1 cup sliced carrots

2 to 3 cloves garlic

5 cups chicken broth

¼ teaspoon ground cumin

¼ teaspoon crushed red pepper flakes

2 cups diced cooked chicken (about
    10 ounces)

½ cup GREY POUPON® Dijon Mustard

¼ cup chopped parsley

Arrange tomatoes, zucchini, onion, bell pepper,
carrots and garlic on large baking sheet. Bake at
325°F for 30 to 45 minutes or until golden and
tender. Remove from oven and cool. Chop
vegetables.

Heat chicken broth, chopped vegetables, cumin
and red pepper flakes to a boil in 3-quart pot, over
high heat; reduce heat. Simmer for 5 minutes. Stir
in chicken and mustard; cook for 5 minutes more.
Stir in parsley and serve warm.

Makes 8 servings

Wild Rice Soup

Seafood Gumbo

1 bag SUCCESS® Rice
1 tablespoon reduced-calorie margarine
¼ cup chopped onion
¼ cup chopped green bell pepper
2 cloves garlic, minced
1 can (28 ounces) whole tomatoes, cut up, undrained
2 cups chicken broth
½ teaspoon ground red pepper
½ teaspoon dried thyme leaves, crushed
½ teaspoon dried basil leaves, crushed
¾ pound white fish, cut into 1-inch pieces
1 package (10 ounces) frozen cut okra, thawed and drained
½ pound shrimp, peeled and deveined

Prepare rice according to package directions.

Melt margarine in large saucepan over medium-high heat. Add onion, green pepper and garlic; cook and stir until crisp-tender. Stir in tomatoes with juices, broth, red pepper, thyme and basil. Bring to a boil. Reduce heat to low; simmer, uncovered, until thoroughly heated, 10 to 15 minutes. Stir in fish, okra and shrimp; simmer until fish flakes easily with fork and shrimp curl and turn pink. Add rice; heat thoroughly, stirring occasionally, 5 to 8 minutes.   *Makes 4 servings*

Corn and Chicken Chowder

3 tablespoons butter *or* margarine, divided
1 pound boneless skinless chicken breasts, cut into chunks
2 medium leeks, sliced (2 cups)
2 medium potatoes, cut into chunks
1 large green pepper, diced
2 tablespoons paprika
2 tablespoons flour
3 cups chicken broth
2½ cups fresh corn kernels
1½ teaspoons TABASCO® brand Pepper Sauce
1 teaspoon salt
1 cup half-and-half

In 4-quart saucepan over medium-high heat, melt 1 tablespoon butter. Cook chicken chunks until well browned on all sides, stirring frequently. With slotted spoon, remove chicken; set aside.

Add 2 tablespoons butter to drippings in saucepan. Over medium heat, cook leeks, potatoes and green pepper until tender, stirring occasionally. Stir in paprika and flour until well blended; cook 1 minute. Add broth, corn, TABASCO® Sauce, salt and chicken. Over high heat, heat to boiling. Reduce heat to low; cover and simmer 20 minutes. Stir in half-and-half; heat.   *Makes 8 cups*

Seafood Gumbo

Napa Valley Chicken Salad

2 cups diced cooked chicken

1 cup seedless red grapes, halved

1 cup diced celery

½ cup chopped toasted pecans

¼ cup thinly sliced green onions

½ cup HIDDEN VALLEY® Original Ranch®
  Dressing

1 teaspoon Dijon mustard

Combine chicken, grapes, celery, pecans and onions in a medium bowl. Stir together dressing and mustard; toss with salad. Cover and refrigerate for 2 hours. *Makes 4 servings*

Grilled Beef Caesar Salad

1 pound flank steak

1 bottle (8 ounces) Caesar salad dressing

⅓ cup *French's®* Dijon Mustard

¼ cup lemon juice

1 tablespoon grated lemon peel

4 anchovy fillets, rinsed and patted dry
  (optional)*

8 thickly cut slices French bread

8 cups washed and torn romaine lettuce
  leaves

1 ripe tomato, chopped

*Anchovies may be omitted. Brush bread slices with mustard mixture; proceed as above.

1. Place steak in large resealable plastic food storage bag. Combine Caesar dressing, mustard, lemon juice and peel in 2-cup measure; mix well. Pour ⅔ cup mustard mixture over steak. Seal bag; marinate in refrigerator 30 minutes.

2. Place anchovies and ¼ cup mustard mixture in food processor. Reserve remaining mustard mixture for dressing. Process until very smooth. Brush anchovy mixture on both sides of bread slices. Grill bread over high heat 2 minutes or until lightly toasted on both sides. Set aside.

3. Place steak on oiled grid, reserving marinade. Grill over high heat 10 to 15 minutes for medium-rare, basting frequently with marinade. *Do not baste with marinade during last 5 minutes of cooking.* Let steak stand 5 minutes. Place lettuce and tomato on serving platter. Slice steak diagonally; arrange over lettuce and tomato. Serve with reserved dressing and anchovy bread slices. *Makes 4 servings*

Prep Time: 20 minutes
Marinate Time: 30 minutes
Cook Time: 17 minutes

Napa Valley Chicken Salad

Golden Gate Chinese Chicken and Cabbage Sesame Salad

1½ **pounds boneless, skinless chicken breast**

1½ **teaspoons salt-free lemon pepper**

¼ **teaspoon salt**

8 **cups thinly sliced Napa cabbage**

1 **medium-size red bell pepper, cut into julienned strips**

1 **medium-size yellow bell pepper, cut into julienned strips**

½ **cup diagonally sliced green onions**

½ **cup sesame seeds, toasted***

½ **cup chopped dried apricots**

1 **tablespoon plus ½ teaspoon grated fresh ginger, divided**

¼ **cup low-sodium chicken broth**

¼ **cup seasoned rice vinegar**

¼ **cup low-sodium soy sauce**

2 **tablespoons sugar**

2 **tablespoons dark sesame oil**

6 **Napa cabbage leaves**

1½ **cups chow mein noodles**

*To toast sesame seeds, place in small skillet. Cook over medium-high heat 1 to 3 minutes or until lightly browned, stirring constantly.

Place chicken in microproof dish; sprinkle with lemon pepper and salt. Cover with wax paper and microwave on HIGH 8 to 10 minutes or until no longer pink in center, rotating dish half turn every 2 minutes. Or, poach chicken**. Remove chicken from dish. Cool; discard liquid. Shred chicken into bite-size pieces. Combine chicken, sliced cabbage, red pepper, yellow pepper, onions, sesame seeds, apricots and 1 tablespoon ginger in large bowl. Toss well; cover and refrigerate until ready to serve.

Combine broth, vinegar, soy sauce, sugar, oil and remaining ½ teaspoon ginger in small jar with lid; shake well. Pour over chicken and cabbage mixture; toss gently. Spoon onto individual plates lined with cabbage leaves. Sprinkle evenly with chow mein noodles. Serve immediately.   *Makes 6 servings*

**To poach chicken, place chicken breasts in saucepan; sprinkle with lemon pepper and salt. Cover with water. Simmer until no longer pink in center.

Favorite recipe from **National Chicken Council**

Holiday Hint:

To grate fresh ginger, first remove the thin outer skin with a vegetable peeler, paring knife or the edge of a spoon. Then grate the ginger on a fine grater or finely chop it with a French chef knife.

Golden Gate Chinese Chicken and Cabbage Sesame Salad

Smoked Chicken Salad with Dried Cherries and Onions

4½ cups diced smoked chicken

2¼ cups diced sweet onions

2¼ cups diced dried tart cherries

  2 cups mayonnaise

1½ cups diced celery

1½ cups pecan pieces, lightly toasted

  ½ cup fresh minced basil

  3 tablespoons fresh orange juice

  1 teaspoon orange zest

  ¾ teaspoon salt

  ¾ teaspoon black pepper

Place all ingredients in mixing bowl; stir gently until well combined. Refrigerate until ready to prepare sandwiches.

Makes 12 sandwiches (9 cups chicken salad)

Favorite recipe from **National Onion Association**

Colorful Turkey Pasta Salad

2½ cups tri-colored rotini pasta, cooked and drained

  2 cups cubed cooked turkey, white meat preferred

  ½ cup thinly sliced green onions

  ¼ cup chopped celery

  ¼ cup chopped fresh parsley

1½ teaspoons chopped fresh tarragon *or*
    ½ teaspoon dried tarragon leaves

  2 tablespoons reduced-calorie mayonnaise

  2 tablespoons tarragon vinegar

  1 tablespoon fresh lemon juice

  1 tablespoon canola or olive oil

1. In large bowl, combine pasta, turkey, onions, celery, parsley and tarragon.

2. In small bowl, mix together mayonnaise, vinegar, lemon juice and oil. Add to turkey mixture.

3. Mix well, coating all surfaces. Cover and refrigerate 1 to 2 hours or until chilled throughout.

Makes 4 servings

Favorite recipe from **California Poultry Federation**

Smoked Chicken Salad with Dried Cherries and Onions

Waldorf Chicken Salad

⅓ cup lemon juice

¼ cup honey

¼ cup vegetable oil

2 tablespoons Dijon-style mustard

1 tablespoon poppy seeds

½ teaspoon grated lemon peel

12 dried apricots, sliced (moist pack preferable)

2 cups cubed cooked chicken or turkey

2 apples, cored and diced

1 cup diced celery

⅓ cup toasted sliced or diced almonds

¼ cup minced green onions

Stir together lemon juice, honey, oil, mustard, poppy seeds and lemon peel in large bowl. Add apricots and let stand 30 minutes. Add chicken and toss lightly. Refrigerate until ready to serve.

To serve, add apples, celery, almonds and green onions to chicken mixture; toss to coat.

Makes 6 servings

Favorite recipe from **National Honey Board**

Marinated Vegetable Spinach Salad

Mustard-Tarragon Marinade (recipe follows)

8 ounces fresh mushrooms, quartered

2 slices purple onion, separated into rings

16 cherry tomatoes, halved

4 cups fresh spinach leaves, washed and stems removed

3 slices (3 ounces) SARGENTO® Light Deli Style Sliced Mozzarella Cheese, cut into julienne strips

Freshly ground black pepper

Prepare Mustard-Tarragon Marinade; set aside. Place mushrooms, onion and tomatoes in bowl. Toss with marinade and let stand 15 minutes. Arrange spinach on 4 individual plates. Divide marinated vegetables among plates and top each salad with ¼ of cheese. Serve with freshly ground black pepper, if desired. *Makes 4 servings*

Mustard-Tarragon Marinade

3 tablespoons red wine vinegar

1 tablespoon Dijon-style mustard

1½ teaspoons dried tarragon

2 tablespoons olive oil

Combine first 3 ingredients in small bowl. Slowly whisk oil into mixture until slightly thickened.

Mandarin Orange and Red Onion Salad

1 cup BLUE DIAMOND® Sliced Natural
    Almonds
1 tablespoon butter
2 tablespoons lemon juice
1 teaspoon Dijon mustard
1/2 teaspoon sugar
1/2 teaspoon salt
1/4 teaspoon white pepper
1/2 cup vegetable oil
1 head romaine lettuce, torn into pieces
1 can (11 ounces) mandarin orange
    segments, drained
1 small red onion, thinly sliced, rings
    separated

Sauté almonds in butter until golden; reserve.
Combine lemon juice, mustard, sugar, salt and
pepper in small bowl. Whisk in oil. Combine
lettuce, oranges, onion and almonds. Toss with
dressing. *Makes 4 to 6 servings*

Roasted Chicken Salad

2 cups cubed TYSON® Roasted Chicken
4 tablespoons mayonnaise
3 tablespoons sweet relish
1 tablespoon finely chopped celery
1 teaspoon finely chopped onion
1/4 teaspoon mustard
1/8 teaspoon garlic salt
    Salt and black pepper to taste

PREP: CLEAN: Wash hands. In large bowl,
combine all ingredients except chicken; mix well.
Stir in chicken. Cover; chill thoroughly.

SERVE: Serve on a bed of lettuce leaves, in tomato
cups or on kaiser rolls.

CHILL: Refrigerate leftovers immediately.
Makes 2 servings

PREP TIME: 5 minutes
COOK TIME: none

Fresh Fruity Chicken Salad

Yogurt Dressing (recipe follows)

2 cups cubed cooked chicken

1 cup cantaloupe balls

1 cup honeydew melon cubes

½ cup chopped celery

⅓ cup cashews

¼ cup sliced green onions

Lettuce leaves

Prepare Yogurt Dressing; set aside. Combine chicken, melon balls, celery, cashews and onions in large bowl. Add dressing; mix lightly. Cover. Refrigerate 1 hour. Serve on bed of lettuce.

Makes 4 servings

Yogurt Dressing

¼ cup plain yogurt

3 tablespoons mayonnaise

3 tablespoons fresh lime juice

¾ teaspoon ground coriander

½ teaspoon salt

Dash black pepper

Combine ingredients in small bowl; mix well.

Makes about ½ cup

Cheery Cherry Chicken Salad

2 cups cubed cooked chicken

½ cup dried tart cherries

¼ cup chopped walnuts

3 green onions, sliced

½ cup mayonnaise

¼ cup plain yogurt

1 tablespoon lemon juice

½ teaspoon dried oregano

Freshly ground black pepper, to taste

Lettuce leaves

Chopped fresh parsley (optional)

In large bowl, combine chicken, cherries, walnuts and onions; mix well. In small bowl, combine mayonnaise, yogurt, lemon juice, oregano and pepper; pour over chicken mixture. Mix gently. Refrigerate, covered, 1 to 2 hours. Serve on lettuce; garnish with parsley, if desired.

Makes 2 main-dish servings

*Favorite recipe from **Cherry Marketing Institute***

Holiday Hint:

This salad, enhanced with tart cherries, is a good use for leftover chicken. Make it ahead, refrigerate it and serve it following a long afternoon of holiday shopping.

Fresh Fruity Chicken Salad

Holiday Sides

Asparagus and Cheese Side Dish

1½ pounds fresh asparagus, trimmed

2 cups crushed saltine crackers

1 can (10¾ ounces) condensed cream of asparagus soup, undiluted

1 can (10¾ ounces) condensed cream of chicken soup, undiluted

¼ pound American cheese, cut into cubes

⅔ cup slivered almonds

1 egg

SLOW COOKER DIRECTIONS
Combine all ingredients in large bowl; stir well. Pour into slow cooker. Cover and cook on High 3 to 3½ hours. *Makes 4 to 6 servings*

Mashed Sweet Potatoes & Parsnips

2 large sweet potatoes (about 1¼ pounds), peeled and cut into 1-inch pieces

2 medium parsnips (about ½ pound), peeled and cut into ½-inch slices

¼ cup evaporated skim milk

1½ tablespoons margarine or butter

½ teaspoon salt

⅛ teaspoon ground nutmeg

¼ cup chopped chives or green onion tops

1. Combine sweet potatoes and parsnips in large saucepan. Cover with cold water and bring to a boil over high heat. Reduce heat; simmer uncovered 15 minutes or until vegetables are tender.

2. Drain vegetables and return to pan. Add milk, margarine, salt and nutmeg. Mash potato mixture over low heat to desired consistency. Stir in chives. *Makes 6 servings*

Asparagus and Cheese Side Dish

Apricot-Glazed Beets

1 large bunch fresh beets *or* 1 pound loose beets

1 cup apricot nectar

1 tablespoon cornstarch

2 tablespoons cider vinegar or red wine vinegar

8 dried apricot halves, cut into strips

¼ teaspoon salt

Additional apricot halves (optional)

Cut tops off beets, leaving at least 1 inch of stems (do not trim root ends). Scrub beets under running water with soft vegetable brush, being careful not to break skins. Place beets in medium saucepan; cover with water. Bring to a boil over high heat; reduce heat. Cover and simmer about 20 minutes or until just barely firm when pierced with fork and skins rub off easily. Transfer to plate; cool. Rinse saucepan.

Combine apricot nectar and cornstarch in same saucepan; stir in vinegar. Add apricot strips and salt. Cook over medium heat until mixture thickens.

Cut roots and stems from beets on plate*. Peel, halve and cut beets into ¼-inch-thick slices. Add beet slices to apricot mixture; toss gently to coat. Transfer to warm serving dish. Garnish as desired. Serve immediately with apricot halves.

Makes 4 side-dish servings

*Do not cut beets on cutting board; the juice will stain the board.

Brussels Sprouts in Mustard Sauce

1½ pounds fresh Brussels sprouts*

1 tablespoon butter or margarine

⅓ cup chopped shallots or onion

⅓ cup half-and-half

1 tablespoon plus 1½ teaspoons Dijon-style mustard or Dusseldorf mustard

¼ teaspoon salt

⅛ teaspoon black pepper or ground nutmeg

1½ tablespoons grated Parmesan cheese

*Or, substitute 2 (10-ounce) packages frozen Brussels sprouts for fresh Brussels sprouts. Cook according to package directions; drain and rinse as directed.

Trim stem from each Brussels sprout; pull off outer bruised leaves. Cut an "X" deep into stem end of each Brussels sprout. Bring 2 quarts salted water to a boil in saucepan large enough to allow Brussels sprouts to fit in a single layer. Add Brussels sprouts; return to a boil. Boil, uncovered, 7 to 10 minutes or until almost tender when pierced with fork. Drain in colander. Rinse under cold water to stop cooking; drain thoroughly.

Melt butter in same saucepan over medium heat. Add shallots; cook 3 minutes, stirring occasionally. Add half-and-half, mustard, salt and pepper. Simmer 1 minute or until thickened. Add drained Brussels sprouts; heat about 1 minute or until heated through, tossing gently with sauce. Sprinkle with cheese.

Makes 6 to 8 servings

Apricot-Glazed Beets

Apple & Carrot Casserole

6 large carrots, sliced
4 large apples, peeled, quartered, cored and sliced
5 tablespoons all-purpose flour
1 tablespoon packed brown sugar
½ teaspoon ground nutmeg
1 tablespoon margarine
½ cup orange juice
½ teaspoon salt (optional)

Preheat oven to 350°F. Cook carrots in large saucepan in boiling water 5 minutes; drain. Layer carrots and apples in large casserole. Combine flour, sugar and nutmeg; sprinkle over top. Dot with margarine; pour orange juice over flour mixture. Bake 30 minutes or until carrots are tender.

Makes 6 servings

Holiday Hint:

For this recipe, choose an apple variety that will hold its shape when baked. Winesap, Granny Smith, Rome Beauty and Golden Delicious apples are excellent choices.

Candied Pineapple Yams

5 pounds yams or sweet potatoes, washed and pierced with fork
½ cup DOLE® Pineapple Juice
¼ cup margarine, melted
½ teaspoon salt
½ teaspoon pumpkin pie spice
½ cup packed brown sugar
1 container (16 ounces) DOLE® Fresh Pineapple, cut into slices

• Place yams on foil-lined baking sheet. Bake at 350°F, 90 minutes or until yams are tender when pricked with fork.

• Spoon out baked yams from skins and place into large mixing bowl. Add pineapple juice, margarine, salt and pumpkin pie spice. Beat until fluffy.

• Spoon mixture into lightly greased 13×9-inch baking dish. Sprinkle with brown sugar. Arrange pineapple slices over yams. Continue baking at 350°F, 15 minutes or until hot. Garnish with fresh rosemary, if desired. Serve with roasted pork tenderloin and green peas. *Makes 10 servings*

Prep Time: 90 minutes

Apple & Carrot Casserole

Double-Baked Potatoes

3 large baking potatoes

4 tablespoons fat-free (skim) milk, warmed

1 cup (4 ounces) shredded reduced-fat
    Cheddar cheese

3/4 cup corn

1/2 teaspoon chili powder

1 tablespoon finely chopped fresh oregano *or*
    1/2 teaspoon dried oregano leaves

1 cup chopped onion

1/2 to 1 cup chopped poblano chili peppers

3 cloves garlic, minced

1/2 teaspoon salt

1/4 teaspoon black pepper

3 tablespoons chopped fresh cilantro

1. Preheat oven to 400°F. Scrub potatoes under running water with soft vegetable brush; rinse. Pierce each potato with fork. Wrap each potato in foil. Bake about 1 hour or until fork-tender. Remove potatoes; cool slightly. *Reduce oven temperature to 350°F.*

2. Cut potatoes in half lengthwise; scoop out inside being careful not to tear shells. Set shells aside. Beat potatoes in bowl with electric mixer until coarsely mashed. Add milk; beat until smooth. Stir in cheese, corn, chili powder and oregano. Set aside.

3. Spray medium skillet with nonstick cooking spray. Add onion, poblano peppers and garlic; cook and stir 5 to 8 minutes or until tender. Stir in salt and pepper.

4. Spoon potato mixture into reserved potato shells. Sprinkle with onion mixture. Place stuffed potatoes in small baking pan. Bake 20 to 30 minutes or until heated through. Sprinkle with cilantro.

Makes 6 servings

Holiday Hint:

Poblano chili peppers are dark green in color, triangular in shape and mild to quite hot in flavor. To reduce the heat of a chili pepper, remove the membranes and seeds. For a milder flavor in this recipe use Anaheim chilies instead.

Double-Baked Potato

Bruschetta

1 can (14½ ounces) DEL MONTE® Diced
   Tomatoes, drained
2 tablespoons chopped fresh basil *or*
   ½ teaspoon dried basil
1 small clove garlic, finely minced
½ French bread baguette, cut into ³⁄₈-inch-
   thick slices
2 tablespoons olive oil

1. Combine tomatoes, basil and garlic in 1-quart
bowl; cover and refrigerate at least ½ hour.

2. Preheat broiler. Place bread slices on baking
sheet; lightly brush both sides of bread with oil.
Broil until lightly toasted, turning to toast both
sides. Cool on wire rack.

3. Bring tomato mixture to room temperature.
Spoon tomato mixture over bread and serve
immediately. Sprinkle with additional fresh basil
leaves, if desired.   *Makes 8 appetizer servings*

NOTE: For a fat-free version, omit olive oil. For a
lower-fat variation, spray the bread with olive oil
cooking spray.

Prep Time: 15 minutes
Cook Time: 30 minutes

Corn Pudding Soufflé

2 tablespoons butter or margarine
2 tablespoons all-purpose flour
   Half-and-half
1 can (17 ounces) whole kernel corn,
   drained, liquid reserved
¼ cup canned chopped green chilies, drained
   Dash garlic powder
2 eggs, separated
¼ cup cream-style cottage cheese

Preheat oven to 350°F. Melt butter in medium
saucepan over medium heat. Stir in flour until
smooth. Add enough half-and-half to corn liquid
to measure 1 cup. Gradually stir liquid into
saucepan. Continue stirring until sauce is smooth
and hot. Stir in corn, chilies and garlic powder.

Bring corn mixture to a boil over medium heat,
stirring constantly. Reduce heat to low. Beat egg
yolks in small bowl. Stir about ¼ cup of hot sauce
into egg yolks, beating constantly. Stir egg yolk
mixture back into sauce. Remove from heat; stir in
cottage cheese. Beat egg whites in narrow bowl
until stiff peaks form. Fold egg whites into corn
mixture. Pour into *ungreased* 1½-quart soufflé dish.
Bake 30 minutes or until toothpick inserted in
center comes out clean.   *Makes 4 to 6 servings*

Eggplant Italiano

1¼ pounds eggplant, cut into 1-inch cubes

2 medium onions, thinly sliced

2 ribs celery, cut into 1-inch pieces

1 can (16 ounces) diced tomatoes, undrained

3 tablespoons tomato sauce

1 tablespoon olive oil, divided

½ cup pitted ripe olives, cut in half

2 tablespoons balsamic vinegar

1 tablespoon sugar

1 tablespoon capers, drained

1 teaspoon dried oregano or basil leaves

Salt and black pepper to taste

SLOW COOKER DIRECTIONS

Combine eggplant, onions, celery, tomatoes, tomato sauce and oil in slow cooker. Cover and cook on LOW 3½ to 4 hours or until eggplant is tender.

Stir in olives, vinegar, sugar, capers and oregano. Season with salt and pepper to taste. Cover and cook 45 minutes to 1 hour or until heated through.

Makes 6 servings

Golden Herb Stuffing

2 tablespoons margarine or butter

1 medium carrot, diced

1 rib celery, diced

1 small onion, finely chopped

1 envelope LIPTON® RECIPE SECRETS® Savory Herb with Garlic Soup Mix

2 cups fresh bread crumbs

½ cup chopped walnuts or pecans (optional)

¼ cup milk or water

In 10-inch skillet, melt margarine over medium heat and cook carrot, celery and onion, stirring occasionally, 4 minutes.

In medium bowl, combine vegetables with remaining ingredients; toss well. Makes enough stuffing for 1 roasting chicken, 2 Cornish hens, 8 pork chops or 8 fish fillets. Or, turn into 1-quart baking dish and bake covered at 375°F for 25 minutes. Remove cover and bake an additional 5 minutes or until top is lightly browned.

Makes 4 servings

Menu Suggestion: Serve as above with whole berry cranberry sauce and baked apples.

Sweet Potato Gratin

3 pounds sweet potatoes (about 5 large)

½ cup butter or margarine, divided

¼ cup plus 2 tablespoons packed light brown sugar, divided

2 eggs

⅔ cup orange juice

2 teaspoons ground cinnamon, divided

½ teaspoon salt

¼ teaspoon ground nutmeg

⅓ cup all-purpose flour

¼ cup uncooked old-fashioned oats

⅓ cup chopped pecans or walnuts

Preheat oven to 350°F. Bake sweet potatoes about 1 hour or until tender. Or, pierce sweet potatoes several times with table fork and place on microwavable plate. Microwave at HIGH 16 to 18 minutes, rotating and turning over potatoes after 9 minutes. Let stand 5 minutes.

Cut hot sweet potatoes lengthwise into halves. Scrape hot pulp from skins into large bowl.

Beat ¼ cup butter and 2 tablespoons sugar into sweet potatoes with electric mixer at medium speed until butter is melted. Add eggs, orange juice,

1½ teaspoons cinnamon, salt and nutmeg. Beat until smooth. Pour mixture into 1½-quart baking dish or gratin dish; smooth top.

For topping, combine flour, oats, remaining ¼ cup sugar and remaining ½ teaspoon cinnamon in medium bowl. Cut in remaining ¼ cup butter until mixture resembles coarse crumbs. Stir in pecans. Sprinkle topping evenly over sweet potatoes.

Bake 25 to 30 minutes or until sweet potatoes are heated through. For crisper topping, broil 5 inches from heat 2 to 3 minutes or until golden brown.

Makes 6 to 8 servings

Holiday Hint:

Sweet Potato Gratin is an excellent side dish for a holiday dinner. Prepare it a day ahead but do not bake it. Cover the baking dish and refrigerate it overnight. Let it stand one hour at room temperature before baking.

Sweet Potato Gratin

Vegetable Rings on Broccoli Spears

1 small bunch broccoli (about 12 ounces), stalks peeled

1 red bell pepper, sliced into thin rings

3 (1/4-inch-thick) center slices mild white onion

2 tablespoons butter or margarine

1/2 teaspoon wine vinegar

1/2 teaspoon dried rosemary

1. To steam broccoli, place steamer basket in large saucepan; add 1 inch of water. (Water should not touch bottom of basket.) Place spears in steamer. Separate onion slices into rings; place on broccoli. Cover. Bring to a boil over high heat; steam about 8 minutes or until broccoli is crisp-tender. Add water, as necessary, to prevent pan from boiling dry.

2. Uncover; place pepper rings on top. Cover; steam briefly until pepper rings brighten in color but still hold their shape. Remove from heat; transfer vegetables with slotted spoon to warm serving dish. Melt butter in small saucepan over medium heat; stir in vinegar and rosemary. Drizzle evenly over vegetables. Serve immediately.

Makes 4 side-dish servings

Escalloped Corn

2 tablespoons butter or margarine

1/2 cup chopped onion

3 tablespoons all-purpose flour

1 cup milk

4 cups frozen corn, thawed, divided

1/2 teaspoon salt

1/2 teaspoon dried thyme leaves

1/4 teaspoon black pepper

1/8 teaspoon ground nutmeg

SLOW COOKER DIRECTIONS

Heat butter in small saucepan over medium heat. Add onion; cook and stir 5 minutes or until tender. Add flour. Cook over medium heat 1 minute, stirring constantly. Stir in milk and heat to a boil. Boil 1 minute or until thickened, stirring constantly.

Process half the corn in food processor or blender until coarsely chopped. Combine milk mixture, processed and whole corn, salt, thyme, pepper and nutmeg in slow cooker. Cover and cook on LOW 3 1/2 to 4 hours or until mixture is bubbly around edge.

Makes 6 servings

Variation: If desired, add 1/2 cup (2 ounces) shredded Cheddar cheese and 2 tablespoons grated Parmesan cheese before serving; stir until melted. Garnish with additional shredded Cheddar cheese, if desired.

Vegetable Rings on Broccoli Spears

Easy Dilled Succotash

1½ cups frozen lima beans

1 small onion, finely chopped

1½ cups frozen corn, thawed

1 teaspoon salt

1 teaspoon sugar

1 teaspoon dried dill weed

1. Bring ½ cup water to a boil in medium saucepan over high heat. Add beans and onion; cover. Reduce heat to low. Simmer 8 minutes.

2. Stir corn into bean mixture; cover. Simmer 5 minutes or until vegetables are tender. Drain bean mixture; discard liquid.

3. Place bean mixture in serving bowl; stir in salt, sugar and dill weed until well blended. Garnish as desired. *Makes 4 servings*

Mrs. Grady's Beans

½ pound lean ground beef

1 small onion, chopped

8 bacon strips, chopped

1 can (about 15 ounces) pinto beans, undrained

1 can (about 15 ounces) butter beans, rinsed and drained, reserve ¼ cup liquid

1 can (about 15 ounces) kidney beans, rinsed and drained

¼ cup ketchup

2 tablespoons molasses

½ teaspoon dry mustard

½ cup granulated sugar

¼ cup packed brown sugar

SLOW COOKER DIRECTIONS

Brown ground beef, onion and bacon in medium saucepan over high heat; drain off fat. Stir in beans and liquid; set aside.

Combine ketchup, molasses and mustard in medium bowl. Mix in sugars. Stir ketchup mixture into beef mixture; mix well. Transfer to slow cooker. Cover and cook on LOW 2 to 3 hours or until heated through. *Makes 6 to 8 servings*

Easy Dilled Succotash

Oven-Roasted Peppers and Onions

Olive oil cooking spray

2 medium green bell peppers

2 medium red bell peppers

2 medium yellow bell peppers

4 small onions

1 teaspoon Italian herb seasoning

½ teaspoon dried basil leaves

¼ teaspoon ground cumin

1. Preheat oven to 375°F. Spray 15×10-inch jelly-roll pan with cooking spray. Cut bell peppers into 1½-inch pieces. Cut onions into quarters. Place vegetables on prepared pan. Spray vegetables with cooking spray. Bake 20 minutes; stir. Sprinkle with herb blend, basil and cumin.

2. *Increase oven temperature to 425°F.* Bake 20 minutes or until edges are darkened and vegetables are crisp-tender. *Makes 6 servings*

Rustic Potatoes au Gratin

½ cup milk

1 can (10¾ ounces) condensed Cheddar cheese soup, undiluted

1 package (8 ounces) cream cheese, softened

1 clove garlic, minced

¼ teaspoon ground nutmeg

⅛ teaspoon black pepper

2 pounds baking potatoes, cut into ¼-inch slices

1 small onion, thinly sliced

Paprika (optional)

SLOW COOKER DIRECTIONS

Heat milk in small saucepan over medium heat until small bubbles form around edge of pan. Remove from heat. Add soup, cream cheese, garlic, nutmeg and pepper. Stir until smooth. Layer ¼ of potatoes and ¼ of onion in bottom of slow cooker. Top with ¼ of soup mixture. Repeat layers 3 times, using remaining potatoes, onion and soup mixture. Cover and cook on LOW 6½ to 7 hours or until potatoes are tender and most of liquid is absorbed. Sprinkle with paprika, if desired.

Makes 6 servings

Oven-Roasted Peppers and Onions

Dry-Cooked Green Beans

4 ounces lean ground pork or turkey

2 tablespoons plus 1 teaspoon light soy sauce, divided

2 tablespoons plus 1 teaspoon rice wine or dry sherry, divided

½ teaspoon sesame oil

2 tablespoons water

1 teaspoon sugar

3 cups vegetable oil

1 pound fresh green beans, trimmed and cut into 2-inch lengths

1 tablespoon sliced green onion (white part only)

Carrot flowers for garnish

1. Combine pork, 1 teaspoon soy sauce, 1 teaspoon rice wine and sesame oil in medium bowl; mix well. Set aside.

2. Combine water, sugar, remaining 2 tablespoons soy sauce and 2 tablespoons rice wine in small bowl; mix well. Set aside.

3. Heat vegetable oil in wok over medium-high heat until oil registers 375°F on deep-fry thermometer. Carefully add ½ of beans and fry 2 to 3 minutes or until beans blister and are crisp-tender. Remove beans with slotted spoon to paper towels; drain. Reheat oil and repeat with remaining beans.

4. Pour off oil; heat wok over medium-high heat 30 seconds. Add pork mixture and stir-fry about 2 minutes or until well browned. Add beans and soy sauce mixture; toss until heated through. Transfer to serving dish. Sprinkle with green onion. Garnish, if desired. Serve immediately.

Makes 4 servings

Savory Matchstick Carrots

½ pound carrots, cut into julienne strips

1 small turnip, cut into julienne strips*

½ cup water

3 tablespoons butter or margarine, cut into chunks

1½ teaspoons fresh thyme leaves *or* ½ teaspoon dried thyme leaves

⅛ teaspoon each salt and black pepper

Green onion tops and edible flowers, such as violets, for garnish

*Or, substitute two extra carrots for turnip.

1. Place carrot and turnip strips in medium saucepan. Add water; cover. Bring to a boil over high heat; reduce heat to medium. Simmer 5 to 8 minutes until crisp-tender.

2. Drain vegetables in colander. Melt butter over medium heat in same saucepan; stir in thyme, salt and pepper. Add carrots; toss gently to coat. Transfer carrot mixture to warm serving dish. Garnish, if desired. Serve immediately.

Makes 4 servings

Dry-Cooked Green Beans

Polenta Triangles

3 cups cold water
1 cup yellow cornmeal
1 envelope LIPTON® RECIPE SECRETS®
Golden Onion or Onion Soup Mix
1 can (4 ounces) mild chopped green chilies,
drained
½ cup thawed frozen or drained canned
whole kernel corn
⅓ cup finely chopped roasted red peppers
½ cup shredded sharp Cheddar cheese (about
2 ounces)

In 3-quart saucepan, bring water to a boil over high
heat. With wire whisk, stir in cornmeal, then
golden onion soup mix. Reduce heat to low and
simmer uncovered, stirring constantly, 25 minutes
or until thickened. Stir in chilies, corn and roasted
red peppers.

Spread into lightly greased 9-inch square baking
pan; sprinkle with cheese. Let stand 20 minutes or
until firm; cut into triangles. Serve at room
temperature or heat in oven at 350°F for 5 minutes
or until warm.   *Makes about 24 triangles*

Country Corn Bake

2 cans (11 ounces each) Mexican-style whole
kernel corn, drained*
1 can (10¾ ounces) condensed cream of
potato soup
1⅓ cups *French's® Taste Toppers*™ French Fried
Onions, divided
½ cup milk
½ cup thinly sliced celery
½ cup (2 ounces) shredded Cheddar cheese
2 tablespoons bacon bits**

*Or, substitute 1 bag (16 ounces) frozen whole kernel corn,
thawed and drained.

**Or, substitute 2 slices crumbled, cooked bacon.

Preheat oven to 375°F. Combine corn, soup, *⅔ cup
Taste Toppers*, milk, celery, cheese and bacon bits
in large bowl. Spoon mixture into 2-quart square
baking dish. Cover; bake 30 minutes or until hot
and bubbly. Stir; sprinkle with remaining *⅔ cup
Taste Toppers*. Bake, uncovered, 3 minutes or until
Taste Toppers are golden.

Makes 4 to 6 servings

Prep Time: 10 minutes
Cook Time: 33 minutes

Honey-Glazed Sweet Potatoes

1½ pounds sweet potatoes or yams, peeled and
    quartered
⅔ cup orange juice, divided
½ teaspoon ground ginger
½ teaspoon ground nutmeg
1 tablespoon butter or margarine
1 tablespoon cornstarch
⅓ cup honey

MICROWAVE DIRECTIONS
Combine sweet potatoes and ⅓ cup orange juice in
2-quart microwave-safe baking dish; sprinkle with
ginger and nutmeg. Dot with butter. Cover and
microwave at HIGH (100%) 7 to 10 minutes or
until sweet potatoes are tender, stirring halfway
through cooking time. Combine cornstarch,
remaining ⅓ cup orange juice and honey in
medium microwave-safe bowl. Microwave at
HIGH 2 minutes or until thickened, stirring every
30 seconds. Drain liquid from sweet potatoes; add
to honey mixture. Microwave at HIGH 1 minute.
Pour sauce over sweet potatoes and microwave at
HIGH 1 minute more or until sweet potatoes are
thoroughly heated. *Makes 4 servings*

Favorite recipe from **National Honey Board**

Swiss Cheese Scalloped Potatoes

2 pounds baking potatoes, peeled and thinly
    sliced
½ cup finely chopped yellow onion
¼ teaspoon salt
¼ teaspoon ground nutmeg
2 tablespoons butter, cut into ⅛-inch pieces
½ cup milk
2 tablespoons all-purpose flour
3 ounces Swiss cheese slices, torn into small
    pieces
¼ cup finely chopped green onion (optional)

1. Layer half the potatoes, ¼ cup onion,
⅛ teaspoon salt, ⅛ teaspoon nutmeg and
1 tablespoon butter in slow cooker. Repeat layers.
Cover and cook on LOW 7 hours or on HIGH
4 hours. Remove potatoes with slotted spoon to
serving dish.

2. Blend milk and flour in small bowl until
smooth. Stir mixture into slow cooker. Add cheese;
stir to combine. If slow cooker is on LOW, turn to
HIGH, cover and cook until slightly thickened,
about 10 minutes. Stir. Pour cheese mixture over
potatoes and serve. Garnish with chopped green
onions, if desired. *Makes 5 to 6 servings*

Hot Hush Puppies

WESSON® Vegetable Oil

1¾ cups cornmeal

½ cup all-purpose flour

1 teaspoon sugar

¾ teaspoon baking soda

½ teaspoon salt

½ teaspoon garlic salt

½ cup diced onion

½ to 1 (4-ounce) can diced jalapeño peppers

1 cup buttermilk

1 egg, beaten

Fill a large deep-fry pot or electric skillet to half its depth with Wesson® Oil. Heat oil to 400°F. Meanwhile, in a large bowl, sift together cornmeal, flour, sugar, baking soda, salt and garlic salt; blend well. Add onion and jalapeño peppers; stir until well blended. In small bowl, combine buttermilk and egg; add to dry ingredients. Stir until batter is moist and *all* ingredients are combined. Working in small batches, carefully drop batter by heaping tablespoons into hot oil. Fry until golden brown, turning once during frying. Remove and drain on paper towels. Serve with your favorite salsa or dipping sauce.

Makes 36 hush puppies

Swiss Vegetable Medley

1 can (10¾ ounces) condensed cream of mushroom soup

⅓ cup sour cream

¼ teaspoon ground black pepper

1 bag (16 ounces) frozen vegetable combination, such as broccoli, cauliflower and red bell pepper, thawed and drained

1⅓ cups *French's® Taste Toppers*™ French Fried Onions, divided

1 cup (4 ounces) shredded Swiss cheese, divided

Preheat oven to 350°F. Combine soup, sour cream and ground pepper in 2-quart shallow baking dish; stir until well blended. Add vegetables, ⅔ cup **Taste Toppers** and ½ cup cheese; mix well.

Cover; bake 30 minutes or until heated through and vegetables are tender. Stir; sprinkle with remaining ⅔ cup **Taste Toppers** and ½ cup cheese. Bake 5 minutes or until **Taste Toppers** are golden.

Makes 6 servings

Prep Time: 10 minutes
Cook Time: 35 minutes

Hot Hush Puppies

Roasted Potatoes and Pearl Onions

3 pounds red potatoes, well-scrubbed and
    cut into 1½-inch cubes
1 package (10 ounces) pearl onions, peeled
2 tablespoons olive oil
2 teaspoons dried basil leaves or thyme leaves
1 teaspoon paprika
¾ teaspoon salt
¾ teaspoon dried rosemary, crushed
¾ teaspoon black pepper

1. Preheat oven to 400°F. Spray large shallow
roasting pan (do not use glass or potatoes will not
brown) with nonstick cooking spray.

2. Add potatoes and onions to pan; drizzle with oil.
Combine basil, paprika, salt, rosemary and pepper
in small bowl; mix well. Sprinkle over potatoes and
onions; toss well to coat lightly with oil and
seasonings.

3. Bake 20 minutes; toss well. Continue baking
15 to 20 minutes or until potatoes are browned and
tender. *Makes 8 servings*

Festive Sweet Potato Combo

2 cans (16 ounces each) sweet potatoes,
    drained
1⅓ cups *French's® Taste Toppers™* French Fried
    Onions, divided
1 large apple, sliced into thin wedges
2 cans (8 ounces each) crushed pineapple,
    undrained
3 tablespoons packed light brown sugar
¾ teaspoon ground cinnamon

Preheat oven to 375°F. Grease 2-quart shallow
baking dish. Layer sweet potatoes, ⅔ cup **Taste
Toppers** and half of the apple wedges in prepared
baking dish.

Stir together pineapple with liquid, sugar and
cinnamon in medium bowl. Spoon pineapple
mixture over sweet potato mixture. Arrange
remaining apple wedges over pineapple layer.

Cover; bake 35 minutes or until heated through.
Uncover; sprinkle with remaining ⅔ cup **Taste
Toppers**. Bake 3 minutes or until **Taste Toppers** are
golden. *Makes 6 servings*

Prep Time: 10 minutes
Cook Time: 38 minutes

*Roasted Potatoes and
Pearl Onions*

Broccoli Timbales

1 pound fresh broccoli

3 eggs

1 cup heavy cream

1 tablespoon lemon juice

1/4 teaspoon salt

   Dash pepper

4 cups boiling water

   Chopped tomato and green onion top
      pieces for garnish

Generously butter six 6-ounce ramekins or custard cups; set in 13×9-inch baking pan. Preheat oven to 375°F.

Cut broccoli into florets; set aside. Peel stalks with vegetable peeler. Cut into 1-inch pieces, then cut each piece lengthwise in half. Bring 1/2 inch of water in medium saucepan to a boil over high heat. Reduce heat to medium-low; add broccoli stem pieces. Cover; simmer about 10 minutes or until fork-tender. Transfer cooked stems with slotted spoon to food processor or blender. Add florets to same pan. Cover; simmer about 5 minutes or until florets turn bright green. Drain.

Add eggs to stem pieces in food processor; process until smooth. Add cream; pulse to blend. Add lemon juice, salt and pepper; pulse once. Set aside 6 small florets for garnish. Chop remaining florets; add to food processor. Pulse several times to blend.

Divide mixture evenly into prepared ramekins. Add boiling water to pan so water comes halfway up sides of ramekins. Bake 25 to 30 minutes or until knife inserted in center comes out clean. Top with reserved florets. Garnish, if desired. Let stand 5 minutes. Serve in ramekins.

Makes 6 servings

German Potato Salad

4 cups sliced peeled Colorado potatoes

4 slices bacon

3/4 cup chopped onion

1/4 cup sugar

3 tablespoons all-purpose flour

1 1/2 teaspoons salt

1 teaspoon celery seeds

1/4 teaspoon black pepper

1 cup water

3/4 cup vinegar

2 hard-cooked eggs, chopped

Cook potatoes in boiling water until tender; drain. Meanwhile, cook bacon in medium skillet. Drain on paper towels; cool and crumble. Cook and stir onion in drippings until tender. Combine sugar, flour, salt, celery seeds and pepper; blend in water and vinegar. Stir into onion in skillet; heat until bubbly. Pour over combined potatoes, bacon and eggs; toss. Serve immediately. *Makes 6 servings*

Favorite recipe from **Colorado Potato Administrative Committee**

Broccoli Timbales

Herbed Mushroom Vegetable Medley

4 ounces button or crimini mushrooms

1 medium red or yellow bell pepper, cut into ¼-inch-wide strips

1 medium zucchini, cut crosswise into ¼-inch-thick slices

1 medium yellow squash, cut crosswise into ¼-inch-thick slices

3 tablespoons butter or margarine, melted

1 tablespoon chopped fresh thyme leaves *or* 1 teaspoon dried thyme leaves

1 tablespoon chopped fresh basil leaves *or* 1 teaspoon dried basil leaves

1 tablespoon chopped fresh chives

1 clove garlic, minced

¼ teaspoon salt

¼ teaspoon black pepper

1. Prepare barbecue grill for direct cooking.

2. Thinly slice mushrooms. Combine mushrooms, bell pepper, zucchini and squash in large bowl. Combine butter, thyme, basil, chives, garlic, salt and black pepper in small bowl. Pour over vegetable mixture; toss to coat well.

3. Transfer mixture to 20×14-inch sheet of heavy-duty foil; wrap. Place foil packet on grid. Grill packet, on covered grill, over medium coals 20 to 25 minutes or until vegetables are tender. Open packet carefully to serve. *Makes 4 to 6 servings*

Green Bean Bundles

8 ounces haricot vert beans or other tiny, young green beans

1 yellow squash, about 1½ inches in diameter

1 tablespoon olive oil

1 clove garlic, minced

¼ teaspoon dried tarragon leaves

Salt and pepper

Place beans in colander; rinse well. Snap off stem end from each bean; arrange beans in 8 stacks, about 10 to 12 beans per stack. Cut eight ½-inch-thick slices of squash; hollow out with spoon to within ¼ inch of rind. Thread bean stacks through squash pieces as if each piece were a napkin ring.

Place steamer basket in large stockpot or saucepan; add 1 inch water. (Water should not touch bottom of basket.) Place bean bundles in steamer basket. Cover. Bring to a boil over high heat; steam 4 minutes or until beans are bright green and crisp-tender. Add water, as necessary, to prevent pan from boiling dry.

Meanwhile, heat oil in small skillet over medium-high heat. Cook and stir garlic and tarragon in hot oil until garlic is soft but not brown. Transfer bean bundles to warm serving plate and pour garlic oil over top. Season to taste with salt and pepper. Garnish, if desired. Serve immediately.

Makes 8 side-dish servings

Herbed Mushroom Vegetable Medley

One-Dish Delights

Spaghetti with Tomatoes and Olives

2 tablespoons extra-virgin olive oil

3 cloves garlic, finely chopped

1½ pounds fresh ripe tomatoes, seeded and chopped (about 3 cups)

1 tablespoon tomato paste

1 teaspoon dried oregano

⅛ teaspoon ground red pepper

½ cup pitted brine-cured black olives, coarsely chopped

2 tablespoons capers

Salt and pepper

1 package (16 ounces) BARILLA® Thin Spaghetti

Grated Parmesan cheese

1. Heat olive oil and garlic in large skillet over low heat until garlic begins to sizzle. Add tomatoes, tomato paste, oregano and red pepper; simmer, uncovered, until sauce is thickened, about 15 minutes. Add olives, capers and salt and pepper to taste.

2. Meanwhile, cook spaghetti according to package directions; drain.

3. Toss spaghetti with sauce. Sprinkle with cheese before serving. *Makes 6 to 8 servings*

Holiday Hint:

Capers are the tiny dark green flower buds of a Mediterrean bush that have been preserved in a vinegary brine. Capers have a spicy, slightly bitter flavor.

Spaghetti with Tomatoes and Olives

Turkey and Rice Quiche

3 cups cooked rice, cooled to room
     temperature
1½ cups chopped cooked turkey
 1 medium tomato, seeded and finely diced
 ¼ cup sliced green onions
 ¼ cup finely diced green bell pepper
 1 tablespoon chopped fresh basil *or*
     1 teaspoon dried basil leaves
 ½ teaspoon seasoned salt
 ⅛ to ¼ teaspoon ground red pepper
 ½ cup skim milk
 3 eggs, beaten
     Vegetable cooking spray
 ½ cup (2 ounces) shredded Cheddar cheese
 ½ cup (2 ounces) shredded mozzarella cheese

Combine rice, turkey, tomato, onions, bell pepper,
basil, salt, red pepper, milk and eggs in 13×9×2-
inch pan coated with cooking spray. Top with
cheeses. Bake at 375°F for 20 minutes or until
knife inserted near center comes out clean. To
serve, cut quiche into 8 squares; cut each square
diagonally into 2 triangles.

Makes 8 servings (2 triangles each)

Favorite recipe from **USA Rice Federation**

Chicken and Zucchini Casserole

 3 cups STOVE TOP® Chicken Flavor or
     Cornbread Stuffing Mix in the Canister
1¼ cups hot water
 3 tablespoons margarine or butter, divided
 ¾ pound boneless skinless chicken breasts,
     cubed
 2 medium zucchini, cut into ½-inch pieces
1½ cups (6 ounces) shredded Cheddar cheese
 1 can (8 ounces) water chestnuts, drained,
     halved (optional)
 ½ teaspoon dried basil leaves
 ¼ teaspoon pepper

MIX stuffing mix, water and 2 tablespoons
margarine in large bowl just until margarine is
melted and stuffing mix is moistened.

PLACE chicken, zucchini and remaining
1 tablespoon margarine in 3-quart microwavable
casserole. Cover loosely with wax paper.

MICROWAVE on HIGH 4 minutes, stirring
halfway through cooking time. Stir in prepared
stuffing, cheese, water chestnuts, basil and pepper
until well mixed. Cover.

MICROWAVE 10 minutes, stirring halfway
through cooking time. Let stand 5 minutes.

Makes 6 servings

Prep Time: 10 minutes
Cook Time: 20 minutes

Turkey and Rice Quiche

Elegant Crabmeat Frittata

  3 tablespoons butter or margarine, divided
1/4 pound fresh mushrooms, sliced
  2 green onions, cut into thin slices
  8 eggs, separated
1/4 cup milk
1/2 teaspoon hot pepper sauce
1/4 teaspoon salt
1/2 pound lump crabmeat or imitation
    crabmeat, flaked and picked over to
    remove any shells
1/2 cup (2 ounces) shredded Swiss cheese

1. Melt 2 tablespoons butter in large ovenproof skillet over medium-high heat. Add mushrooms and onions; cook and stir 3 to 5 minutes or until vegetables are tender. Remove from skillet; set aside.

2. Beat egg yolks with electric mixer at high speed until slightly thickened and lemon color. Stir in milk, hot pepper sauce and salt.

3. Beat egg whites in clean large bowl with electric mixer at high speed until foamy. Gradually add to egg yolk mixture, whisking just until blended.

4. Melt remaining 1 tablespoon butter in skillet. Pour egg mixture into skillet. Cook until egg is almost set. Remove from heat.

5. Preheat broiler. Broil frittata 4 to 6 inches from heat until top is set. Top with crabmeat, mushroom mixture and cheese. Return frittata to broiler; broil until cheese is melted. Garnish, if desired. Serve immediately. *Makes 4 servings*

Family Baked Bean Dinner

  1 can (20 ounces) DOLE® Pineapple Chunks
1/2 DOLE® Green Bell Pepper, julienne-cut
1/2 cup chopped onion
  1 pound Polish sausage or frankfurters, cut
    into 1-inch chunks
1/3 cup packed brown sugar
  1 teaspoon dry mustard
  2 cans (16 ounces each) baked beans

MICROWAVE DIRECTIONS

• Drain pineapple; reserve juice for beverage. Add green pepper and onion to 13×9-inch microwavable dish.

• Cover; microwave on HIGH (100% power) 3 minutes. Add sausage, arranging around edges of dish. Cover; continue microwaving on HIGH (100% power) 6 minutes.

• In bowl, combine brown sugar and mustard; stir in beans and pineapple. Add to sausage mixture. Stir to combine. Microwave, uncovered, on HIGH (100% power) 8 to 10 minutes, stirring after 4 minutes. *Makes 6 servings*

Elegant Crabmeat Frittata

Barley with Chicken and Belgioioso® Parmesan Cheese

5 cups water

⅔ cup pearl barley

½ pound boneless skinless chicken breasts

¾ cup chopped carrots

¾ cup chopped celery

¾ cup chopped leeks (white and pale green parts only)

1 tablespoon plus 1½ teaspoons chopped onion

½ cup chopped fresh parsley

¼ cup chicken stock or canned broth

6 tablespoons grated BELGIOIOSO® Parmesan Cheese, divided

Pepper to taste

Bring water and barley to boil in heavy medium saucepan. Reduce heat, cover and simmer until barley is tender, stirring occasionally, about 45 minutes. Drain. Transfer to large bowl. Set aside.

Preheat broiler. Broil chicken breasts until cooked through, about 3 minutes per side. Transfer chicken to plate; cool. Shred chicken into pieces.

Combine carrots, celery, leeks and onion in heavy, large nonstick skillet. Cover and cook over low heat until tender, stirring frequently and adding small amount of water if vegetables begin to stick, about 25 minutes. Add barley, chicken, parsley, stock and 3 tablespoons BelGioioso Parmesan Cheese; stir until heated through. Season with pepper. Divide barley mixture among plates. Sprinkle with remaining 3 tablespoons cheese and serve.

Makes 4 servings

Cheesy Pork and Potatoes

½ pound ground pork, cooked and crumbled

½ cup finely crushed saltine crackers

⅓ cup barbecue sauce

1 egg

3 tablespoons margarine

1 tablespoon vegetable oil

4 potatoes, peeled and thinly sliced

1 onion, thinly sliced

1 cup grated mozzarella cheese

⅔ cup evaporated milk

1 teaspoon salt

¼ teaspoon paprika

⅛ teaspoon black pepper

Chopped fresh parsley

SLOW COOKER DIRECTIONS

Combine pork, crackers, barbecue sauce and egg in large bowl; shape mixture into 6 patties. Heat margarine and oil in medium skillet. Sauté potatoes and onion until lightly browned. Drain and place in slow cooker.

Combine cheese, milk, salt, paprika and pepper in small bowl. Pour into slow cooker. Layer pork patties on top. Cover and cook on LOW 3 to 5 hours. Garnish with parsley. *Makes 6 servings*

Country-Style Lasagna

9 lasagna noodles (2 inches wide)
2 cans (14½ ounces each) DEL MONTE®
   Italian Recipe Stewed Tomatoes
  Milk
2 tablespoons butter or margarine
3 tablespoons all-purpose flour
1 teaspoon dried basil, crushed
1 cup diced cooked ham
2 cups (8 ounces) shredded mozzarella cheese

1. Cook noodles according to package directions; rinse, drain and separate noodles.

2. Meanwhile, drain tomatoes, reserving liquid; pour liquid into measuring cup. Add milk to measure 2 cups.

3. Melt butter in large saucepan; stir in flour and basil. Cook over medium heat 3 minutes, stirring constantly. Stir in reserved liquid; cook until thickened, stirring constantly. Season to taste with salt and pepper, if desired. Stir in tomatoes.

4. Spread thin layer of sauce on bottom of 11×7-inch or 2-quart baking dish. Top with 3 noodles and ⅓ each of sauce, ham and cheese; repeat layers twice, ending with cheese.

5. Bake, uncovered, at 375°F 25 minutes. Serve with grated Parmesan cheese and garnish, if desired.
Makes 6 servings

Prep Time: 15 minutes
Cook Time: 25 minutes

Easy Beef and Rice Stew

2 tablespoons flour
½ teaspoon salt
¼ teaspoon pepper
1 pound boneless beef top round, cut into
   ¾-inch chunks
1 tablespoon oil
2 medium carrots, diagonally sliced
1 medium onion, coarsely chopped
1 jar (4½ ounces) sliced mushrooms, drained
1 can (14½ ounces) whole tomatoes,
   undrained, coarsely chopped
1 can (10¼ ounces) beef gravy
¼ cup burgundy or other dry red wine
1½ cups MINUTE® Original Rice, uncooked

MIX flour, salt and pepper in large bowl. Add meat; toss to coat.

HEAT oil in large skillet on medium-high heat. Add meat; cook and stir until browned. Add carrots, onion and mushrooms; cook and stir 2 minutes.

STIR in tomatoes, gravy and wine. Bring to a boil. Reduce heat to low; cover and simmer 10 minutes.

STIR in rice; cover. Remove from heat. Let stand 5 minutes. Stir. *Makes 4 servings*

Prep Time: 10 minutes
Cook Time: 20 minutes

Fettuccine Gorgonzola with Sun-Dried Tomatoes

8 ounces uncooked spinach or tri-color fettuccine

1 cup low-fat cottage cheese

½ cup plain nonfat yogurt

½ cup (2 ounces) crumbled Gorgonzola cheese

⅛ teaspoon white pepper

2 cups rehydrated sun-dried tomatoes (4 ounces dry), cut into strips

1. Cook pasta according to package directions, omitting salt. Drain well. Cover to keep warm.

2. Combine cottage cheese and yogurt in food processor or blender; process until smooth. Heat cottage cheese mixture in small saucepan over low heat. Add Gorgonzola and white pepper; stir until cheese is melted.

3. Return pasta to saucepan; add tomatoes. Pour cheese mixture over pasta; mix well. Garnish as desired. Serve immediately.   *Makes 4 servings*

Herbed Chicken over Spinach Fettuccine

10 ounces uncooked spinach fettuccine

1 tablespoon olive oil

8 boneless skinless chicken thighs (1¼ pounds), cut into 1-inch pieces

1½ teaspoons dried oregano leaves

1½ teaspoons dried thyme leaves

1 cup dry white wine

½ cup water

1 teaspoon chicken bouillon granules

Pinch sugar

2 tablespoons cold butter, cut into cubes

1. Cook pasta according to package directions; drain.

2. While pasta is cooking, heat oil in large nonstick skillet over medium heat. Add chicken, oregano and thyme; cook 3 minutes or until chicken is no longer pink in center. Remove chicken; keep warm.

3. Add wine, water, bouillon and sugar to skillet; bring to a boil over high heat, scraping particles from bottom of skillet. Boil 2 minutes or until liquid is reduced by half. Gradually stir butter into simmering sauce.

4. Serve chicken over pasta; spoon sauce over chicken and pasta.   *Makes 4 servings*

Prep and Cook Time: 20 minutes

Fettuccine Gorgonzola with Sun-Dried Tomatoes

Homestyle Tuna Pot Pie

1 package (15 ounces) refrigerated pie crusts
1 can (12 ounces) STARKIST® Solid White
    or Chunk Light Tuna, drained and
    chunked
1 package (10 ounces) frozen peas and
    carrots, thawed and drained
½ cup chopped onion
1 can (10¾ ounces) cream of potato or
    cream of mushroom soup
⅓ cup milk
½ teaspoon poultry seasoning or dried thyme
    Salt and pepper to taste

Line 9-inch pie pan with one crust; set aside.
Reserve second crust. In medium bowl, combine
remaining ingredients; mix well. Pour tuna mixture
into pie shell; top with second crust. Crimp edges
to seal. Cut slits in top crust to vent. Bake in 375°F
oven 45 to 50 minutes or until golden brown.

Makes 6 servings

Prep & Cook Time: 55 to 60 minutes

Veal Escallops with Fruited Wild Rice Stuffing

3⅓ cups cooked U.S. wild rice
1 cup chopped dried apricots
½ cup butter, softened, divided
½ cup fresh bread crumbs
½ cup chopped nuts, toasted (optional)
2 egg whites
4 tablespoons raisins
    Salt and black pepper to taste
10 boned veal cutlets (3 ounces each),
    pounded thin
½ pound shiitake mushrooms, sliced
½ cup minced shallots
2 teaspoons minced fresh thyme
    All-purpose flour
2 cups dry white wine

Mix wild rice, apricots, ¼ cup butter, bread
crumbs, nuts, if desired, egg whites, raisins, salt and
pepper in medium bowl. Spread approximately
½ cup mixture on each cutlet; roll each cutlet and
tie with string. Set aside. Sauté mushrooms and
shallots in remaining ¼ cup butter 5 minutes in
large saucepan. Season with thyme, salt and pepper.
Remove mushroom mixture from pan; set aside.
Flour rolled cutlets; brown in same pan. Add wine
and mushroom mixture; cover and braise
15 minutes over low heat. Slice and serve with
mushroom sauce. *Makes 10 servings*

*Favorite recipe from **California Wild Rice Advisory Board***

Homestyle Tuna Pot Pie

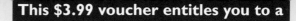

BUSINESS REPLY MAIL
FIRST-CLASS MAIL PERMIT NO. 24 MT. MORRIS, IL

POSTAGE WILL BE PAID BY ADDRESSEE

EASY HOME COOKING
PO BOX 520
MT MORRIS IL 61054-7451

|.|I......|III......|.|..|.|.||...|.|.|.|.||...|II...II

Lasagna Florentine

2 tablespoons olive or vegetable oil
3 medium carrots, finely chopped
1 package (8 to 10 ounces) sliced
   mushrooms
1 medium onion, finely chopped
2 cloves garlic, finely chopped
1 jar (28 ounces) RAGÚ® Hearty Robusto!
   Pasta Sauce
1 container (15 ounces) ricotta cheese
2 cups shredded mozzarella cheese, divided
1 box (10 ounces) frozen chopped spinach,
   thawed and squeezed dry
$\frac{1}{4}$ cup grated Parmesan cheese
2 eggs
1 teaspoon salt
1 teaspoon dried Italian seasoning
16 lasagna noodles, cooked and drained

Preheat oven to 375°F. In 12-inch skillet, heat oil
over medium heat and cook carrots, mushrooms,
onion and garlic until carrots are almost tender,
about 5 minutes. Stir in Ragú® Hearty Robusto!
Pasta Sauce; heat through.

Meanwhile, in medium bowl, combine ricotta
cheese, 1$\frac{1}{2}$ cups mozzarella cheese, spinach,
Parmesan cheese, eggs, salt and Italian seasoning;
set aside.

In 13×9-inch baking dish, evenly spread $\frac{1}{2}$ cup
sauce mixture. Arrange 4 lasagna noodles,
lengthwise over sauce, overlapping edges slightly.

Spread $\frac{1}{3}$ of the ricotta mixture over noodles;
repeat layers, ending with noodles. Top with
remaining sauce and $\frac{1}{2}$ cup mozzarella cheese.
Cover with foil and bake 40 minutes. Remove foil
and continue baking 10 minutes or until bubbling.

Makes 8 servings

Prize Potluck Casserole

1 cup lentils, rinsed and drained
2 cups water
1 can (16 ounces) tomatoes
$\frac{1}{4}$ cup minced onion
$\frac{1}{4}$ cup chopped green pepper
1 teaspoon salt
$\frac{1}{2}$ teaspoon dry mustard
$\frac{1}{4}$ teaspoon Worcestershire sauce
$\frac{1}{4}$ teaspoon pepper
$\frac{1}{8}$ teaspoon dried thyme leaves
1 pound Polish sausage, cut into 1$\frac{1}{2}$-inch-
   thick slices

Cook lentils in water until tender, about
30 minutes; drain if necessary. Combine lentils
with tomatoes, onion, green pepper and seasonings;
spoon into 13×9-inch casserole. Top with sausage.
Cover casserole and bake 45 minutes at 350°F.
Remove cover and bake 15 minutes longer.

Makes 6 servings

Favorite recipe from **USA Dry Pea & Lentil Council**

Lasagna Florentine

Fancy Chicken Puff Pie

4 tablespoons butter or margarine

¼ cup chopped shallots

¼ cup all-purpose flour

1 cup chicken stock or broth

¼ cup sherry

Salt to taste

⅛ teaspoon white pepper

Pinch ground nutmeg

¼ pound ham, cut into 2×¼-inch strips

3 cups cooked PERDUE® Chicken, cut into
    2¼-inch strips

1½ cups fresh asparagus pieces or 1 (10-ounce)
    package frozen asparagus pieces

1 cup (½ pint) heavy cream

Chilled pie crust for a 1-crust pie or
    1 sheet frozen puff pastry

1 egg, beaten

In medium saucepan, melt butter over medium-high heat. Add shallots; cook and stir until tender. Stir in flour; cook 3 minutes, stirring constantly. Add broth and sherry. Heat to boiling, stirring constantly; season to taste with salt, pepper and nutmeg. Reduce heat to low; simmer 5 minutes, stirring occasionally. Stir in ham, chicken, asparagus and cream. Pour chicken mixture into ungreased 9-inch pie plate.

Preheat oven to 425°F. Cut 8-inch circle from crust. Cut hearts from extra dough with cookie cutter, if desired. Place circle on cookie sheet moistened with cold water; pierce with fork. Brush with egg. Decorate pastry with hearts; brush hearts with egg.

Bake crust and filled pie plate 10 minutes. Reduce heat to 350°F. Bake additional 10 to 15 minutes or until pastry is golden brown and filling is hot and set. With spatula, place pastry over hot filling and serve immediately.   *Makes 4 servings*

Holiday Hint:

Shallots are a member of the onion family. They have a mild onion-garlic flavor. Each shallot head is made up of two or three cloves, and each clove is covered in a papery skin.

Curried Chicken, Vegetables and Couscous Skillet

1 package (16 ounces) frozen vegetable medley, such as broccoli, carrots and cauliflower or bell pepper and onion strips
1 pound chicken tenders
2 teaspoons curry powder, divided
¾ teaspoon garlic salt
⅛ teaspoon ground red pepper
4½ teaspoons vegetable oil
1 can (about 14 ounces) chicken broth
1 cup uncooked couscous

1. Thaw vegetables according to package directions.

2. While vegetables are thawing, place chicken in bowl. Sprinkle with 1 teaspoon curry powder, garlic salt and ground red pepper; toss to coat.

3. Heat oil in large deep skillet over medium-high heat until hot. Add chicken mixture, spreading in one layer. Cook 5 to 6 minutes or until chicken is no longer pink in center, turning occasionally.

4. Transfer chicken to plate; set aside. Add broth and remaining 1 teaspoon curry powder to skillet; bring to a boil over high heat, scraping up browned bits on bottom of skillet.

5. Stir thawed vegetables into skillet; return to a boil. Stir in couscous; top with chicken. Cover and remove from heat. Let stand 5 minutes or until liquid is absorbed. *Makes 4 servings*

Rocky Mountain Hash with Smoked Chicken

1½ pounds Colorado russet variety potatoes, unpeeled
2 tablespoons olive oil, divided
1 teaspoon salt, divided
¼ teaspoon black pepper
Nonstick cooking spray
2 cups chopped red or yellow onions
2 tablespoons bottled minced garlic
2 cups diced red bell pepper
⅛ to ¼ teaspoon cayenne pepper
2 cups shredded smoked chicken or turkey
1 can (11 ounces) whole kernel corn

Cut potatoes into ½- to ¾-inch chunks. Toss with 1 tablespoon oil, ½ teaspoon salt and black pepper. Spray 15×10×1-inch baking pan with nonstick cooking spray. Arrange potato chunks in single layer; roast at 450°F for 20 to 30 minutes or until tender, stirring and tossing occasionally. In large skillet heat remaining 1 tablespoon oil. Sauté onions and garlic until tender. Add red bell pepper, remaining ½ teaspoon salt and cayenne pepper. Cook and stir until peppers are crisp-tender. Stir in chicken, corn and potatoes. Cook and stir until heated through. *Makes 6 to 8 servings*

*Favorite recipe from **Colorado Potato Administrative Committee***

Louisiana Jambalaya

1½ pounds chicken tenders

½ teaspoon salt

½ teaspoon ground black pepper

1 tablespoon vegetable oil

¾ pound smoked turkey sausage, cut into
   ¼-inch slices

2 medium onions, chopped

1 large green bell pepper, chopped

1 cup chopped celery

1 clove garlic, minced

2 cups uncooked long grain white rice (not
   converted)

¼ to ½ teaspoon ground red pepper

2½ cups chicken broth

1 cup sliced green onions

1 medium tomato, chopped

Celery leaves for garnish

Season chicken with salt and black pepper. Heat oil in large saucepan or Dutch oven over high heat until hot. Add chicken, stirring until brown on all sides. Add sausage; cook 2 to 3 minutes. Remove chicken and sausage from saucepan; set aside. Add chopped onions, green pepper, celery and garlic to same saucepan; cook and stir over medium-high heat until crisp-tender. Stir in rice, red pepper, broth, and reserved chicken and sausage; bring to a boil. Reduce heat to low; cover and simmer 30 minutes. Stir in green onions and tomato. Garnish with celery leaves. Serve immediately.

Makes 8 servings

Microwave Directions: Season chicken with salt and black pepper. Place oil in deep 3-quart microwavable baking dish. Add chicken; cover with wax paper and cook on HIGH 3 minutes, stirring after 2 minutes. Add sausage; cover with wax paper and cook on HIGH 1 minute. Remove chicken and sausage with slotted spoon; set aside. Add chopped onions, green pepper, celery and garlic to same dish. Cover and cook on HIGH 4 minutes, stirring after 2 minutes. Stir in rice, red pepper, broth, and reserved chicken and sausage; cover and cook on HIGH 8 minutes or until boiling. Reduce setting to MEDIUM (50% power); cover and cook 30 minutes, stirring after 15 minutes. Stir in green onions and tomato. Let stand 5 minutes before serving. Garnish with celery leaves.

Favorite recipe from **USA Rice Federation**

Holiday Hint:

Louisiana Jambalaya is a festive dish that holiday guests are sure to enjoy. No one needs to know how easy it is to prepare. For a milder flavor add only a portion of the ground red pepper. Taste the jambalaya, then add more pepper if you wish.

Louisiana Jambalaya

Hearty Beef Bourguignonne

4 slices bacon, chopped

1 medium onion, chopped

1 large carrot, chopped

2 pounds boneless sirloin steak, cut into
    ¾-inch cubes

½ cup dry red wine or beef broth

1 jar (26 to 28 ounces) RAGÚ® Hearty
    Robusto! Pasta Sauce

In 6-quart saucepan or Dutch oven, cook bacon over medium heat, stirring occasionally, 4 minutes or until crisp. Stir in onion and carrot and cook, stirring occasionally, 5 minutes. Stir in steak and cook over medium-high heat, stirring occasionally, 5 minutes or until steak is no longer pink. Add wine and Ragú® Hearty Robusto! Pasta Sauce; bring to a boil over high heat. Reduce heat to low and simmer covered, stirring occasionally, 30 minutes. Serve, if desired, with hot cooked rice or noodles. *Makes 4 servings*

Recipe Tip: If cooking with wine, use the quality of wine which you would also enjoy drinking. For this classic dinner—your best Burgundy!

Rice Lasagna

1 bag SUCCESS® Rice

    Vegetable cooking spray

2 tablespoons reduced-calorie margarine

1 pound ground turkey

1 cup chopped onion

1 cup sliced fresh mushrooms

1 clove garlic, minced

2 cans (8 ounces each) no-salt-added tomato
    sauce

1 can (6 ounces) no-salt-added tomato paste

1 teaspoon dried oregano leaves, crushed

1 carton (15 ounces) lowfat cottage cheese

½ cup (2 ounces) grated Parmesan cheese

2 cups (8 ounces) shredded mozzarella cheese

1 tablespoon dried parsley flakes

Prepare rice according to package directions. Preheat oven to 350°F.

Spray 13×9-inch baking dish with cooking spray; set aside. Melt margarine in large skillet over medium heat. Add ground turkey, onion, mushrooms and garlic; cook until turkey is no longer pink and vegetables are tender, stirring occasionally to separate turkey. Drain. Stir in tomato sauce, tomato paste and oregano; simmer 15 minutes, stirring occasionally. Layer half each of rice, turkey mixture, cottage cheese, Parmesan cheese and mozzarella cheese in prepared baking dish; repeat layers. Sprinkle with parsley; cover. Bake 30 minutes. Uncover; continue baking 15 minutes. *Makes 8 servings*

Hearty Beef Bourguignonne

Florentine Strata

8 ounces BARILLA® Spaghetti or Linguine

1 jar (26 ounces) BARILLA® Roasted Garlic and Onion Pasta Sauce, divided

1 package (12 ounces) frozen spinach soufflé, thawed

2 cups (8 ounces) shredded mozzarella cheese, divided

¼ cup (1 ounce) grated Parmesan cheese, divided

1. Cook spaghetti according to package directions until partially done but still firm, 5 to 8 minutes. Drain.

2. Meanwhile, coat microwave-safe 13×9×2-inch baking dish with nonstick cooking spray. Pour 1½ cups pasta sauce into baking dish; top with half of drained spaghetti, half of spinach soufflé, 1 cup mozzarella cheese and 2 tablespoons Parmesan. Repeat layers of spaghetti, pasta sauce and cheeses.

3. Cover with plastic wrap and microwave on HIGH, turning every 4 minutes, until strata is bubbly and cheese is melted, 8 to 10 minutes. Let stand 3 minutes before serving.

Makes 8 servings

Tip: When preparing pasta that will be used in a casserole, it's important to reduce the suggested cooking time on the package by about one third. The pasta will continue to cook and absorb liquid while the casserole is cooking.

Beef Pot Roast

2½ pounds beef eye of round roast

1 can (14 ounces) beef broth

2 cloves garlic

1 teaspoon herbs de Provence *or* ¼ teaspoon *each* rosemary, thyme, sage and savory

4 small turnips, peeled and cut into wedges

10 ounces fresh brussels sprouts, trimmed

8 ounces baby carrots

4 ounces pearl onions, skins removed

1 tablespoon water

2 teaspoons cornstarch

1. Heat large nonstick skillet over medium-high heat. Place roast, fat side down, in skillet. Cook until evenly browned. Remove roast from skillet; place in Dutch oven.

2. Pour broth into Dutch oven; bring to a boil over high heat. Add garlic and herbs de Provence. Cover and reduce heat; simmer 1½ hours.

3. Add turnips, brussels sprouts, carrots and onions to Dutch oven. Cover; cook 25 to 30 minutes or until vegetables are tender. Remove meat and vegetables and arrange on serving platter; cover with foil to keep warm.

4. Strain broth; return to Dutch oven. Stir water into cornstarch until smooth. Stir cornstarch mixture into broth. Bring to a boil over medium-high heat; cook and stir 1 minute or until thick and bubbly. Serve immediately with pot roast and vegetables. Garnish as desired. *Makes 8 servings*

Florentine Strata

Creamy Turkey & Broccoli

1 package (6 ounces) stuffing mix, plus ingredients to prepare mix*

1⅓ cups *French's®* *Taste Toppers*™ French Fried Onions, divided

1 package (10 ounces) frozen broccoli spears, thawed and drained

1 package (about 1⅛ ounces) cheese sauce mix

1¼ cups milk

½ cup sour cream

2 cups (10 ounces) cubed cooked turkey or chicken

*Substitute 3 cups leftover stuffing for stuffing mix. If stuffing is dry, stir in water, 1 tablespoon at a time, until moist but not wet.

Preheat oven to 350°F. In medium saucepan, prepare stuffing mix according to package directions; stir in ⅔ *cup* **Taste Toppers**. Spread stuffing over bottom of greased 9-inch round baking dish. Arrange broccoli spears over stuffing with flowerets around edge of dish. In medium saucepan, prepare cheese sauce mix according to package directions using 1¼ cups milk. Remove from heat; stir in sour cream and turkey. Pour turkey mixture over broccoli stalks. Bake, covered, at 350°F for 30 minutes or until heated through. Sprinkle remaining ⅔ *cup* **Taste Toppers** over turkey; bake, uncovered, 5 minutes or until **Taste Toppers** are golden brown.

Makes 4 to 6 servings

Microwave Directions: In 9-inch round microwave-safe dish, prepare stuffing mix according to package microwave directions; stir in ⅔ *cup* **Taste Toppers**. Arrange stuffing and broccoli spears in dish as above; set aside. In medium microwave-safe bowl, prepare cheese sauce mix according to package microwave directions using 1¼ cups milk. Add turkey and microwave, covered, on HIGH 5 to 6 minutes, stirring turkey halfway through cooking time. Stir in sour cream. Pour turkey mixture over broccoli stalks. Microwave, covered, 8 to 10 minutes or until heated through. Rotate dish halfway through cooking time. Top turkey with remaining ⅔ *cup* **Taste Toppers;** microwave, uncovered, 1 minute. Let stand 5 minutes.

Holiday Hint:

Do you have leftover turkey from Christmas dinner? Everyone will love it recycled in this tasty casserole. Or purchase a thick slice or two of turkey breast from the supermarket deli.

Pollo Verde Casserole

2 boneless skinless chicken breast halves
    (about 4 ounces each)
1 teaspoon canola oil
1 medium onion, chopped
½ medium bell pepper, chopped
1 teaspoon chopped garlic
1 cup GUILTLESS GOURMET® Salsa
    (Roasted Red Pepper or Southwestern
    Grill), divided
½ cup low fat sour cream, divided
    Nonstick cooking spray
1 cup (3.5 ounces) crushed GUILTLESS
    GOURMET® Unsalted Baked Tortilla
    Chips, divided

Cut chicken into 1-inch cubes. Heat oil in large skillet over medium-high heat until hot. Add chicken cubes, onion, pepper and garlic; cook and stir about 5 to 10 minutes or until chicken turns white and onion is translucent. Remove from heat.

Combine ½ cup salsa and ¼ cup sour cream in small bowl until blended. Stir salsa mixture into chicken mixture.

Preheat oven to 325°F. Coat 2-quart glass casserole dish with cooking spray. Sprinkle ½ cup crushed chips into prepared casserole dish. Spread chicken mixture over crushed chips. Top with remaining crushed chips, then with remaining ½ cup salsa.

Bake 30 minutes or cover with plastic wrap and microwave on HIGH (100% power) 12 minutes or until heated through. Let stand 5 minutes before serving. To serve, divide mixture among 4 serving plates. Top each serving with a dollop of remaining ¼ cup sour cream. *Makes 4 servings*

Herbed Chicken and Potatoes

2 medium all-purpose potatoes, thinly sliced
    (about 1 pound)
4 bone-in chicken breast halves (about
    2 pounds)*
1 envelope LIPTON® RECIPE SECRETS®
    Savory Herb with Garlic Soup Mix
⅓ cup water
1 tablespoon olive or vegetable oil

*Substitution: Use 1 (2½- to 3-pound) chicken, cut into serving pieces.

1. Preheat oven to 425°F. In 13×9-inch baking or roasting pan, add potatoes; arrange chicken over potatoes.

2. Pour soup mix blended with water and oil over chicken and potatoes.

3. Bake uncovered 40 minutes or until chicken is no longer pink and potatoes are tender.

Makes 4 servings

Chicken Tetrazzini with Roasted Red Peppers

6 ounces uncooked egg noodles

3 tablespoons butter or margarine

¼ cup all-purpose flour

1 can (14½ ounces) chicken broth

1 cup whipping cream

2 tablespoons dry sherry

2 cans (6 ounces each) sliced mushrooms, drained

1 jar (7½ ounces) roasted red peppers, drained and cut into ½-inch strips

2 cups chopped cooked chicken

1 teaspoon dried Italian seasoning

½ cup (2 ounces) grated Parmesan cheese

1. Cook egg noodles according to package directions. Drain well.

2. While noodles are cooking, melt butter in medium saucepan over medium heat. Add flour and whisk until smooth. Add chicken broth; bring to a boil over high heat. Remove from heat. Gradually add whipping cream and sherry; stir to combine.

3. Combine mushrooms, red peppers and noodles in large bowl; toss to combine. Add half the chicken broth mixture to noodle mixture. Combine remaining chicken broth mixture, chicken and Italian seasoning in large bowl.

4. Spoon noodle mixture into serving dish. Make a well in center of noodles and spoon in chicken mixture. Sprinkle cheese over top.

Makes 6 servings

Cheesy Sausage Strata

½ pound bulk pork sausage

¾ cup mushroom slices

¼ cup green onion slices

½ pound VELVEETA® Pasteurized Prepared Cheese Product, cubed

4 cups (¾-inch) crustless sourdough bread cubes

1 cup milk

4 eggs, beaten

• Brown sausage; drain. Add vegetables. Continue cooking 5 minutes; drain. Let cool 10 minutes.

• Stir in prepared cheese product and bread cubes; spoon into greased 8-inch square baking dish.

• Beat milk and eggs. Pour over sausage mixture; cover. Refrigerate several hours or overnight.

• Preheat oven to 350°F.

• Remove cover. Bake 50 to 55 minutes or until golden brown. Let stand 10 minutes before serving. Garnish with fresh rosemary.   *Makes 6 servings*

Prep Time: 20 minutes plus chilling
Cooking Time: 55 minutes plus standing

Chicken Tetrazzini with Roasted Red Peppers

Spaghetti Pie

4 ounces uncooked thin spaghetti

1 egg

¼ cup grated Parmesan cheese

1 teaspoon dried Italian seasoning

⅔ cup reduced-fat ricotta cheese

½ pound 93% lean ground turkey

1 teaspoon chili powder

¼ teaspoon crushed fennel seeds

¼ teaspoon black pepper

⅛ teaspoon ground coriander

1 can (14½ ounces) diced tomatoes, undrained

1½ cups sliced fresh mushrooms

1 cup chopped onion

1 can (8 ounces) tomato sauce

¼ cup tomato paste

1 clove garlic, minced

2 teaspoons dried basil leaves

1 cup (4 ounces) shredded part-skim mozzarella cheese

1. Cook spaghetti according to package directions, omitting salt. Drain and rinse well under cold water until pasta is cool; drain well.

2. Beat egg, Parmesan cheese and Italian seasoning lightly in medium bowl. Add spaghetti; blend well. Spray deep 9-inch pie plate with nonstick cooking spray. Place spaghetti mixture in pie plate. Press onto bottom and up side of pie plate. Spread ricotta cheese on spaghetti layer.

3. Preheat oven to 350°F. Combine turkey, chili powder, fennel seeds, pepper and coriander in medium bowl. Spray large nonstick skillet with nonstick cooking spray; heat over medium heat until hot. Brown turkey mixture until turkey is no longer pink, stirring to break up meat. Add remaining ingredients except mozzarella cheese. Cook and stir until mixture boils. Spoon mixture over ricotta cheese in pie plate.

4. Cover pie plate with foil. Bake 20 minutes. Remove foil. Sprinkle with mozzarella cheese; bake 5 minutes or until cheese is melted. Let stand before cutting and serving.   *Makes 6 servings*

Holiday Hint:

Ricotta cheese is a soft, fresh white Italian cheese typically used in lasagna, manicotti and cannoli. Ricotta has a short shelf life so use it soon after you purchase it.

Spaghetti Pie

Meatless Medley

Triple-Decker Vegetable Omelet

1 cup finely chopped broccoli

½ cup diced red bell pepper

½ cup shredded carrot

⅓ cup sliced green onions

1 clove garlic, minced

2½ teaspoons FLEISCHMANN'S® Original Margarine, divided

¾ cup low fat cottage cheese (1% milkfat), divided

1 tablespoon plain dry bread crumbs

1 tablespoon grated Parmesan cheese

½ teaspoon Italian seasoning

1½ cups EGG BEATERS® Healthy Real Egg Product, divided

⅓ cup chopped tomato

Chopped fresh parsley, for garnish

In 8-inch nonstick skillet, over medium-high heat, sauté broccoli, bell pepper, carrot, green onions and garlic in 1 teaspoon margarine until tender. Remove from skillet; stir in ½ cup cottage cheese. Keep warm. Combine bread crumbs, Parmesan cheese and Italian seasoning; set aside.

In same skillet, over medium heat, melt ½ teaspoon margarine. Pour ½ cup Egg Beaters into skillet. Cook, lifting edges to allow uncooked portion to flow underneath. When almost set, slide unfolded omelet onto ovenproof serving platter. Top with half each of the vegetable mixture and bread crumb mixture; set aside.

Prepare 2 more omelets with remaining Egg Beaters and margarine. Layer 1 omelet onto serving platter over vegetable and bread crumb mixture; top with remaining vegetable mixture and bread crumb mixture. Layer with remaining omelet. Top omelet with remaining cottage cheese and tomato. Bake at 425°F for 5 to 7 minutes or until hot. Garnish with parsley. Cut into wedges.   *Makes 4 servings*

Prep Time: 20 minutes
Cook Time: 30 minutes

Triple-Decker Vegetable Omelet

Angel Hair with Roasted Red Pepper Sauce

1 package (16 ounces) BARILLA® Angel Hair

1 jar (12 ounces) roasted red peppers with juice, divided

1 tablespoon olive or vegetable oil

3 cloves garlic, minced

2 cups heavy cream

1½ teaspoons salt

1 teaspoon pepper

½ cup (2 ounces) grated Romano cheese, divided

3 tablespoons fresh basil leaves, cut into thin strips (optional)

1. Cook angel hair according to package directions; drain.

2. Meanwhile, chop ¼ cup roasted peppers; set aside. Purée remaining peppers and juice in food processor or blender.

3. Heat oil in large nonstick skillet. Add garlic; cook and stir 2 minutes over medium-low heat. Add pepper purée, cream, salt and pepper; cook over medium heat, stirring frequently, about 6 minutes or until hot and bubbly. Stir in ¼ cup cheese.

4. Combine hot drained angel hair with pepper mixture. Top with reserved chopped peppers, ¼ cup cheese and basil, if desired.

Makes 6 to 8 servings

Artichoke Frittata

1 can (14 ounces) artichoke hearts, drained and rinsed

Olive oil

½ cup minced green onions

5 eggs

½ cup (2 ounces) shredded Swiss cheese

2 tablespoons grated Parmesan cheese

1 tablespoon minced fresh savory *or* 1 teaspoon dried savory leaves

1 tablespoon minced fresh parsley

1 teaspoon salt

Black pepper to taste

1. Chop artichoke hearts; set aside.

2. Heat 1 tablespoon olive oil in 10-inch skillet over medium heat. Add green onions; cook until tender. Remove with slotted spoon; set aside.

3. Beat eggs in medium bowl until light. Stir in artichokes, green onions, cheeses, herbs, salt and pepper.

4. Heat 1½ teaspoons olive oil in same skillet over medium heat. Pour egg mixture into skillet.

5. Cook 4 to 5 minutes or until bottom is lightly browned. Place large plate over skillet. Invert frittata onto plate. Return frittata, uncooked side down, to skillet. Cook about 4 minutes more or until center is just set. Cut into 6 wedges to serve.

Makes 6 servings

Angel Hair with Roasted Red Pepper Sauce

Polenta with Pasta Sauce & Vegetables

1 can (about 14 ounces) reduced-sodium chicken broth

1½ cups water

1 cup yellow cornmeal

2 teaspoons olive oil

12 ounces assorted cut vegetables, such as broccoli florets, bell peppers, red onions, zucchini squash and julienned carrots

2 teaspoons fresh or bottled minced garlic

2 cups prepared tomato-basil pasta sauce

½ cup grated Asiago cheese

¼ cup chopped fresh basil (optional)

1. To prepare polenta, whisk together chicken broth, water and cornmeal in large microwavable bowl. Cover with waxed paper; microwave at HIGH 5 minutes. Whisk well and microwave at HIGH 2 to 3 minutes more or until polenta is very thick. Whisk again; cover and keep warm.

2. Meanwhile, heat oil in a large deep nonstick skillet over medium heat. Add vegetables and garlic; cook and stir 5 minutes. Add pasta sauce; reduce heat, cover and simmer 5 to 8 minutes or until vegetables are tender.

3. Spoon polenta onto serving plates; top with pasta sauce mixture. Sprinkle with cheese and basil, if desired. *Makes 4 servings*

Vegetables in Garlic Cream Sauce

1 cup water

4 cups cut-up vegetables such as DOLE® Asparagus, Bell Peppers, Broccoli, Carrots, Cauliflower or Sugar Peas

1 teaspoon olive or vegetable oil

4 cloves garlic, finely chopped

⅓ cup fat free or reduced fat mayonnaise

⅓ cup nonfat or low fat milk

2 tablespoons chopped fresh parsley

• Place water in large saucepan; bring to a boil. Add vegetables; reduce heat to low. Cook, uncovered, 9 to 12 minutes or until vegetables are tender-crisp; meanwhile, prepare sauce.

• Heat oil in small saucepan over medium heat. Add garlic; cook and stir garlic until golden brown. Remove from heat; stir in mayonnaise and milk.

• Drain vegetables; place in serving bowl. Pour in garlic sauce; toss to evenly coat. Sprinkle with parsley. *Makes 4 servings*

Prep Time: 10 minutes
Cook Time: 15 minutes

Polenta with Pasta Sauce & Vegetables

Pasta with Pieces of Jade

1 cup frozen peas, thawed

1 cup heavy cream

½ cup grated Parmesan cheese

½ teaspoon salt

½ teaspoon dried thyme leaves

½ teaspoon black pepper

2 dashes hot pepper sauce

8 ounces uncooked linguine

1 tablespoon vegetable oil

6 ounces green beans, stemmed and cut into halves

6 ounces broccoli florets, cut into bite-size pieces

4 ounces snow peas, stemmed and cut into halves

½ red bell pepper, roasted, peeled and cut into thin strips

1 clove garlic, minced

Additional grated Parmesan cheese

1. Purée peas in blender or food processor. Add cream, ½ cup cheese, salt, thyme, black pepper and pepper sauce; blend until smooth. Set aside.

2. Place 6 cups water in wok or large saucepan; bring to a boil over high heat. Add linguine; cook 8 minutes or until *al dente,* stirring occasionally. Drain, set aside.

3. Heat oil in wok over high heat. Add green beans and broccoli; stir-fry 5 to 6 minutes or until crisp-tender. Add snow peas, roasted bell pepper and garlic; stir-fry 1 to 2 minutes or until all vegetables are crisp-tender.

4. Pour pea mixture over vegetables, stirring until hot. Add linguine to wok; toss to combine. Sprinkle with additional cheese.

Makes 4 servings

Holiday Hint:

When buying green beans for a stir-fry, always choose slender beans because they are the most tender. Store green beans, unwashed, in a plastic bag in the refrigerator. It is best to stir-fry them within a day or two of purchase.

Spinach Lasagna

5 lasagna noodles
    Nonstick cooking spray
2 cups sliced fresh mushrooms
1 cup chopped onion
1 cup chopped green bell pepper
2 cloves garlic, minced
2 cans (8 ounces each) no-salt-added tomato
    sauce
1 teaspoon chopped fresh basil *or*
    ¼ teaspoon dried basil leaves
1 teaspoon chopped fresh oregano *or*
    ¼ teaspoon dried oregano leaves
¼ teaspoon ground red pepper
2 egg whites
1½ cups low-fat (1%) cottage cheese or light
    ricotta cheese
¼ cup grated Romano or Parmesan cheese
3 tablespoons fine dry bread crumbs
1 package (10 ounces) frozen chopped
    spinach, thawed and well drained
¾ cup (3 ounces) shredded part-skim
    mozzarella cheese
¼ cup chopped fresh parsley

Prepare noodles according to package directions, omitting salt; drain. Rinse under cold water; drain.

Coat large skillet with cooking spray. Add mushrooms, onion, bell pepper and garlic; cook and stir over medium heat until vegetables are tender. Stir in tomato sauce, basil, oregano and red pepper. Bring to a boil over medium-high heat. Reduce heat to medium-low. Simmer, uncovered, 10 minutes, stirring occasionally.

Preheat oven to 350°F. Combine egg whites, cottage cheese, Romano cheese and bread crumbs in medium bowl. Stir spinach into cottage cheese mixture.

Cut noodles in half crosswise. Spread ½ cup sauce in ungreased 8- or 9-inch square baking dish. Top with half the noodles, half the spinach mixture and half the remaining sauce. Repeat layers.

Cover and bake 45 minutes or until hot and bubbly. Sprinkle with mozzarella cheese. Bake, uncovered, 2 to 3 minutes more or until cheese melts. Sprinkle with parsley. Let stand 10 minutes before serving. *Makes 4 servings*

Hot and Spicy Spuds

4 medium baking potatoes
   Nonstick cooking spray
1 cup chopped onion
½ cup chopped green bell pepper
2 cloves garlic, minced
1 teaspoon olive oil
1 can (15½ ounces) reduced-sodium kidney
   beans, rinsed and drained
1 can (14½ ounces) no-salt-added tomatoes,
   cut up and undrained
1 can (4 ounces) diced mild green chilies
¼ cup chopped fresh cilantro or parsley
1 teaspoon ground cumin
1 teaspoon chili powder
¼ teaspoon ground red pepper
¼ cup reduced-fat sour cream
¼ cup (1 ounce) shredded reduced-fat
   Cheddar cheese

Preheat oven to 350°F. Scrub potatoes; pierce with fork. Bake 1¼ to 1½ hours or until tender.

Meanwhile, spray 2-quart saucepan with cooking spray; heat saucepan over medium heat. Cook and stir onion, bell pepper and garlic in oil until vegetables are tender. Stir in beans, tomatoes with juice, chilies, cilantro, cumin, chili powder and red pepper. Bring to a boil over high heat. Reduce heat to medium-low. Cover; simmer 8 minutes, stirring occasionally.

Gently roll potatoes under your hand using hot pad to loosen pulp. Cut crisscross slit in each potato. Place potatoes on four plates. Press potato ends to open slits. Spoon bean mixture over potatoes. Top with sour cream and sprinkle with cheese.

Makes 4 servings

Cheesy Rice Casserole

2 cups hot cooked rice
1⅓ cups *French's® Taste Toppers*™ French Fried
   Onions, divided
1 cup sour cream
1 jar (16 ounces) medium salsa, divided
1 cup (4 ounces) shredded Cheddar or taco
   blend cheese, divided

Combine rice and ⅔ cup *Taste Toppers* in large bowl. Spoon half of the rice mixture into microwavable 2-quart shallow casserole. Spread sour cream over rice mixture.

Layer half of the salsa and half of the cheese over sour cream. Sprinkle with remaining rice mixture, salsa and cheese. Cover loosely with plastic wrap. Microwave on HIGH 8 minutes or until heated through. Sprinkle with remaining ⅔ cup *Taste Toppers*. Microwave 1 minute or until *Taste Toppers* are golden.   *Makes 6 servings*

Prep Time: 15 minutes
Cook Time: 9 minutes

Cheesy Rice Casserole

Wild Rice with Dried Apricots and Cranberries

½ **cup uncooked wild rice**

3 **cups chicken broth, divided**

1 **cup apple juice**

¾ **cup uncooked long-grain white rice**

½ **cup golden raisins**

½ **cup chopped dried apricots**

½ **cup dried cranberries**

2 **tablespoons butter**

¾ **cup chopped onion**

½ **cup coarsely chopped pecans**

⅓ **cup chopped fresh parsley**

1. Rinse wild rice in fine strainer under cold running water. Drain.

2. Combine wild rice, 1½ cups chicken broth and apple juice in 2-quart saucepan. Bring to a boil over medium-high heat. Reduce heat to low; simmer, covered, about 45 minutes or until rice is tender. Drain; set aside.

3. Combine white rice and remaining 1½ cups broth in separate 2-quart saucepan. Bring to a boil over medium-high heat. Reduce heat to low; simmer, covered, 12 to 15 minutes.

4. Stir in raisins, apricots and cranberries; simmer 5 minutes or until rice is tender and fluffy and liquid is absorbed. Remove from heat. Let stand covered 5 minutes or until fruit is tender; set aside.

5. Melt butter in large skillet over medium heat. Add onion; cook and stir 5 to 6 minutes until tender. Stir in pecans. Cook and stir 2 minutes.

6. Add wild rice and white rice mixtures to skillet. Stir in parsley; cook and stir over medium heat about 2 minutes or until heated through. Garnish with fresh thyme, orange slices and whole cranberries, if desired. *Makes 6 to 8 servings*

Holiday Hint:

Always rinse wild rice before cooking to remove any debris left after processing. Place raw wild rice in a bowl and cover with cold water. Let it stand until debris floats to the surface. Remove the debris and drain.

Wild Rice with Dried Apricots and Cranberries

Savory Lentil Casserole

1¼ cups uncooked dried brown or green
     lentils, rinsed and sorted
2 tablespoons olive oil
1 large onion, chopped
3 cloves garlic, minced
8 ounces fresh shiitake or button
     mushrooms, sliced
2 tablespoons all-purpose flour
1½ cups beef broth
1 tablespoon Worcestershire sauce
1 tablespoon balsamic vinegar
½ teaspoon salt
½ teaspoon black pepper
½ cup grated Parmesan cheese
2 to 3 plum tomatoes, seeded and chopped

1. Preheat oven to 400°F. Place lentils in medium saucepan; cover with 1 inch water. Bring to a boil over high heat. Reduce heat to low. Simmer, covered, 20 to 25 minutes until lentils are barely tender; drain.

2. Meanwhile, heat oil in large skillet over medium heat. Add onion and garlic; cook and stir 10 minutes. Add mushrooms; cook and stir 10 minutes or until liquid is evaporated and mushrooms are tender. Sprinkle flour over mushroom mixture; stir well. Cook and stir 1 minute. Stir in beef broth, Worcestershire, vinegar, salt and pepper. Cook and stir until mixture is thick and bubbly.

3. Grease 1½-quart casserole. Stir lentils into mushroom mixture. Spread evenly into prepared casserole. Sprinkle with cheese. Bake 20 minutes.

4. Sprinkle tomatoes over casserole just before serving. Garnish with thyme and Italian parsley, if desired. *Makes 4 servings*

Holiday Hint:

Before cooking lentils carefully look through them and discard any shriveled or broken lentils or pieces of gravel. Place lentils in a colander and rinse with cold running water.

Cheesy Baked Barley

2 cups water

½ cup medium pearled barley

½ teaspoon salt, divided

Nonstick cooking spray

½ cup diced onion

½ cup diced zucchini

½ cup diced red bell pepper

1½ teaspoons all-purpose flour

Seasoned pepper

¾ cup fat-free (skim) milk

1 cup (4 ounces) shredded reduced-fat Italian blend cheese, divided

1 tablespoon Dijon mustard

1. Bring water to a boil in 1-quart saucepan. Add barley and ¼ teaspoon salt. Cover; reduce heat and simmer 45 minutes or until tender and most water is evaporated. Let stand covered, 5 minutes.

2. Preheat oven to 375°F. Spray medium skillet with cooking spray. Cook onion, zucchini and bell pepper over medium-low heat about 10 minutes or until soft. Stir in flour, remaining ¼ teaspoon salt and seasoned pepper to taste; cook 1 to 2 minutes. Add milk, stirring constantly; cook and stir until slightly thickened. Remove from heat and add barley, ¾ cup cheese and mustard; stir until cheese is melted.

3. Spread in even layer in casserole. Sprinkle with remaining ¼ cup cheese. Bake 20 minutes or until hot. Preheat broiler. Broil casserole 1 to 2 minutes or until cheese is lightly browned. *Makes 2 servings*

Harveys® Bristol Cream® Fettuccine and Vegetables

1 pound fresh asparagus

1 cup sliced fresh mushrooms

½ cup finely chopped red bell pepper

¼ cup chopped onion

1 clove garlic, minced

3 tablespoons butter or margarine

2 tablespoons all-purpose flour

½ teaspoon salt

¼ teaspoon white pepper

1 cup milk

¼ cup HARVEYS® Bristol Cream®

¼ cup grated Parmesan cheese

8 ounces uncooked fettuccine, cooked and drained

Snap off tough ends of asparagus. Cut asparagus into ¾-inch pieces. Cook in small amount of boiling water 2 to 3 minutes or until crisp-tender. Drain and set aside.

In small saucepan, sauté mushrooms, bell pepper, onion and garlic in butter until tender. Combine flour, salt and white pepper in small bowl; stir into vegetable mixture. Add milk and Harveys® Bristol Cream®. Cook and stir over medium heat until thickened and bubbly, stirring constantly. Stir in cheese.

Place hot fettuccine in serving bowl. Add sauce and asparagus. Toss gently to coat evenly.

Makes 4 to 6 servings

Three Mushroom Ratatouille

1 package (3½ ounces) fresh shiitake
    mushrooms*
1 tablespoon olive oil
1 large onion, chopped
4 cloves garlic, minced
1 package (8 ounces) button mushrooms,
    chopped
1 package (6 ounces) crimini mushrooms,
    chopped
1 cup chicken broth
½ cup chopped fresh tomato
2 tablespoons chopped fresh parsley
2 tablespoons grated Parmesan cheese
3 pita breads (6 inches each)
    Italian parsley for garnish

*Or, substitute 1 ounce dried black Chinese mushrooms. Place dried mushrooms in small bowl; cover with warm water. Soak 20 minutes to soften. Drain; squeeze out excess moisture. Prepare as directed in Step 1.

1. Remove stems from shiitake mushrooms; discard stems and chop caps.

2. Preheat broiler. Heat oil in large skillet over medium heat until hot. Add onion and garlic. Cook 5 minutes, stirring occasionally. Add mushrooms; cook 5 minutes more, stirring often.

3. Add chicken broth; bring to a boil. Cook about 10 minutes or until liquid is absorbed. Remove from heat. Stir in tomato, chopped parsley and cheese. Spoon into bowl.

4. Meanwhile, split each pita bread horizontally in half. Stack halves; cut stack into 6 wedges. Arrange wedges in single layer on baking sheet. Broil 4 inches from heat 1 to 3 minutes or until wedges are toasted.

5. Arrange toasted pita bread triangles and warm dip in basket. Garnish, if desired.

Makes about 2¼ cups

Three Mushroom Ratatouille

Spaghetti Squash Primavera

1 teaspoon olive oil
¼ cup diced green bell pepper
¼ cup diced zucchini
¼ cup sliced mushrooms
¼ cup diced carrot
¼ cup sliced green onions
2 cloves garlic, minced
1 plum tomato, diced
1 tablespoon red wine or water
½ teaspoon dried basil leaves
¼ teaspoon salt
⅛ teaspoon black pepper
2 cups cooked spaghetti squash
2 tablespoons grated Parmesan cheese

1. Heat oil in medium skillet over low heat. Add bell pepper, zucchini, mushrooms, carrot, green onions and garlic; cook 10 to 12 minutes or until crisp-tender, stirring occasionally. Stir in tomato, wine, basil, salt and black pepper; cook 4 to 5 minutes, stirring once or twice.

2. Serve vegetables over spaghetti squash. Top with cheese.   *Makes 2 servings*

Spinach Tortellini with Roasted Red Peppers

2 packages (9 ounces each) fresh spinach tortellini
1 jar (7 ounces) roasted red peppers or pimientos
2 tablespoons butter or olive oil
4 cloves garlic, minced
¼ cup chopped fresh basil *or* 2 teaspoons dried basil, crushed
½ cup chopped walnuts or pine nuts, toasted
1 cup **HIDDEN VALLEY® ORIGINAL RANCH® Dressing**
Fresh basil leaves (optional)

Cook tortellini according to package directions; drain and set aside. Slice red peppers into strips; set aside. In a medium saucepan, melt butter; add garlic and sauté about 2 minutes. Add red pepper strips, basil and tortellini. Stir to coat; add walnuts. Stir in enough dressing so that mixture is creamy and tortellini are coated. Garnish with fresh basil, if desired. Serve hot.   *Makes 4 to 6 servings*

Spaghetti Squash Primavera

Savory Roasted Vegetables & Pasta

4 carrots, thinly sliced

2 red bell peppers, cut into strips

2 zucchini, cut into ½-inch chunks

2 yellow squash, cut into ½-inch chunks

4 cloves garlic, peeled

½ cup half-and-half

3 tablespoons *French's*® Dijon Mustard

8 ounces penne pasta, cooked

  Shaved Parmesan cheese

1. Preheat oven to 425°F. In roasting pan, toss vegetables and garlic with *2 tablespoons olive oil, 1 teaspoon salt* and *¼ teaspoon black pepper.* Bake, uncovered, 20 minutes or until tender, stirring occasionally.

2. Spoon half of vegetables into blender or food processor. Add half-and-half, mustard and *2 tablespoons water.* Process until mixture is smooth.

3. Toss pasta with vegetable purée in large serving bowl. Spoon remaining vegetables on top. Sprinkle with Parmesan cheese.   *Makes 4 servings*

Prep Time: 20 minutes
Cook Time: 20 minutes

Valley Eggplant Parmigiano

2 eggplants (about 1 pound each)

⅓ cup olive or vegetable oil

1 container (15 ounces) ricotta cheese

2 packages (1 ounce each) HIDDEN VALLEY® Milk Recipe Original Ranch® Salad Dressing Mix

2 eggs

2 teaspoons dry bread crumbs

1 cup tomato sauce

½ cup shredded mozzarella cheese

1 tablespoon grated Parmesan cheese

  Chopped parsley

Preheat oven to 350°F. Cut eggplants into ½-inch slices. Brush some of the oil onto two large baking sheets. Arrange eggplant slices in single layer on sheets and brush tops with additional oil. Bake until eggplant is fork-tender, about 20 minutes.

In large bowl, whisk together ricotta cheese and salad dressing mix; whisk in eggs. In 13×9×2-inch baking dish, layer half the eggplant. Sprinkle 1 teaspoon of the bread crumbs over eggplant; spread all the ricotta mixture on top. Arrange remaining eggplant in another layer. Sprinkle with remaining 1 teaspoon bread crumbs; top with tomato sauce. Sprinkle cheeses on top. Bake until cheeses begin to brown, about 30 minutes. Sprinkle with parsley.   *Makes 6 to 8 servings*

Savory Roasted Vegetables & Pasta

Southwestern Lasagna

1 tablespoon vegetable oil
1 medium onion, thinly sliced
1 clove garlic, finely chopped
1 tablespoon chili powder
1 tablespoon paprika
¾ cup water
1 can (6 ounces) tomato paste
¼ cup honey
¼ cup fresh lime juice
1 can (15 ounces) black beans, undrained
1 can (12 ounces) whole kernel corn
6 medium corn tortillas, cut in quarters
1 package (15 ounces) part skim ricotta
    cheese
1 can (7 ounces) whole mild green chilies,
    cut lengthwise into ½-inch strips
½ cup (2 ounces) shredded Monterey Jack
    cheese

In medium saucepan, heat oil over medium-high heat until hot; cook and stir onions and garlic 3 to 5 minutes or until onion is tender. Add chili powder and paprika; cook and stir 1 minute. Stir in water, tomato paste, honey and lime juice until well mixed. Stir in black beans and corn. Bring to a boil; reduce heat and simmer 5 minutes.

Spoon ⅓ of sauce into 1½-quart rectangular baking pan; arrange ½ of tortilla quarters evenly over sauce in pan. Spread with ½ of ricotta cheese and arrange ½ of green chile strips evenly over cheese. Repeat with ⅓ of sauce, remaining tortillas, ricotta cheese and green chilies. Spread remaining sauce evenly over top of lasagna; sprinkle evenly with shredded cheese. Bake at 350°F 20 to 25 minutes, or until heated through. *Makes 6 servings*

Broccoli & Cheese Strata

2 cups chopped broccoli florets
4 slices firm white bread, ½-inch thick
4 teaspoons butter
1½ cups (6 ounces) shredded Cheddar cheese
3 eggs
1½ cups low-fat (2%) milk
½ teaspoon salt
½ teaspoon hot pepper sauce
⅛ teaspoon black pepper

SLOW COOKER DIRECTIONS

1. Cook broccoli in boiling water 10 minutes or until tender. Drain. Spread one side of each bread slice with 1 teaspoon butter.

2. Arrange 2 slices bread, buttered sides up in greased 1-quart casserole. Layer cheese, broccoli and remaining 2 bread slices, buttered sides down.

3. Beat together eggs, milk, salt, hot pepper sauce and pepper in medium bowl. Gradually pour over bread.

4. Place small wire rack in 5-quart slow cooker. Pour in 1 cup water. Place casserole on rack. Cover and cook on HIGH 3 hours. *Makes 4 servings*

Vegetable & Tofu Gratin

  Nonstick cooking spray
 1 teaspoon olive oil
 ¾ cup thinly sliced fennel bulb
 ¾ cup thinly sliced onion
 2 cloves garlic, minced
 ¾ cup cooked brown rice
 2 tablespoons balsamic vinegar, divided
 2 teaspoons dried Italian seasoning, divided
 3 ounces firm tofu, crumbled
 ¼ cup crumbled feta cheese
 2 to 3 ripe plum tomatoes, sliced ¼ inch
    thick
 1 medium zucchini, sliced ¼ inch thick
 ⅛ teaspoon salt
 ⅛ teaspoon black pepper
 ¼ cup fresh bread crumbs
 2 tablespoons grated fresh Parmesan cheese

1. Preheat oven to 400°F. Spray 1-quart shallow baking dish with nonstick cooking spray.

2. Spray medium skillet with cooking spray. Heat oil in skillet over medium heat until hot. Add fennel and onion. Cook about 10 minutes or until tender and lightly browned, stirring frequently. Add garlic; cook and stir 1 minute. Spread over bottom of prepared baking dish.

3. Combine rice, 1 tablespoon vinegar and ½ teaspoon Italian seasoning in small bowl. Spread over onion mixture.

4. Combine tofu, feta cheese, remaining 1 tablespoon vinegar and 1 teaspoon Italian seasoning in same small bowl; toss to combine. Spoon over rice.

5. Top with alternating rows of tomato and zucchini slices. Sprinkle with salt and pepper.

6. Combine bread crumbs, Parmesan cheese and remaining ½ teaspoon Italian seasoning in small bowl. Sprinkle over top. Spray bread crumb topping lightly with nonstick cooking spray. Bake 30 minutes or until heated through and topping is browned. *Makes 2 servings*

Holiday Hint:

Balsamic vinegar, made from sweet white grapes, is expensive because it is aged for years to develop its brown color and mellow sweet flavor. You may substitute red wine vinegar and a pinch of sugar for balsamic vinegar.

Two Cheese Mediterranean Stir-Fry

6 ounces uncooked penne pasta

2 tablespoons extra-virgin olive oil, divided

4 cloves garlic, minced

$\frac{1}{2}$ pound mushrooms, cut into quarters

2 cups diced eggplant

$1\frac{1}{2}$ cups matchstick-size zucchini strips

1 green bell pepper, cut into 1-inch pieces

1 cup chopped onion

$1\frac{1}{2}$ teaspoons dried basil leaves

$\frac{3}{4}$ teaspoon salt or to taste

$\frac{1}{8}$ teaspoon black pepper

4 plum tomatoes, cut into quarters and seeded

2 to 3 tablespoons capers, well-drained (optional)

3 ounces provolone cheese, shredded

$\frac{1}{4}$ cup grated Parmesan cheese, divided

1. Cook pasta according to package directions.

2. Meanwhile, place 1 tablespoon oil in large nonstick skillet or wok. Heat over medium-high heat 1 minute. Add garlic; cook 1 minute. Add mushrooms, eggplant, zucchini, bell pepper, onion, basil, salt and black pepper. Cook 15 minutes or until eggplant is tender.

3. Gently stir in tomatoes and capers, if desired. Reduce heat, cover tightly and simmer 5 minutes.

4. Remove skillet from heat; toss with remaining 1 tablespoon oil, provolone cheese and 2 tablespoons Parmesan cheese.

5. Place cooked pasta on serving platter. Spoon vegetable mixture over pasta and top with remaining 2 tablespoons Parmesan cheese.

Makes 4 servings

Holiday Hint:

Young eggplants have tender edible skin, but it is best to peel older, large eggplants. The skin can be removed with a vegetable peeler or paring knife. Since the flesh of eggplant discolors rapidly, peel and cut it just before cooking.

Two Cheese Mediterranean Stir-Fry

Vegetable Melange Couscous

¾ cups mesquite chips

4 small new potatoes, cut into eighths

½ pound fresh green beans, trimmed and halved

2 carrots, peeled and diagonally cut into 1-inch pieces

2 plum tomatoes, chopped

1 clove garlic, minced

4 tablespoons dry white wine or water, divided

¼ teaspoon salt, divided

1 can (15 ounces) pinto beans, drained and rinsed

1 package (10 ounces) couscous

½ teaspoon ground cumin

½ teaspoon ground cinnamon

¼ teaspoon crushed red pepper

1 can (14½ ounces) vegetable broth, heated

¼ cup chopped fresh cilantro

Lemon peel strips for garnish

1. Cover mesquite chips with water and soak for 20 minutes.

2. Combine vegetables and garlic in large bowl. Divide between 2 sheets of heavy-duty foil. Sprinkle each with 2 tablespoons wine and ⅛ teaspoon salt; seal using Drugstore Wrap technique.*

3. Drain mesquite; sprinkle over coals. Grill packets on covered grill over medium coals 20 to 25 minutes or until vegetables are tender, turning once. Meanwhile, combine beans and 3 tablespoons water in saucepan. Bring to a boil and boil 2 to 3 minutes, stirring occasionally; remove from heat. Remove packets from grill to cool.

4. Combine couscous, cumin, cinnamon and red pepper in 8-inch square baking dish and add hot vegetable broth; cover immediately with foil. Allow to stand 5 minutes; fluff with fork and arrange on platter. Top with vegetables and beans; sprinkle with cilantro. Garnish with strips of lemon peel, if desired. *Makes 4 servings*

*Place food in the center of an oblong piece of heavy-duty foil, leaving at least a two-inch border around the food. Bring the two long sides together above the food; fold down in a series of locked folds, allowing for heat circulation and expansion. Fold short ends up and over again. Press folds firmly to seal the foil packet.

Note: Vegetable packets may be baked in a prepared 350°F oven for 20 to 25 minutes. Omit mesquite chips.

Vegetable Melange Couscous

Brown Rice Spinach Quiche

1 bag SUCCESS® Brown Rice

6 egg whites, divided

¼ cup (1 ounce) grated Parmesan cheese, divided

Vegetable cooking spray

1 tablespoon reduced-calorie margarine

½ cup chopped onion

1 package (10 ounces) frozen chopped spinach, thawed and drained

1 teaspoon black pepper

½ teaspoon salt

½ teaspoon ground nutmeg

½ cup fat-free sour cream

2 tablespoons flour

1 cup skim milk

Prepare rice according to package directions. Cool.

Preheat oven to 425°F.

Combine rice, three egg whites and 2 tablespoons cheese; mix well. Spray 9-inch pie plate with cooking spray. With back of spoon, firmly press rice mixture onto bottom and up side of prepared pie plate to form shell. Bake 5 minutes. Remove from oven. Melt margarine in small skillet. Add onion; cook and stir until tender. Combine onion, spinach, pepper, salt and nutmeg in medium bowl; mix well. Spoon spinach mixture into rice shell; sprinkle with remaining 2 tablespoons cheese. Slightly beat remaining three egg whites in medium bowl. Stir in sour cream, flour and milk. Pour over spinach mixture. Bake 10 minutes. *Reduce oven temperature to 350°F.* Continue baking until quiche is firm, about 30 minutes. *Makes 6 servings*

7 Veggie Mac 'n Cheese

1 can (15 ounces) VEG•ALL® Original Mixed Vegetables, drained

1 box (7¼ ounces) macaroni and cheese mix, prepared

1 teaspoon onion powder

1 teaspoon prepared mustard

1 tomato, sliced

1 teaspoon dried parsley

Preheat oven to 350°F. Combine Veg•All, prepared macaroni and cheese, onion powder and mustard; mix well. Pour into greased 1-quart casserole. Bake for 20 to 25 minutes. Garnish with tomato slices and dried parsley. Serve hot. *Makes 6 servings*

Prep Time: 7 minutes
Cook Time: 20 minutes

Greek White Bean Risotto

3 teaspoons low-sodium chicken flavor bouillon granules

Nonstick cooking spray

3 cloves garlic, minced

1½ cups uncooked arborio rice

2 teaspoons dried oregano leaves

⅓ cup finely chopped dry-pack sun-dried tomatoes

1 cup rinsed, drained canned cannellini beans (white kidney beans)

¾ cup (3 ounces) crumbled feta cheese

⅓ cup grated Parmesan cheese

1 teaspoon lemon juice

½ teaspoon black pepper

1. Combine 5½ cups water and bouillon granules in large saucepan; cover. Bring to a simmer over medium-low heat.

2. Spray large saucepan with cooking spray; heat over medium heat until hot. Add garlic; cook and stir 1 minute. Add rice and oregano; reduce heat to medium-low.

3. Stir 1 cup hot chicken broth into rice mixture; cook until broth is absorbed, stirring constantly. Stir ½ cup hot chicken broth into rice mixture, stirring constantly until broth is absorbed. Stir tomatoes into rice mixture.

4. Stir remaining hot chicken broth into rice mixture, ½ cup at a time, stirring constantly until all broth is absorbed before adding next ½ cup. (Total cooking time for chicken broth absorption is about 35 to 40 minutes or until rice is just tender but still firm to the bite.)

5. Stir beans into rice mixture; cook 1 minute, stirring constantly. Remove from heat. Stir in cheeses, lemon juice and pepper. Cover; let stand 5 minutes. Stir once. Serve with breadsticks, if desired. Garnish as desired.   *Makes 5 servings*

Brunch-Time Best

Cranberry Sausage Quiche

1 (9-inch) frozen deep-dish pie shell

½ pound BOB EVANS® Savory Sage Roll Sausage

¼ cup chopped yellow onion

¾ cup dried cranberries

1½ cups (6 ounces) shredded Monterey Jack cheese

3 eggs, lightly beaten

1½ cups half-and-half

Fresh parsley or sage leaves for garnish

Preheat oven to 400°F. Let frozen pie shell stand at room temperature 10 minutes; do not prick shell. Bake 7 minutes. Remove from oven and set aside. Reduce oven temperature to 375°F. Crumble and cook sausage and onion in large skillet over medium-high heat until sausage is browned. Drain off any drippings. Remove from heat; stir in cranberries. Sprinkle cheese on bottom of pie shell; top evenly with sausage mixture. Combine eggs and half-and-half in medium bowl; whisk until blended but not frothy. Pour egg mixture over sausage mixture in pie shell. Bake 40 to 45 minutes or until knife inserted into center comes out clean. Let stand 10 minutes before serving. Garnish with fresh parsley. Refrigerate leftovers. *Makes 6 servings*

Holiday Hint:

A quiche is a savory tart or pie that is served most often as an entrée and sometimes as an appetizer. Quiches originated in the Alsace-Lorraine region of France.

Cranberry Sausage Quiche

Spiced Pancakes with Apple Topping

¼ cup I CAN'T BELIEVE IT'S NOT BUTTER!® Spread

¼ cup sugar

3 large Gala, Braeburn or Fuji apples, peeled, cored and cut into ½-inch slices

1 cup original pancake and waffle mix *or* 1 container (16 ounces) frozen pancake batter, thawed

½ teaspoon ground cinnamon

½ teaspoon vanilla extract

¼ teaspoon ground ginger (optional)

1 tablespoon cornstarch

1¼ cup apple juice

⅓ cup pure maple syrup or pancake syrup

In 12-inch nonstick skillet, melt I Can't Believe It's Not Butter! Spread and sugar over medium heat and cook apples, stirring occasionally, 15 minutes or until apples are tender.

Meanwhile, prepare pancake mix according to package directions, blending in cinnamon, vanilla and ginger. In another 12-inch skillet or on griddle, cook pancakes until done, turning once.

In small bowl, with wire whisk, blend cornstarch, apple juice and syrup. Add to apples; bring to a boil. Boil, stirring occasionally, 1 minute or until thickened. To serve, pour apple topping over hot pancakes. *Makes 4 servings*

Breakfast in a Cup

3 cups cooked rice

1 cup (4 ounces) shredded Cheddar cheese, divided

1 can (4 ounces) diced green chilies

1 jar (2 ounces) diced pimientos, drained

⅓ cup skim milk

2 eggs, beaten

½ teaspoon ground cumin

½ teaspoon salt

½ teaspoon ground black pepper

Vegetable cooking spray

Combine rice, ½ cup cheese, chilies, pimientos, milk, eggs, cumin, salt and pepper in large bowl. Evenly divide mixture into 12 muffin cups coated with cooking spray. Sprinkle with remaining ½ cup cheese. Bake at 400°F for 15 minutes or until set. *Makes 12 servings*

Tip: Breakfast cups may be stored in the freezer in a freezer bag or tightly sealed container. To reheat frozen breakfast cups, microwave each cup on HIGH 1 minute.

Favorite recipe from **USA Rice Federation**

Spiced Pancakes with Apple Topping

Spicy Sausage Skillet Breakfast

2 bags SUCCESS® Rice
   Vegetable cooking spray
1 pound bulk turkey sausage
½ cup chopped onion
1 can (10 ounces) tomatoes with green
   chilies, undrained
1 tablespoon chili powder
1 cup (4 ounces) shredded reduced-fat
   Monterey Jack cheese

Prepare rice according to package directions.

Lightly spray large skillet with cooking spray. Crumble sausage into prepared skillet. Cook over medium heat until lightly browned, stirring occasionally. Add onion; cook until tender. Stir in tomatoes, chili powder and rice; simmer 2 minutes. Reduce heat to low. Simmer until no liquid remains, about 8 minutes, stirring occasionally. Sprinkle with cheese. *Makes 6 to 8 servings*

Brunch Sandwiches

4 English muffins, split, lightly toasted
8 thin slices CURE 81® ham
8 teaspoons Dijon mustard
8 large eggs, fried or poached
8 slices SARGENTO® Deli Style Sliced Swiss
   Cheese

1. Top each muffin half with a slice of ham, folding to fit. Spread mustard lightly over ham; top with an egg and one slice cheese.

2. Transfer to foil-lined baking sheet. Broil 4 to 5 inches from heat source until cheese is melted and sandwiches are hot, 2 to 3 minutes.
Makes 4 servings

Preparation Time: 5 minutes
Cooking Time: 10 minutes

Honey Custard French Toast

½ cup honey
1 cup milk
6 eggs
1½ teaspoon cinnamon
⅛ teaspoon salt
12 slices (¾-inch thick) French bread
   Butter
   Honey and toasted pecan pieces

In large bowl, beat together honey, milk, eggs, cinnamon and salt. Dip bread slices in egg mixture, turning to coat. Brown soaked slices in butter over medium heat, turning once. Serve with honey and sprinkle with pecans, if desired.
Makes 6 servings

Baked French Toast Wedges

4 whole BAYS® English muffins, cut into 1-inch cubes

3 large eggs

½ cup sugar

1 teaspoon cinnamon

1 teaspoon vanilla

¼ teaspoon salt

1⅔ cups half-and-half, whipping cream or whole milk

2 tablespoons butter or margarine, melted

⅛ teaspoon nutmeg, preferably freshly grated

Spray 10-inch quiche dish or deep dish pie plate with non-stick cooking spray. Arrange muffins in a single layer in dish. In a medium bowl, beat together eggs and combined sugar and cinnamon. Stir in vanilla and salt; mix well. Add half-and-half and melted butter or margarine, mixing well. Pour evenly over muffins; press down on muffins to moisten with liquid. Sprinkle nutmeg evenly over mixture. Cover and refrigerate overnight, if desired, or bake immediately.

Bake in 350°F oven for 40 to 45 minutes or until puffed and golden brown. Transfer to cooling rack; cool at least 10 minutes before serving.* Cut into wedges and serve warm with desired fruit topping or heated maple syrup.   *Makes 6 servings*

*At this point, French toast may be cooled completely, cut into wedges, placed between sheets of waxed paper in a plastic freezer storage bag and frozen up to 1 month. Place wedges on baking sheet and bake in 350°F oven for 8 to 10 minutes or until thawed and heated through.

Mixed Fruit Topping: Combine 1 kiwifruit, peeled and diced, ½ cup fresh raspberries and 1 ripe small banana, sliced with 2 tablespoons honey and 2 teaspoons fresh lime juice. Let stand 5 minutes.

Strawberry Topping: Combine 1¼ cups thinly sliced strawberries, ¼ cup strawberry jam or currant jelly and 1 teaspoon orange juice** in a microwave-safe bowl. Cover and cook at high power 1 minute or until warm. (Or, heat in a small saucepan over medium heat until warm.)

**Almond or orange-flavored liqueur may be substituted, if desired.

Peachy Keen Topping: Combine ¼ cup peach or apricot preserves and 1 tablespoon pineapple or apple juice.*** Add 1 peeled and diced ripe peach or 1 cup diced thawed frozen sliced peaches and ¼ cup fresh or partially thawed frozen blueberries, mixing well. Serve at room temperature or heat as for Strawberry Topping above.

***Almond or orange-flavored liqueur may be substituted, if desired.

Gala Apple Tart

1 cup all-purpose flour

4 teaspoons plus 3 tablespoons granulated sugar

¼ teaspoon baking powder

¼ teaspoon salt

9 tablespoons I CAN'T BELIEVE IT'S NOT BUTTER!® Spread, divided

2½ tablespoons cold water

2 Gala or Granny Smith apples, peeled, cored and cut into ¼-inch slices

½ cup whipping or heavy cream

1 tablespoon confectioners' sugar

1 tablespoon rum (optional)

In food processor, process flour, 4 teaspoons granulated sugar, baking powder and salt. Add 6 tablespoons I Can't Believe It's Not Butter! Spread, cut in pieces, and process until mixture is size of small peas. Sprinkle water over flour mixture and process until dough forms. Wrap in plastic wrap and refrigerate until firm, about 30 minutes.

Preheat oven to 400°F. Meanwhile, in 10-inch oven-proof* nonstick skillet, melt remaining 3 tablespoons I Can't Believe It's Not Butter! Spread with remaining 3 tablespoons granulated sugar over medium heat. Add apples, arranging in two layers, and cook uncovered 12 minutes or until apples are tender and golden brown.

Meanwhile, on lightly floured surface, roll dough into 10-inch circle. Lift and arrange over apples in skillet. Bake 25 minutes or until crust is golden.

Meanwhile, in large bowl, with electric mixer, beat cream with confectioners' sugar until soft peaks form. Add rum and beat until stiff. To serve, turn tart onto serving plate. Cut into wedges.

Makes 6 servings

*Suggestion: If oven-proof skillet is not available, before baking, thoroughly wrap handle of skillet with heavy-duty aluminum foil.

Holiday Hint:

For a festive touch, top individual servings of this apple tart with a dollop of whipped cream, sprinkled with ground nutmeg and garnished with a few bright red raspberries.

Ham Stromboli

1 can (10 ounces) refrigerated pizza dough
1 tablespoon prepared mustard
½ pound thinly sliced deli ham
1 package (3½ ounces) sliced pepperoni
1 teaspoon dried Italian seasoning
2 cups (8 ounces) shredded part-skim
    mozzarella cheese

1. Preheat oven to 425°F. Unroll pizza dough on greased jelly-roll pan; pat dough into 12-inch square. Spread mustard over dough to within ½ inch of edges. Layer ham slices down center 6 inches of dough, leaving 3-inch border on either side and ½-inch border at top and bottom. Top ham with pepperoni slices. Sprinkle with Italian seasonings and cheese.

2. Fold sides of dough over filling, pinching center seam and each end to seal. Bake 15 to 20 minutes or until lightly browned. *Makes 6 servings*

Serving Suggestion: To make this meal complete, just add a tossed salad and fresh fruit for dessert.

Prep & Cook Time: 22 minutes

Raspberry Wine Punch

1 package (10 ounces) frozen red raspberries
    in syrup, thawed
1 bottle (750 ml) white Zinfandel or blush
    wine
¼ cup raspberry-flavored liqueur
    Empty ½ gallon milk or juice carton
3 to 4 cups distilled water, divided
    Sprigs of pine and tinsel
    Fresh cranberries

Process raspberries with syrup in food processor or blender until smooth; press through strainer, discarding seeds. Combine wine, raspberry purée and liqueur in pitcher; refrigerate until serving time. Rinse out wine bottle and remove label.

Fully open top of carton. Place wine bottle in center of carton. Tape bottle securely to carton so bottle will not move when adding water. Pour 2 cups distilled water into carton. Carefully push pine sprigs, cranberries and tinsel into water between bottle and carton to form decorative design. Add remaining water to almost fill carton. Freeze until firm, 8 hours or overnight.

Just before serving, peel carton from ice block. Using funnel, pour punch back into wine bottle. Wrap bottom of ice block with white cotton napkin or towel to hold while serving.

Makes 8 servings

Note: Punch may also be served in punch bowl if desired.

Ham Stromboli

Sausage Vegetable Frittata

5 eggs
¼ cup milk
2 tablespoons grated Parmesan cheese
½ teaspoon dried oregano leaves
½ teaspoon black pepper
1 (10-ounce) package BOB EVANS® Skinless
    Link Sausage
2 tablespoons butter or margarine
1 small zucchini, sliced (about 1 cup)
½ cup shredded carrots
⅓ cup sliced green onions with tops
¾ cup (3 ounces) shredded Swiss cheese
    Carrot curls (optional)

Whisk eggs in medium bowl; stir in milk, Parmesan cheese, oregano and pepper. Set aside. Cook sausage in large skillet over medium heat until browned, turning occasionally. Drain off any drippings. Remove sausage from skillet and cut into ½-inch lengths. Melt butter in same skillet. Add zucchini, shredded carrots and onions; cook and stir over medium heat until tender. Top with sausage, then Swiss cheese. Pour egg mixture over vegetable mixture. Stir gently to combine. Cook, without stirring, over low heat 8 to 10 minutes or until center is almost set. Remove from heat. Let stand 5 minutes before cutting into wedges; serve hot. Garnish with carrot curls, if desired. Refrigerate leftovers.   *Makes 4 to 6 servings*

Nutty Bacon Cheeseball

1 package (8 ounces) cream cheese, softened
½ cup milk
2 cups (8 ounces) shredded sharp Cheddar
    cheese
2 cups (8 ounces) shredded Monterey Jack
    cheese
¼ cup (1 ounce) crumbled blue cheese
¼ cup finely minced green onions (white
    parts only)
1 jar (2 ounces) diced pimiento, drained
10 slices bacon, cooked, drained, finely
    crumbled and divided
¾ cup finely chopped pecans, divided
    Salt and black pepper to taste
¼ cup minced parsley
1 tablespoon poppy seeds

Beat cream cheese and milk on low speed in large bowl until blended. Add cheeses. Beat on medium speed until well combined. Add onions, pimiento, ½ of bacon and ½ of pecans. Beat until well mixed. Add salt and pepper to taste. Transfer ½ of mixture to large piece of plastic wrap. Form into ball; wrap tightly. Repeat with remaining mixture. Refrigerate until chilled, at least two hours.

Combine remaining bacon and pecans with parsley and poppy seeds in pie plate or large dinner plate. Remove plastic wrap from each ball; roll each in bacon mixture until well coated. Wrap each ball tightly in plastic wrap and refrigerate until ready to use, up to 24 hours.   *Makes about 24 servings*

Sausage Vegetable Frittata

Cinnamon-Nut Bubble Ring

DOUGH

¾ cup apple juice, room temperature

1 egg

2 tablespoons butter, softened

1 teaspoon salt

3 cups bread flour

½ cup finely chopped walnuts

¼ cup granulated sugar

2 tablespoons nonfat dry milk powder

¼ teaspoon ground cinnamon

2 teaspoons active dry yeast

CINNAMON COATING

½ cup granulated sugar

4 teaspoons ground cinnamon

3 tablespoons butter, melted

APPLE GLAZE

1 cup powdered sugar

4 to 5 teaspoons apple juice

1. Measuring carefully, place all dough ingredients in bread machine pan in order specified by owner's manual. Program dough cycle setting; press start. (Do not use delay cycle.) Lightly grease 10-inch tube pan; set aside.

2. When cycle is complete, remove dough to lightly floured surface. If necessary, knead in additional bread flour to make dough easy to handle. For cinnamon topping, combine granulated sugar and cinnamon in shallow bowl. Shape dough into 2-inch balls. Roll in melted butter; coat evenly with cinnamon-sugar mixture. Place in prepared pan. Cover with clean towel; let rise in warm, draft-free place 1 to 1½ hours or until doubled in size.

3. Preheat oven to 350°F. Bake bread 30 minutes or until golden brown. Let cool in pan on wire rack 10 minutes; carefully remove from pan. Cool completely.

4. For apple glaze, combine powdered sugar and apple juice in medium bowl until smooth; drizzle over bubble ring. *Makes 12 servings*

Note: To warm apple juice, place in 2-cup microwavable glass measure and heat at HIGH 10 to 15 seconds or until of desired temperature.

Ham and Rice Pie

1 bag SUCCESS® Rice

Vegetable cooking spray

1 cup (4 ounces) shredded low-fat Cheddar cheese

8 ounces egg substitute, divided

2 tablespoons reduced-calorie margarine

1 cup sliced fresh mushrooms

½ cup chopped green onions

½ cup chopped red bell pepper

½ teaspoon salt

¼ teaspoon dried tarragon leaves, crushed

¼ teaspoon black pepper

6 ounces turkey ham, cut into strips

1 cup broccoli flowerets, cooked

¼ cup flour

½ cup fat-free sour cream

Prepare rice according to package directions.

Preheat oven to 350°F. Spray 10-inch pie plate with cooking spray; set aside.

Place hot rice in medium bowl. Add cheese; stir until melted. Stir in ½ of the egg substitute. With back of spoon, spread rice mixture onto bottom and up side of prepared pie plate to form shell.

Melt margarine in large saucepan over medium heat. Add mushrooms, green onions, red pepper, salt, tarragon and black pepper. Cook, stirring occasionally, until vegetables are crisp-tender. Remove from heat. Stir in ham and broccoli. In small bowl, beat remaining egg substitute, flour and sour cream until blended. Add to ham mixture; mix well. Pour into rice shell. Bake just until center is set, about 30 minutes. Let stand 5 minutes before cutting into wedges to serve. *Makes 8 servings*

Silver Dollar Pancakes with Mixed Berry Topping

1¼ **cups all-purpose flour**

  2 **tablespoons sugar**

  2 **teaspoons baking soda**

1½ **cups buttermilk**

  ½ **cup EGG BEATERS® Healthy Real Egg Product**

  3 **tablespoons FLEISCHMANN'S® Original Margarine, melted, divided**

    Mixed Berry Topping (recipe follows)

In large bowl, combine flour, sugar and baking soda. Stir in buttermilk, Egg Beaters® and 2 tablespoons margarine just until blended.

Brush large nonstick griddle or skillet with some of remaining margarine; heat over medium-high heat. Using 1 heaping tablespoon batter for each pancake, spoon batter onto griddle. Cook until bubbly; turn and cook until lightly browned. Repeat with remaining batter using remaining margarine as needed to make 28 pancakes. Serve hot with Mixed Berry Topping.

Makes 28 (2-inch) pancakes

Mixed Berry Topping: In medium saucepan, over medium-low heat, combine 1 (12-ounce) package frozen mixed berries,* thawed, ¼ cup honey and ½ teaspoon grated gingerroot (or ⅛ teaspoon ground ginger). Cook and stir just until hot and well blended. Serve over pancakes.

*Three cups mixed fresh berries may be substituted.

Prep Time: 20 minutes
Cook Time: 20 minutes

┌─ *Holiday Hint:* ─────────────

Sour milk may be substituted for the buttermilk in this recipe. For sour milk, place 1 tablespoon cider vinegar in a 1-cup glass measuring cup. Add enough milk to measure 1 cup. Let this mixture stand for five minutes.

French Breakfast Crêpes

1 cup all-purpose flour
1 cup fat-free (skim) milk
⅔ cup EGG BEATERS® Healthy Real Egg
**   Product**
1 tablespoon FLEISCHMANN'S® Original
**   Margarine, melted**

In medium bowl, combine flour, milk, Egg Beaters and margarine; let stand 30 minutes.

Heat lightly greased 8-inch nonstick skillet or crêpe pan over medium-high heat. Pour in scant ¼ cup batter, tilting pan to cover bottom. Cook for 1 to 2 minutes; turn and cook for 30 seconds to 1 minute more. Place on waxed paper. Stir batter and repeat to make 10 crêpes. Fill with desired fillings or use in recipes calling for prepared crêpes.

Makes 10 crêpes

Strawberry Yogurt Crêpes: In medium bowl, combine 1 pint low fat vanilla yogurt and 2 tablespoons orange-flavored liqueur or orange juice; reserve ½ cup. Stir 2 cups sliced strawberries into remaining yogurt mixture. Spoon ¼ cup strawberry mixture down center of each prepared crêpe; roll up. Top with reserved yogurt mixture.

Blueberry Crêpes: In medium saucepan, combine 2 cups fresh or frozen blueberries, ⅓ cup water, 2 teaspoons lemon juice and 2 teaspoons cornstarch. Cook over medium-high heat, stirring frequently until mixture thickens and begins to boil. Reduce heat; simmer 1 minute. Chill.

Spoon 2 tablespoons low fat vanilla yogurt down center of each prepared crêpe; roll up. Top with blueberry sauce.

Prep Time: 10 minutes
Cook Time: 40 minutes

Coconut Snowball Cocoa

1 pint vanilla ice cream
1 cup flaked coconut
½ cup unsweetened cocoa powder
1 quart milk
½ cup dark rum (optional)
¾ to 1 cup cream of coconut
1 teaspoon coconut extract
½ cup chocolate-flavored ice cream sauce
**   (optional)**
8 maraschino cherries (optional)

Scoop ice cream into 8 small balls; immediately roll in coconut. Place on waxed paper-lined baking sheet; freeze until ready to use.

Whisk cocoa into milk in large saucepan. Stir in rum, if desired, cream of coconut and coconut extract. Bring to a simmer over medium-high heat. Pour into 8 large heatproof mugs.

Float ice cream balls in cocoa. If desired, drizzle each ice cream ball with chocolate sauce and top with cherry.

Makes 8 servings

French Breakfast Crêpe

French Toast Eggnog Style

1¼ cups half-and-half

1 cup milk

5 eggs, slightly beaten

3 tablespoons sugar

1 teaspoon rum extract

1 teaspoon vanilla

⅛ teaspoon ground nutmeg

1 loaf (1 pound) hearty-style white bread,
   cut into ¾- to 1-inch slices

2 tablespoons butter or margarine, divided
   Powdered sugar

Preheat oven to 200°F.

Combine half-and-half, milk, eggs, sugar, rum and vanilla extracts and nutmeg in large bowl. Beat until thoroughly blended. Dip 2 to 3 bread slices into mixture. Soak 1 to 2 minutes to allow liquid to completely penetrate bread. Remove carefully to avoid tearing bread. Set aside. Repeat with remaining slices.

Heat large skillet over medium heat. Add ½ tablespoon butter; melt. Add 3 to 4 bread slices. Cook over medium heat 5 minutes or until browned on both sides. Place cooked slices on baking sheet; keep warm in oven. Repeat with remaining bread. Arrange on serving platter and dust lightly with powdered sugar. Serve immediately.   *Makes 4 to 6 servings*

Crabmeat Quiche

1 (9-inch) unbaked pastry shell

4 eggs

1½ cups light cream or half-and-half

1 envelope LIPTON® RECIPE SECRETS®
   Savory Herb with Garlic Soup Mix*

1 cup flaked crabmeat (about 6 ounces)

1 to 2 tablespoons dry sherry (optional)

2 cups shredded Swiss cheese (about
   8 ounces)

*Also terrific with Lipton® Recipe Secrets® Onion-Mushroom or Golden Onion Soup Mix.

Preheat oven to 400°F.

Bake pastry shell 10 minutes. Remove from oven; *reduce oven temperature to 375°F.*

In large bowl, beat eggs. Blend in cream, soup mix, crabmeat and sherry. Sprinkle cheese in pastry shell; pour in egg mixture. Bake 40 minutes or until knife inserted in center comes out clean and pastry is golden. Garnish, if desired, with orange slices, grapes and fresh herbs. Serve hot or cold.

Makes 6 servings

Eggstra Special Omelets for Two

6 eggs
3 tablespoons half-and-half, light cream or milk
¼ teaspoons salt
⅛ teaspoon ground black pepper
2 tablespoons I CAN'T BELIEVE IT'S NOT BUTTER!® Spread, divided
Special Omelet Fillings*

*Fillings are for 2 omelets.

In small bowl, with wire whisk or fork, beat eggs, half-and-half, salt and pepper; set aside.

In 8-inch nonstick skillet, melt 1 tablespoon I Can't Believe It's Not Butter! Spread; add ½ of the egg mixture. With spatula, lift edges of omelet, tilting pan to allow uncooked mixture to flow to bottom. When omelet is set and slightly moist, add desired Special Omelet Filling. With spatula, fold omelet and cook 30 seconds. Repeat with remaining 1 tablespoon I Can't Believe It's Not Butter! Spread and egg mixture.   *Makes 2 servings*

Springtime Asparagus Omelet Filling: In 10-inch skillet, melt 2 tablespoons I CAN'T BELIEVE IT'S NOT BUTTER!® Spread over medium-high heat and cook ¼ cup chopped shallots or onions until tender. Add 1½ cups cut-up asparagus and salt and ground black pepper to taste. Cook until asparagus is tender. Spoon into omelets, then evenly sprinkle with ¼ cup grated Parmesan cheese.

Western Omelet Filling: In 10-inch skillet, melt 1 tablespoon I CAN'T BELIEVE IT'S NOT BUTTER!® Spread over medium-high heat and cook 1 cup chopped bell pepper, 1 cup diced potatoes, ½ cup chopped onion and salt and ground black pepper to taste, stirring occasionally, until vegetables are tender. Spoon into omelets.

Florentine Omelet Filling: In 10-inch skillet, melt 2 tablespoons I CAN'T BELIEVE IT'S NOT BUTTER!® Spread over medium-high heat and cook ¼ cup chopped shallots or onions until tender. Add 4 cups baby spinach leaves and cook, stirring occasionally, until wilted. Stir in ½ cup chopped prosciutto (optional) and ground black pepper to taste. Spoon into omelets, then evenly sprinkle, if desired, with ½ cup crumbled goat cheese.

Salmon Omelet Filling: Fill omelets with 2 thin slices smoked salmon, 2 tablespoons chopped red onion, 2 teaspoons chopped drained capers, ¼ cup cream cheese and salt and ground black pepper to taste.

Fresh Tomato-Basil Omelet Filling: Fill omelets with 2 chopped plum tomatoes, ⅔ cup chopped fresh mozzarella cheese, 4 fresh basil leaves, cut in thin strips, and salt and ground black pepper to taste.

Eggstra Special Omelet

Corned Beef Hash

2 large russet potatoes, peeled and cut into
    ½-inch cubes
½ teaspoon salt
¼ teaspoon black pepper
¼ cup butter or margarine
1 large onion, chopped
8 ounces corned beef, finely chopped
1 tablespoon prepared horseradish, drained
¼ cup whipping cream (optional)
4 poached or fried eggs

1. Place potatoes in 10-inch skillet. Cover potatoes with water. Bring to a boil over high heat. Reduce heat to low; simmer 6 minutes. (Potatoes will be firm.) Drain potatoes in colander; sprinkle with salt and pepper.

2. Wipe out skillet with paper towel. Add butter and onion; cook and stir over medium-high heat 5 minutes. Stir in corned beef, horseradish and potatoes; mix well. Press down mixture with spatula to flatten into compact layer.

3. Reduce heat to low. Drizzle cream evenly over mixture. Cook 10 to 15 minutes. Turn mixture with spatula; pat down and continue cooking 10 to 15 minutes or until bottom is well browned. Top each serving with poached egg. Serve immediately. Garnish, if desired. *Makes 4 servings*

Ham-Egg-Brie Strudel

4 eggs
1 tablespoon minced green onion
1 tablespoon minced parsley
¼ teaspoon salt
⅛ teaspoon black pepper
1 tablespoon vegetable oil
4 sheets phyllo pastry
2 tablespoons butter or margarine, melted
3 ounces sliced ham
3 ounces Brie cheese

1. Preheat oven to 375°F. Lightly beat eggs; add green onion, parsley, salt and pepper. Heat oil in medium skillet over medium-low heat. Add egg mixture; cook and stir until softly scrambled. Set aside.

2. Place 1 phyllo sheet on large piece of waxed paper. Brush lightly with butter. Top with second phyllo sheet; brush with butter. Repeat with remaining phyllo sheets. Arrange half of ham slices near short end of pastry, leaving 2-inch border around short end and sides. Place scrambled eggs over ham. Cut cheese into small pieces. Place over eggs; top with remaining ham.

3. Fold in long sides of phyllo; fold short end over ham. Use waxed paper to roll pastry to enclose filling. Place on lightly greased baking sheet, seam side down. Brush with remaining butter. Bake about 15 minutes or until lightly browned. Slice and serve immediately. *Makes 4 servings*

Corned Beef Hash

Festive Yule Loaf

2¾ cups all-purpose flour, divided
⅓ cup sugar
1 teaspoon salt
1 package active dry yeast
1 cup milk
½ cup butter or margarine
1 egg
½ cup golden raisins
½ cup chopped candied red and green
    cherries
½ cup chopped pecans
    Vanilla Glaze (recipe follows, optional)

Combine 1½ cups flour, sugar, salt and yeast in large bowl. Heat milk and butter over medium heat until very warm (120° to 130°F). Gradually stir into flour mixture. Add egg. Mix with electric mixer on low speed 1 minute. Beat on high speed 3 minutes, scraping sides of bowl frequently. Toss raisins, cherries and pecans with ¼ cup flour in small bowl; stir into yeast mixture. Stir in enough of remaining 1 cup flour to make a soft dough. Turn out onto lightly floured surface. Knead about 10 minutes or until smooth and elastic. Place in greased bowl; turn to grease top of dough. Cover with towel. Let rise in warm, draft-free place about 1 hour or until double in volume.

Punch dough down. Divide in half. Roll out each half on lightly floured surface to form 8-inch circle. Fold in half; press only folded edge firmly. Place on ungreased cookie sheet. Cover with towel. Let rise in warm, draft-free place about 30 minutes or until double in volume.

Preheat oven to 375°F. Bake 20 to 25 minutes until golden brown. Remove from cookie sheet and cool completely on wire rack. Frost with Vanilla Glaze, if desired. Store in airtight containers.

Makes 2 loaves

Vanilla Glaze: Combine 1 cup sifted powdered sugar, 4 to 5 teaspoons light cream or half-and-half and ½ teaspoon vanilla extract in small bowl; stir until smooth.

Southwest Tuna Sandwiches

  2 cans (6 ounces each) tuna in water, drained
    or 2 cups diced cooked chicken
  1 can (4 ounces) chopped mild green chilies
½ cup reduced-fat mayonnaise
½ cup finely chopped seeded peeled
    cucumber
½ cup chopped red bell pepper
¼ cup chopped green onions
¼ cup finely chopped fresh cilantro
½ teaspoon cumin
¼ teaspoon garlic powder
    Salt and pepper to taste
  4 small pita breads (6-inch size)
  1 cup shredded leaf lettuce
½ cup sliced pitted ripe olives
½ cup chopped tomatoes
½ cup (2 ounces) shredded Cheddar cheese

Combine tuna, chilies, mayonnaise, cucumber, bell pepper, green onions, cilantro, cumin and garlic powder in medium bowl. Toss to mix. Break up large chunks of tuna. Do not flake finely.

Add salt and pepper to taste. Cover and refrigerate 1 hour or until chilled.

Cut each pita in half crosswise and fill with tuna salad. Add lettuce, olives, tomatoes and Cheddar cheese to each pita half and serve.

Makes 4 servings

Banana Nog

2 cups milk

1 large ripe banana, cut into pieces

½ cup sugar

1 tablespoon cornstarch

2 egg yolks*

⅔ cup light rum

¼ cup crème de cacao

1 teaspoon vanilla

2 cups half-and-half, chilled

Whipped cream

Unsweetened cocoa powder

6 miniature candy canes

*Use only grade A clean, uncracked eggs.

1. Process milk and banana in blender or food processor until smooth. Mix sugar and cornstarch in medium saucepan; stir in milk mixture. Heat to simmering over medium heat, stirring occasionally.

2. Lightly beat egg yolks in small bowl; whisk about ½ cup milk mixture into egg yolks. Whisk yolk mixture back into saucepan. Cook over medium heat, stirring constantly, until thick enough to coat the back of a spoon. *Do not boil.*

3. Remove from heat; stir in rum, liqueur and vanilla. Pour into large heatproof pitcher or bowl. Cover; refrigerate until chilled.

4. Just before serving, stir half-and-half into eggnog mixture. Serve in mugs or punch cups; garnish with dollops of whipped cream and sprinkles of cocoa. Tie pieces of red and green ribbon around candy canes; use as stirrers.

Makes 6 servings (about 6 ounces each)

Holiday Hint:

Eggnog was traditionally made with raw eggs, but now raw eggs introduce the risk of bacterial contamination. So be sure to choose a recipe like this one that uses a cooked egg custard base.

Potato Straw Cake with Ham & Gruyère

4 medium Colorado russet variety potatoes

1 tablespoon water

2 teaspoons lemon juice

2 teaspoons Dijon mustard

1 cup (4 ounces) thinly sliced ham, cut into strips

¾ cup (3 ounces) shredded Gruyère cheese

½ teaspoon dried tarragon, crushed *or*
    ¼ teaspoon ground nutmeg

3 to 4 green onions, thinly sliced, white parts separated from dark green tops

3 teaspoons oil, divided

Salt and black pepper

Peel and grate potatoes. Place in bowl with water to cover; let stand at room temperature about ½ hour while preparing other ingredients. Blend 1 tablespoon water, lemon juice and mustard in bowl. Stir in ham, cheese, tarragon and white parts of onions. Reserve green onion tops. Drain potatoes, wrap in several thicknesses of paper towels or clean dish towel and squeeze to wring out much of liquid.

Heat 1½ teaspoons oil in heavy 8- or 10-inch nonstick skillet over high heat. Add half the potatoes, pressing into skillet with back of spoon. Season to taste with salt and pepper. Spread evenly with ham mixture. Cover with remaining potatoes. Season to taste with salt and pepper. Reduce heat to medium-low. Cover and cook 20 to 30 minutes or until potatoes are crisp and golden brown on bottom. Uncover and place rimless baking sheet over skillet. Invert skillet onto baking sheet to release potato cake. Add remaining 1½ teaspoons oil to skillet. Slide cake into skillet, uncooked side down. Cook, uncovered, over medium-low heat 10 to 15 minutes. Increase heat to medium-high and cook until brown and crisp, shaking pan several times to prevent sticking. Slide potato cake onto serving plate. Garnish with reserved green onion tops. Cut into wedges.

Makes 5 to 6 servings

Favorite recipe from **Colorado Potato Administrative Committee**

Harvest Rice Breakfast Cereal

1 bag SUCCESS® Rice

1 cup evaporated skim milk

¼ cup skim milk

⅓ cup packed brown sugar

¼ cup golden raisins

½ teaspoon pumpkin pie spice

½ teaspoon vanilla

Prepare rice according to package directions.

Combine rice and milk in medium saucepan. Cook over medium heat 5 minutes, stirring occasionally. Add all remaining ingredients *except* vanilla. Reduce heat to low. Simmer 20 minutes, stirring frequently. Stir in vanilla. Serve hot.   *Makes 4 servings*

Potato Straw Cake with Ham & Gruyère

216

Denver Spoonbread

3 tablespoons butter, divided

2 tablespoons grated Parmesan cheese

½ cup chopped onion

¼ cup chopped green bell pepper

¼ cup chopped red bell pepper

2½ cups milk

1 cup yellow cornmeal

1 teaspoon salt

1½ cups (6 ounces) shredded Cheddar cheese

4 eggs, separated*

*Egg whites must be free from any yolk to reach proper volume when beaten.

1. Preheat oven to 350°F.

2. Grease 1½-quart soufflé dish with 1 tablespoon butter. Sprinkle bottom and side of dish evenly with Parmesan cheese.

3. Melt remaining 2 tablespoons butter in medium, heavy saucepan over medium heat. Add onion and bell peppers; cook 5 to 7 minutes or until tender, stirring occasionally. Transfer mixture to small bowl; set aside.

4. Combine milk, cornmeal and salt in same saucepan. Bring to a boil over high heat. Reduce heat to medium; cook and stir 5 minutes or until mixture thickens. Remove from heat. Stir in Cheddar cheese until cheese is melted. Stir in onion mixture.

5. Beat egg whites in clean large bowl using clean beaters with electric mixer at high speed until stiff but not dry; set aside.

6. Beat egg yolks in separate large bowl. Stir into cornmeal mixture. Stir ⅓ of egg whites into cornmeal mixture. Fold remaining egg whites into cornmeal mixture until evenly incorporated. Pour into prepared soufflé dish.

7. Bake about 50 minutes or until puffed and golden brown. Serve immediately. Garnish, if desired. *Makes 6 servings*

Holiday Hint:

Spoonbread is a soft, moist egg-based dish made with cornmeal. It is baked in a casserole or soufflé dish. The result is a side dish that is more like a pudding than a bread. Spoonbread, attributed to early settlers of Virginia, remains a favorite Southern dish often served at holiday meals.

Denver Spoonbread

Puffy Orange Omelets

5 eggs, separated
2 tablespoons all-purpose flour
1 tablespoon grated orange peel
4 tablespoons sugar, divided
¾ cup orange juice
2 tablespoons butter or margarine
2 tablespoons brown sugar

1. Preheat oven to 375°F. Whisk together egg yolks, flour and orange peel in large bowl until well blended.

2. Combine egg whites and 2 tablespoons sugar in medium bowl. Beat egg white mixture on high speed of electric mixer 3 to 5 minutes or until stiff, but not dry, peaks form. Fold into egg yolk mixture. Set aside.

3. Combine orange juice, butter and brown sugar in small saucepan. Cook and stir over medium heat 3 to 5 minutes or until butter melts and sauce is heated through.

4. Grease 6 (5-ounce) soufflé dishes or custard cups; lightly sprinkle with remaining 2 tablespoons sugar, shaking out excess. Place 1 tablespoon orange sauce in bottom of each soufflé dish, reserving remaining sauce. Spoon egg mixture equally into dishes.

5. Place soufflé dishes in shallow baking pan. Bake 15 to 20 minutes or until tops are golden brown. Serve immediately with reserved warm orange sauce. *Makes 6 servings*

Ham Scramble

¼ cup butter or margarine
2 cups (12 ounces) chopped CURE 81® ham
2 tablespoons sliced green onion
8 eggs, beaten
½ cup sour cream
2 tablespoons grated Parmesan cheese
½ teaspoon salt
¼ teaspoon black pepper
3 English muffins, split, toasted and buttered

In large skillet melt butter. Add ham and green onion. Cook over medium-high heat, stirring constantly until onion is tender. In bowl, beat together eggs, sour cream, Parmesan cheese, salt and black pepper. Add to ham mixture. Cook, without stirring, until mixture begins to set on bottom. Draw a spatula across bottom of pan to form large curds. Continue cooking until eggs are thickened but still moist; do not stir constantly. Serve immediately over toasted English muffin halves. *Makes 6 servings*

Puffy Orange Omelet

Rainbow Fruit Salad with Yogurt Sauce

1 medium pear, sliced

1 medium navel orange, peeled and cut into segments

1 cup sliced strawberries

¾ cup seedless red grapes

1 kiwifruit, peeled and chopped

2 tablespoons lemon juice

1 container (8 ounces) plain nonfat yogurt

2 tablespoons packed brown sugar

¼ teaspoon ground cinnamon

1 medium cantaloupe

1. Combine pear, orange, strawberries, grapes and kiwi in large bowl. Pour lemon juice over fruit; toss gently to coat.

2. Blend yogurt, brown sugar and cinnamon in small bowl until smooth.

3. Cut cantaloupe in half between stem and blossom ends. Scoop out and discard seeds. Carefully slice cantaloupe into 4 rings about 1 inch thick.

4. Place cantaloupe rings on each of 4 plates. Fill center of each ring with fruit salad; drizzle with yogurt mixture.   *Makes 4 servings*

Prep Time: 15 minutes

Hot Crab and Cheese on Muffins

4 English muffins, split

1 tablespoon butter or margarine

3 green onions, chopped

⅓ cup chopped red bell pepper

½ pound fresh crabmeat, drained and flaked*

1 to 2 teaspoons hot pepper sauce

1 cup (4 ounces) shredded Cheddar cheese

1 cup (4 ounces) shredded Monterey Jack cheese

*Two cans (6 ounces each) fancy crabmeat, drained, can be substituted for fresh crabmeat.

1. Preheat broiler. Place muffin halves on lightly greased baking sheet. Broil 4 inches from heat 2 minutes or until muffins are lightly toasted. Place on large microwavable plate.

2. Melt butter in medium skillet over medium heat. Add green onions and bell pepper; cook and stir 3 to 4 minutes or until tender. Remove from heat; stir in crabmeat, hot pepper sauce and cheeses. Spoon about ⅓ cup crab mixture onto muffin halves.

3. Microwave at HIGH 2 to 3 minutes, rotating platter once, or until crab mixture is heated through.   *Makes 8 servings*

Prep and Cook Time: 12 minutes

Rainbow Fruit Salad with Yogurt Sauce

Make-Ahead Breakfast Casserole

2½ cups seasoned croutons

1 pound BOB EVANS® Original Recipe Roll Sausage

4 eggs

2¼ cups milk

1 (10½-ounce) can condensed cream of mushroom soup

1 (10-ounce) package frozen chopped spinach, thawed and squeezed dry

1 (4-ounce) can mushrooms, drained and chopped

1 cup (4 ounces) shredded sharp Cheddar cheese

1 cup (4 ounces) shredded Monterey Jack cheese

¼ teaspoon dry mustard

Fresh herb sprigs and carrot strips (optional)

Picante sauce or salsa (optional)

Spread croutons on bottom of greased 13×9-inch baking dish. Crumble sausage into medium skillet. Cook over medium heat until browned, stirring occasionally. Drain off any drippings. Spread over croutons. Whisk eggs and milk in large bowl until blended. Stir in soup, spinach, mushrooms, cheeses and mustard. Pour egg mixture over sausage and croutons. Refrigerate overnight. Preheat oven to 325°F. Bake egg mixture 50 to 55 minutes or until set and lightly browned on top. Garnish with herb sprigs and carrot, if desired. Serve hot with picante sauce, if desired. Refrigerate leftovers.

Makes 10 to 12 servings

Wisconsin Spicy Apple Eggnog

3 cups milk

2 cups light cream or half-and-half

2 beaten eggs*

⅓ cup sugar

½ teaspoon ground cinnamon

Dash salt

¾ cup apple brandy

Ground nutmeg

*Use clean, uncracked eggs.

In large saucepan combine milk, light cream, eggs, sugar, cinnamon and salt. Cook and stir over medium heat until mixture is slightly thickened and heated through. *Do not boil.* Remove from heat; stir in apple brandy. To serve, ladle mixture into 12 heatproof glasses or cups. Sprinkle each serving with nutmeg. Serve warm.

Makes 12 servings

Prep Time: 25 minutes

*Favorite recipe from **Wisconsin Milk Marketing Board***

Make-Ahead Breakfast Casserole

Bountiful Breads

Nutty Cinnamon Sticky Buns

⅓ cup margarine or butter

½ cup packed brown sugar

½ cup PLANTERS® Pecans, chopped

1 teaspoon ground cinnamon

1 (17.3-ounce) package refrigerated biscuits
   (8 large biscuits)

1. Melt margarine or butter in 9-inch round baking pan in 350°F oven.

2. Mix brown sugar, pecans and cinnamon in small bowl; sprinkle over melted margarine or butter in pan. Arrange biscuits in pan with sides touching (biscuits will fit tightly in pan).

3. Bake at 350°F for 25 to 30 minutes or until biscuits are golden brown and center biscuit is fully cooked. Invert pan immediately onto serving plate. Spread any remaining topping from pan on buns. Serve warm.   *Makes 8 buns*

Preparation Time: 10 minutes
Cook Time: 25 minutes
Total Time: 35 minutes

Holiday Hint:

When the holiday season gets hectic, you can still prepare a breakfast treat for your family with this quick and easy recipe for sticky buns. The secret is to start with a refrigerated biscuit dough.

Nutty Cinnamon Sticky Buns

Cherry Zucchini Bread

2 eggs
¾ cup sugar
⅓ cup vegetable oil
⅓ cup lemon juice
¼ cup water
2 cups all-purpose flour
2 teaspoons baking powder
1 teaspoon ground cinnamon
½ teaspoon baking soda
¼ teaspoon salt
⅔ cup shredded unpeeled zucchini
⅔ cup dried tart cherries
1 tablespoon grated lemon peel

Put eggs in large mixing bowl. Beat with an electric mixer on medium speed 3 to 4 minutes or until eggs are thick and lemon colored. Add sugar, oil, lemon juice and water; mix well. Combine flour, baking powder, cinnamon, baking soda and salt. Add flour mixture to egg mixture; mix well. Stir in zucchini, cherries and lemon peel.

Grease and flour bottom of 8½×4½-inch loaf pan. Pour batter into prepared pan. Bake in preheated oven to 350°F 55 to 65 minutes or until wooden toothpick inserted in center comes out clean. Let cool in pan on wire rack 10 minutes. Loosen edges with a metal spatula. Remove from pan. Let cool completely. Wrap tightly in plastic wrap and store in refrigerator. *Makes 1 loaf, about 16 servings*

Favorite recipe from **Cherry Marketing Institute**

Mexican Corn Bread

¼ pound VELVEETA® Mexican Pasteurized Process Cheese Spread with Jalapeño Peppers, cubed
2 tablespoons milk
1 egg, beaten
1 (8½-ounce) package corn muffin mix

• PREHEAT oven to 350°F.

• STIR together process cheese spread and milk in saucepan over low heat until process cheese spread is melted. Add with egg to muffin mix, mixing just until moistened. Pour into greased 8-inch square pan.

• BAKE 20 minutes. *Makes 6 to 8 servings*

Variation: Substitute VELVEETA® Pasteurized Prepared Cheese Product for VELVEETA® Pasteurized Process Cheese Spread with Jalapeño Peppers.

Prep Time: 10 minutes
Cook Time: 20 minutes

Cherry Zucchini Bread

Whole Wheat Herbed Bread Wreath

4 cups all-purpose flour, divided

2 packages active dry yeast

2 tablespoons sugar

4 teaspoons dried rosemary, crushed

1 tablespoon salt

2½ cups water

2 tablespoons olive oil

3 cups whole wheat flour, divided

1 egg, beaten

Combine 2½ cups all-purpose flour, yeast, sugar, rosemary and salt in large bowl. Heat water until very warm (120° to 130°F). Gradually add water and oil to flour mixture, beating with electric mixer on medium speed 2 minutes until blended. Add 1 cup whole wheat flour. Beat on high speed 2 minutes. By hand, stir in enough of remaining flours to make a soft, sticky dough. Place in greased bowl; turn to grease top of dough. Cover with towel. Let rise in warm, draft-free place about 1½ hours or until doubled in volume.

Punch down dough. Turn out onto well-floured surface. Knead about 10 minutes or until smooth and elastic. Divide into thirds. Roll each piece to form 24-inch rope. Place on large greased cookie sheet. Braid ropes beginning at center and working toward ends. Seal edges. Shape into circle around greased 10-ounce ovenproof round bowl. Seal ends well. Cover with towel. Let rise in warm, draft-free place about 30 minutes or until doubled in volume.

Preheat oven to 450°F. Carefully brush wreath with egg. Bake 25 to 30 minutes until wreath sounds hollow when tapped and top is golden brown. Cool on cookie sheet 10 minutes. Carefully remove from cookie sheet and bowl; cool completely on wire rack. Store tightly wrapped in plastic wrap at room temperature. *Makes one 12-inch wreath*

Tip: If desired, fill center of bread with watercress, radish roses and star-shaped cut-outs of flavored cheese.

Biscuits

2 cups sifted all-purpose flour

3 teaspoons baking powder

1 teaspoon salt

⅓ CRISCO® Stick or ⅓ cup CRISCO®
    all-vegetable shortening

¾ cup milk

1. Heat oven to 425°F. Combine flour, baking powder and salt in bowl. Cut in ⅓ cup shortening using pastry blender (or 2 knives) until mixture resembles coarse meal. Add milk; stir with fork until blended.

2. Transfer dough to lightly floured surface. Knead gently 8 to 10 times. Roll dough ½ inch thick. Cut with floured 2-inch-round cutter.

3. Bake at 425°F 12 to 15 minutes. *Do not overbake.*   *Makes 12 to 16 (2-inch) biscuits*

Whole Wheat Herbed Bread Wreath

Spicy Mincemeat Bread

6 tablespoons butter

1 cup packed light brown sugar

2 eggs

1 teaspoon vanilla

2½ cups all-purpose flour

1½ teaspoons baking soda

1 teaspoon ground cinnamon

¾ teaspoon baking powder

½ teaspoon ground nutmeg

¼ teaspoon salt

¾ cup sour cream

1 cup prepared mincemeat

¾ cup chopped pecans

Preheat oven to 350°F. Grease 9×5-inch loaf pan.

Beat butter and brown sugar in large bowl with electric mixer on medium speed until light and fluffy. Beat in eggs and vanilla until blended. Combine flour, baking soda, cinnamon, baking powder, nutmeg and salt. Add flour mixture to butter mixture on low speed alternately with sour cream, beginning and ending with flour mixture. Mix well after each addition. Stir in mincemeat and pecans on low speed until blended. Spoon into prepared pan.

Bake 55 to 60 minutes or until wooden pick inserted in center comes out clean. Cool in pan 15 minutes. Remove from pan and cool completely on wire rack. Store tightly wrapped in plastic wrap at room temperature. *Makes 1 loaf*

Mini Sticky Pecan Buns

1 package BOB EVANS® Frozen White Dinner Roll Dough

½ cup packed brown sugar

2 teaspoons ground cinnamon

½ cup finely chopped pecans

½ cup melted butter

Thaw dough at room temperature 45 minutes to 1 hour; do not allow dough to begin rising. Divide each piece of dough into 4 equal pieces; roll each piece in tight circle to form a ball with smooth surface. Combine sugar, cinnamon and pecans in shallow dish. Dip dough balls in melted butter and roll in sugar mixture. Arrange in 2 layers in well-greased 10-inch tube pan, allowing space for dough to rise. Combine any remaining butter and sugar mixture; pour over rolls. Cover pan with damp towel; allow to rise at room temperature until doubled in bulk. Preheat oven to 350°F. Bake 30 minutes or until light golden in color. Let stand 10 to 15 minutes before turning out of pan onto serving plate. Serve warm.

Makes 8 to 10 servings

Anadama Bread

7¾ to 8¼ cups all-purpose flour, divided
2 packages (¼ ounce each) active dry yeast
1½ teaspoons salt
2¾ cups water
¾ cup molasses
¼ cup butter
1¼ cups yellow cornmeal

1. Combine 4 cups flour, yeast and salt in large bowl. Combine water, molasses and butter in 2-quart saucepan. Heat over low heat until mixture is 120° to 130°F. (Butter does not need to completely melt.)

2. Gradually beat water mixture into flour mixture with electric mixer at low speed. Increase speed to medium; beat 2 minutes. Beat in cornmeal and 2 cups flour at low speed. Increase speed to medium; beat 2 minutes.

3. Stir in enough additional flour, about 1¾ cups to make soft dough. Turn out dough onto floured surface; flatten slightly. Knead dough 8 to 10 minutes or until smooth and elastic, adding remaining ½ cup flour to prevent sticking, if necessary.

4. Shape dough into a ball; place in large greased bowl. Turn dough over so that top is greased. Cover with towel; let rise in warm place about 1 hour or until doubled in bulk.

5. Punch down dough. Knead dough on well-floured surface 1 minute. Cut dough into halves. Cover with towel; let rest 10 minutes.

6. Grease 2 (1½-quart) soufflé or casserole dishes or 2 (9×5-inch) loaf pans. For soufflé dishes, shape each half of dough into a ball; place in prepared pans. For loaf pans, roll out one half of dough into 12×8-inch rectangle with well-floured rolling pin. Starting with one 8-inch side, roll up dough jelly-roll style. Pinch seam and ends to seal. Place loaf, seam side down, in prepared pan, tucking ends under. Repeat with remaining dough. Cover and let rise in warm place about 40 minutes or until doubled in bulk.

7. Preheat oven to 375°F. Bake 35 to 40 minutes or until loaves are browned and sound hollow when tapped. Immediately remove from soufflé dishes; cool on wire racks.   *Makes 2 loaves*

Cinnamon Bubble Ring

¼ cup sugar

½ teaspoon ground cinnamon

1 can (11 ounces) refrigerated French bread
    dough

1½ tablespoons margarine or butter, melted

1. Preheat oven to 350°F. Grease 9-inch tube pan.
Combine sugar and cinnamon in small bowl.

2. Cut dough into 16 slices; roll into balls. Arrange
12 balls evenly spaced against outer wall of pan.
Arrange remaining 4 balls evenly spaced against
tube of pan. Brush with margarine. Sprinkle sugar
mixture evenly over balls.

3. Bake 20 to 25 minutes or until golden brown.
Serve warm.   *Makes 8 servings*

Tip: For a fast start to your morning, prepare the
cinnamon buns in the pan, cover and refrigerate
overnight. All you have to do in the morning is
bake them for a quick, delicious treat.

Prep and Cook Time: 30 minutes

Orange Coconut Muffins

¾ cup all-purpose flour

¾ cup whole wheat flour

⅔ cup toasted wheat germ

½ cup sugar

½ cup coconut

1½ teaspoons baking soda

½ teaspoon salt

1 cup dairy sour cream

2 eggs

1 can (11 ounces) mandarin oranges, drained

½ cup chopped nuts

Preheat oven to 400°F. Butter 12 (2½-inch) muffin
cups.

Combine flours, wheat germ, sugar, coconut,
baking soda and salt in large bowl. Blend sour
cream, eggs and oranges in small bowl; stir into
flour mixture just until moistened. Fold in nuts.
Spoon into prepared muffin cups, filling ¾ full.

Bake 18 to 20 minutes or until wooden pick
inserted in center comes out clean. Remove from
pan. Cool on wire rack.   *Makes 12 muffins*

Favorite recipe from **Wisconsin Milk Marketing Board**

Cinnamon Bubble Ring

Grandma's® Bran Muffins

2½ cups bran flakes, divided
1 cup raisins
1 cup boiling water
½ cup canola oil
1 cup GRANDMA'S® Molasses
2 eggs, beaten
2 cups buttermilk
2¾ cups all-purpose flour
2½ teaspoons baking soda
½ teaspoon salt

Heat oven to 400°F. In medium bowl, mix 1 cup bran flakes, raisins and water. Set aside. In large bowl, combine remaining ingredients. Mix in bran-raisin mixture. Pour into greased muffin pan cups. Fill ⅔ full and bake for 20 minutes. Remove muffins and place on rack to cool.

Makes 48 muffins

─ Holiday Hint: ─────────

When preparing muffin batter, stir just until the dry ingredients are moistened. A few lumps may remain. Overbeating will result in muffins with a tough texture.

Apricot Holiday Bread

⅔ cup milk
1 teaspoon salt
1 egg
2 tablespoons butter, softened
3 cups all-purpose flour
2 tablespoons sugar
1 tablespoon active dry yeast
½ cup pecan or walnut pieces
½ cup dried apricots or peaches, chopped
¼ teaspoon ground ginger
¼ teaspoon ground nutmeg

1. Measuring carefully, place all ingredients in bread machine pan in order specified by owner's manual.

2. Program basic or white cycle and desired crust setting; press start. *(Do not use delay cycles.)* Remove baked bread from pan; cool on wire rack.

Makes 1 (1½-pound) loaf (12 to 16 servings)

Crispy Ranch Breadsticks

2 tablespoons dry ranch party dip mix
2 tablespoons sour cream
1 package (10 ounces) refrigerated pizza
    dough
Butter, melted

1. Preheat oven to 400°F. Grease baking sheets or line with parchment paper. Combine dip mix and sour cream in small bowl; set aside.

2. Unroll pizza dough on lightly floured work surface. Shape dough into 16×10-inch rectangle. Brush with melted butter. Spread dip mixture evenly over top of dough; cut into 24 (10-inch) strips. Shape into desired shapes.

3. Place breadsticks ½ inch apart on prepared baking sheets. Bake 10 minutes or until golden brown. Serve immediately or place on wire rack to cool.   *Makes 24 breadsticks*

Crispy Spiced Nut Breadsticks: Place 1 cup finely chopped pecans and 1 tablespoon vegetable oil in plastic bag; toss to coat. Combine ¼ teaspoon chili powder, ¼ teaspoon ground cumin, ¼ teaspoon curry powder, ⅛ teaspoon ground cinnamon and dash of ground red pepper in small bowl. Add to nuts; toss to coat. Place nuts in small pan over medium heat and stir constantly until nuts are lightly toasted. Sprinkle nut mixture with 1 teaspoon garlic salt; cool to room temperature. Instead of spreading dough with sour cream mixture, sprinkle ½ cup spiced nuts over dough.

Store remaining nuts in tightly covered container. Cut into 24 (10-inch) strips. Shape into desired shapes. Bake as directed.

Kikko-Style French Rolls

4 tablespoons butter or margarine
1 tablespoon KIKKOMAN® Teriyaki
    Marinade & Sauce
¼ teaspoon garlic powder
4 French rolls

Combine butter, teriyaki sauce and garlic powder in small saucepan with heatproof handle; heat on grill until butter melts. Slice each roll in half lengthwise. Place rolls, cut side down, on grill 3 to 4 inches from hot coals; cook about 2 minutes, or until golden brown. Brush butter mixture equally on each toasted roll half.   *Makes 4 servings*

Note: Rolls also may be toasted under a broiler.

Top to bottom: Crispy Spiced Nut Breadsticks and Crispy Ranch Breadsticks

Apricot-Filled Coffee Cakes

COFFEE CAKES

- 1 cup sugar
- 1 teaspoon cinnamon
- 1/2 cup butter
- 1 can (12 ounces) evaporated milk
- 1 1/2 teaspoons salt
- 2 packages active dry yeast
- 1/4 cup warm water (105° to 115°F)
- 1/2 cup sour cream
- 3 eggs
- 6 to 7 cups all-purpose flour, divided

FILLING

- 2 1/4 to 2 3/4 cups water
- 1 package (6 ounces) dried apricots (2 cups)
- 1 egg, lightly beaten
- 2 tablespoons milk
- Additional sugar

For coffee cakes, combine sugar and cinnamon in medium saucepan; stir in butter, evaporated milk and salt. Cook over medium heat 5 to 8 minutes or until butter is melted, stirring occasionally. Remove from heat; let cool slightly.

Dissolve yeast in 1/4 cup water in large bowl; stir in warm milk mixture, sour cream, 3 eggs and 3 cups flour. Beat at medium spead with electric mixer 1 to 2 minutes or until smooth. Stir in enough remaining flour, by hand, to make dough easy to handle. Turn dough out onto lightly floured surface; knead about 5 minutes or until smooth and elastic. Place dough in greased bowl; turn dough over so that top is greased. Cover and let rise in warm place 1 to 1 1/2 hours or until double in size.

For filling, combine 2 1/4 cups water and apricots in medium saucepan. Cook over low heat about 45 minutes or until apricots are tender and mixture has thickened. Add small amounts of additional water if neccesary. Stir occasionally.

Punch down dough and divide in half; let rest 10 minutes. Roll half of dough on lightly floured surface into 20×9-inch rectangle; cut into 3 (3-inch-wide) strips. Spread each strip with 1/4 cup apricot mixture to within 1/2 inch of edges. Bring 20-inch sides up together; pinch sides and ends tightly to seal well. Gently braid filled strips together. Place on large greased cookie sheet. Form into wreath; pinch ends to seal well. Repeat with remaining dough and apricot mixture. Cover and let rise in warm place 30 minutes.

Meanwhile, preheat oven to 350°F. Bake 25 to 30 minutes or until lightly browned. (Cover with foil if coffee cakes brown too quickly.) Blend beaten egg and milk in small bowl. Brush coffee cakes with egg mixture; sprinkle with additional sugar. Continue baking 5 to 10 minutes or until golden brown. Remove from cookie sheets; cool on wire racks.

Makes 2 coffeecakes

Apricot-Filled Coffee Cake

Thyme-Cheese Bubble Loaf

1 package active dry yeast

1 teaspoon sugar

1 cup warm water, 105° to 115°F

3 cups all-purpose flour

1 teaspoon salt

2 tablespoons vegetable oil

1 cup (4 ounces) shredded Monterey Jack cheese

4 tablespoons butter or margarine, melted

¼ cup chopped fresh parsley

3 teaspoons finely chopped fresh thyme *or* ¾ teaspoon dried thyme leaves, crushed

1. Sprinkle yeast and sugar over warm water in small bowl; stir until yeast is dissolved. Let stand 5 minutes or until mixture is bubbly.

2. Combine flour and salt in food processor. With food processor running, add yeast mixture and oil. Process until mixture forms dough that leaves side of bowl. If dough is too dry, add 1 to 2 tablespoons water. If dough is too wet, add 1 to 2 tablespoons additional flour until dough leaves side of bowl. Dough will be sticky.

3. Place dough in large greased bowl. Turn dough over so that top is greased. Cover with towel; let rise in warm place about 1 hour or until doubled in bulk.

4. Punch down dough. Knead cheese into dough on lightly floured surface until evenly distributed. Cover with towel; let rest 10 minutes.

5. Grease 1½-quart casserole dish or 8½×4½-inch loaf pan; set aside. Combine butter, parsley and thyme in small bowl.

6. Roll out dough into 8×6-inch rectangle with lightly floured rolling pin. Cut dough into 48 (1-inch) squares with pizza cutter. Shape each square into a ball. Dip into parsley mixture. Place in prepared pan.

7. Cover with towel; let rise in warm place about 45 minutes or until doubled in bulk. Preheat oven to 375°F.

8. Bake 35 to 40 minutes or until top is golden and loaf sounds hollow when tapped. Immediately remove from casserole dish; cool on wire rack 30 minutes. Serve warm. Store leftover bread in refrigerator. *Makes 1 loaf*

Orange Cranberry Bread

2 cups flour

¾ cup sugar

1 teaspoon baking soda

¾ cup MIRACLE WHIP® *or* MIRACLE WHIP LIGHT® Dressing

2 eggs, beaten

¼ cup orange juice

2 teaspoons grated orange peel

1 cup cranberries, chopped

• MIX flour, sugar and baking soda in large bowl. Add dressing, eggs, juice and peel; stir just until moistened. Gently stir in cranberries.

• POUR batter into greased 9×5-inch loaf pan.

• BAKE at 350°F for 55 to 60 minutes or until toothpick inserted in center comes out clean. Cool 10 minutes. Remove from pan. Cool completely on wire rack. *Makes 1 loaf*

Tip: Garnish plate with orange peel and fresh or dried cranberries.

Prep Time: 15 minutes
Bake Time: 1 hour

Cherry Orange Poppy Seed Muffins

2 cups all-purpose flour

¾ cup granulated sugar

1 tablespoon baking powder

1 tablespoon poppy seeds

¼ teaspoon salt

1 cup milk

¼ cup (½ stick) butter, melted

1 egg, slightly beaten

½ cup dried tart cherries

3 tablespoons grated orange peel

Combine flour, sugar, baking powder, poppy seeds and salt in large mixing bowl. Add milk, melted butter and egg, stirring just until dry ingredients are moistened. Gently stir in cherries and orange peel. Fill paper-lined muffin cups three-fourths full.

Bake in preheated 400°F oven 18 to 22 minutes or until wooden pick inserted in center comes out clean. Let cool in pan 5 minutes. Remove from pan and serve warm or let cool completely.

Makes 12 muffins

Favorite recipe from **Cherry Marketing Institute**

Chocolate Walnut Coffee Rings

6½ to 7 cups all-purpose flour, divided
 ½ cup granulated sugar
1½ teaspoons salt
1½ teaspoons ground cinnamon
 2 packages active dry yeast
 1 cup butter or margarine
 1 cup milk
 ½ cup water
 2 eggs
 2 egg yolks
 2 cups (12-ounce package) NESTLÉ® TOLL
    HOUSE® Semi-Sweet Chocolate Morsels
 1 cup chopped walnuts
 ⅓ cup packed brown sugar
    Vegetable oil
    Glaze (recipe follows)

In large mixer bowl, combine 2 cups flour, granulated sugar, salt, cinnamon and yeast. In small saucepan over low heat, warm butter, milk and water until very warm (120° to 130°F.). On low speed of electric mixer, gradually beat milk mixture into dry ingredients; beat for 2 minutes. Add eggs, egg yolks and 1 cup flour. Beat on high speed for 2 minutes. Stir in about 2½ cups flour to make a stiff dough. Cover; let stand for 20 minutes.

In medium bowl, combine morsels, walnuts and brown sugar. Sprinkle work surface with ½ cup flour. Turn dough onto work surface; sprinkle with additional ½ cup flour. Knead for 2 to 3 minutes; cut dough in half. On floured surface, roll out one dough half into 16×10-inch rectangle. Sprinkle one half morsel mixture to within ½ inch of edges. Starting at wide end, roll up jelly-roll fashion; pinch seam to seal. Place, seam side down, on large greased baking sheet, joining ends to form a circle. Cut outside edge at 1-inch intervals, two thirds of way through. Turn each slice on its side to overlap. Brush with oil; cover with plastic wrap.

Repeat with remaining dough and filling. Chill for 2 to 24 hours.

Let coffee rings stand uncovered at room temperature for 10 minutes. Bake in preheated 375°F. oven for 25 to 30 minutes or until golden. Remove from baking sheets; cool on wire racks. Drizzle with Glaze.   *Makes 2 coffee rings*

Glaze: In small bowl, combine 1 cup powdered sugar, 5 to 6 teaspoons milk, ½ teaspoon vanilla extract and dash ground cinnamon; blend until smooth.

Chocolate Walnut
Coffee Rings

Orange Marmalade Bread

3 cups all-purpose flour
4 teaspoons baking powder
1 teaspoon salt
½ cup chopped walnuts
¾ cup milk
¾ cup SMUCKER'S® Sweet Orange
    Marmalade
2 eggs, lightly beaten
¼ cup honey
2 tablespoons oil

Grease 9×5×3-inch loaf pan. Combine flour, baking powder and salt in large bowl. Stir in nuts. Combine milk, marmalade, eggs, honey and oil; blend well. Add to flour mixture; stir only until dry ingredients are moistened (batter will be lumpy). Turn into prepared pan.

Bake at 350°F for 65 to 70 minutes or until lightly browned and toothpick inserted in center comes out clean. *Makes 8 to 10 servings*

Pumpkin Apple Streusel Muffins

2½ cups all-purpose flour
2 cups granulated sugar
1 tablespoon pumpkin pie spice
1 teaspoon baking soda
½ teaspoon salt
2 eggs, lightly beaten
1 cup LIBBY'S® Solid Pack Pumpkin
½ cup vegetable oil
2 cups peeled, finely chopped apples
Streusel Topping (recipe follows)

COMBINE flour, sugar, pumpkin pie spice, baking soda and salt in large bowl. Combine eggs, pumpkin and oil in medium bowl, mix well. Stir into flour mixture just until moistened. Stir in apples. Spoon batter into greased or paper-lined muffin cups, filling ¾ full. Sprinkle with Streusel Topping.

BAKE in preheated 350°F. oven for 35 to 40 minutes or until wooden pick inserted in muffin comes out clean. Remove from pan to wire rack; cool slightly. Serve warm. *Makes 18 muffins*

Streusel Topping: COMBINE ⅓ cup granulated sugar, 3 tablespoons all-purpose flour and ½ teaspoon ground cinnamon in medium bowl. Cut in 2 tablespoons butter with pastry blender or two knives until mixture is crumbly.

Orange Marmalade Bread

Fast Pesto Focaccia

1 can (10 ounces) pizza crust dough
2 tablespoons prepared pesto
4 sun-dried tomatoes packed in oil, drained

1. Preheat oven to 425°F. Lightly grease 8×8×2-inch pan. Unroll pizza dough; fold in half and pat into pan.

2. Spread pesto evenly over dough. Chop tomatoes or snip with kitchen scissors; sprinkle over pesto. Press tomatoes into dough. Make indentations in dough every 2 inches using wooden spoon handle.

3. Bake 10 to 12 minutes or until golden brown. Cut into squares and serve warm or at room temperature. *Makes 16 appetizers*

Prep and Cook Time: 20 minutes

Holiday Hint:

Pesto, a green uncooked sauce from Italy, is made from fresh basil leaves, garlic, pine nuts (or walnuts), Parmesan cheese and olive oil. Pesto is most commonly served with pasta, but its intense flavor also is used to season soups, salad dressings and focaccia.

Country Recipe Biscuits

2 cups all-purpose flour
1 tablespoon baking powder
½ cup prepared **HIDDEN VALLEY®** Original Ranch® salad dressing
½ **cup buttermilk**

Preheat oven to 425°F. In small bowl, sift together flour and baking powder. Make a well in flour mixture; add salad dressing and buttermilk. Stir with fork until dough forms a ball. Drop by rounded spoonfuls onto ungreased baking sheet. Bake until lightly browned, 12 to 15 minutes.
Makes 12 biscuits

Fast Pesto Focaccia

Herb-Cheese Biscuit Loaf

1½ cups all-purpose flour

¼ cup grated Parmesan cheese

2 tablespoons yellow cornmeal

2 teaspoons baking powder

½ teaspoon salt

¼ cup butter

2 eggs

½ cup heavy cream

¾ teaspoon dried basil leaves

¾ teaspoon dried oregano leaves

⅛ teaspoon garlic powder

Additional grated Parmesan cheese (optional)

1. Preheat oven to 425°F. Grease large baking sheet; set aside.

2. Combine flour, ¼ cup cheese, cornmeal, baking powder and salt in large bowl. Cut in butter with pastry blender or two knives until mixture resembles coarse crumbs.

3. Beat eggs in medium bowl. Add cream, basil, oregano and garlic powder; beat until well blended. Add cream mixture to flour mixture; stir until mixture forms soft dough that clings together and forms a ball.

4. Turn out dough onto well-floured surface. Knead dough gently 10 to 12 times. Place dough on prepared baking sheet. Roll or pat dough into 7-inch round, about 1 inch thick.

5. Starting from center, score top of dough into 8 wedges with tip of sharp knife, taking care not to cut completely through dough. Sprinkle with additional cheese, if desired.

6. Bake 20 to 25 minutes or until wooden toothpick inserted in center comes out clean. Cool on baking sheet on wire rack 10 minutes. Serve warm. *Makes 8 servings*

Holiday Hint:

As with any biscuit dough, take care not to overwork it. Knead the dough gently 10 to 12 times just to incorporate dry ingredients and distribute fat. Overworking will produce tough biscuits.

Onion Dill Bread

2 cups bread flour
1 cup whole wheat flour
½ cup instant non-fat dry milk
½ teaspoon salt
1 package active dry yeast
2 tablespoons sugar
1¼ cups water (110° to 115°F)
1 cup KELLOGG'S® ALL-BRAN® cereal
2 egg whites
¼ cup reduced-calorie margarine
¼ cup chopped green onions
¼ cup chopped red onion
1 tablespoon dill weed
1 tablespoon skim milk
2 tablespoons finely chopped onion

1. Stir together flours, dry milk and salt.

2. In large electric mixer bowl, combine yeast, sugar and water. Stir in Kellogg's® All-Bran® cereal; let stand 2 minutes or until cereal is soft.

3. Add egg whites, margarine and ½ of flour mixture. Beat at medium speed for 2 minutes or about 200 strokes by hand.

4. Mix in green onions, red onion and dill weed. Stir in remaining flour mixture by hand to form stiff, sticky dough. Cover lightly. Let rise in warm place until double in volume (about 1 hour).

5. Stir down dough to original volume. Spoon into 2-quart round casserole dish or 9¼×5¼×2¾-inch loaf pan coated with nonstick cooking spray. Brush surface with milk and sprinkle evenly with 2 tablespoons chopped onion.

6. Bake at 350°F for 55 minutes or until loaf is golden brown and sounds hollow when lightly tapped. Place on wire rack; cool.   *Makes 1 loaf*

Cinnamon-Pecan Pull-Apart Bread

1½ cups water

¾ cup butter, divided

3¾ cups all-purpose flour

1¼ cups sugar, divided

2 teaspoons active dry yeast

1 teaspoon salt

¾ cup finely chopped pecans

1½ teaspoons ground cinnamon

½ cup raisins

Measuring carefully, place water, ¼ cup butter, flour, ¼ cup sugar, yeast and salt in bread machine pan in order specified by owner's manual. Program dough cycle setting; press start.

Melt remaining ½ cup butter. Combine remaining 1 cup sugar, pecans and cinnamon in small bowl. Divide dough in half; shape each half into twenty balls. Dip balls first in butter, then in sugar mixture. Arrange 20 balls in bottom of greased 12-cup tube pan; sprinkle with raisins. Top with remaining 20 balls. Cover and let rise in warm place 45 minutes or until doubled.

Preheat oven to 350°F. Bake 35 to 40 minutes or until evenly browned. Invert onto heatproof serving plate; let stand 1 minute before removing pan. Serve warm. *Makes 8 to 12 servings*

Whole Wheat Popovers

2 eggs

1 cup milk

2 tablespoons butter, melted

½ cup all-purpose flour

½ cup whole wheat flour

¼ teaspoon salt

Position rack in lower third of oven. Preheat oven to 450°F. Grease 6 (6-ounce) custard cups. Set custard cups in jelly-roll pan for easier handling; set aside.

Beat eggs in large bowl with electric mixer at low speed 1 minute. Beat in milk and butter until blended. Beat in flours and salt until batter is smooth. Pour evenly into prepared custard cups.

Bake 20 minutes. Reduce oven temperature to 350°F. Bake 15 minutes; quickly make small slit in top of each popover to let out steam. Bake 5 to 10 minutes or until browned. Remove from cups. Cool on wire rack 10 minutes. Serve warm or cool completely. *Makes 6 popovers*

Dresden Stollen

¼ cup golden raisins

¼ cup chopped candied cherries

¼ cup slivered almonds

¼ cup candied orange peel

 2 tablespoons brandy or rum

¼ cup warm water (105° to 115°F)

 4 tablespoons sugar, divided

 2 packages (¼ ounce each) active dry yeast

 4 pieces pared lemon peel (each about 2×½-inch)

2¾ cups all-purpose flour

 ⅓ cup cold butter, cut into 5 pieces

 ½ teaspoon salt

 1 large egg

 ½ teaspoon almond extract

 2 to 5 tablespoons milk

 All-purpose flour

 2 tablespoons butter, melted and divided

 1 large egg white, lightly beaten

 3 tablespoons powdered sugar

1. Mix raisins, cherries, almonds, orange peel and brandy. Reserve.

2. Combine water, 1 tablespoon of the sugar and yeast. Stir to dissolve yeast and let stand until bubbly, about 5 minutes.

3. Fit processor with steel blade. Add remaining 3 tablespoons sugar and lemon peel to work bowl. Process until peel is minced. Add 2¾ cups flour, butter and salt to sugar mixture in work bowl. Process until mixed, about 15 seconds. Add yeast mixture, egg and almond extract; process until blended, about 10 seconds.

4. Turn on processor and very slowly drizzle just enough milk through feed tube so dough forms a ball that cleans the sides of the bowl. Process until ball turns around bowl about 25 times. Turn off processor and let dough stand 1 to 2 minutes.

5. Turn on processor and gradually drizzle in enough remaining milk to make dough soft, smooth and satiny but not sticky. Process until dough turns around bowl about 15 times.

6. Turn dough onto lightly floured surface. Shape into ball, cover with inverted bowl or plastic wrap and let stand 20 minutes.

7. Uncover dough and knead fruit mixture into dough on well floured surface. Sprinkle with additional flour, if necessary, to keep dough from becoming sticky. Shape dough into ball and place in lightly greased bowl, turning to grease all sides. Cover loosely with plastic wrap and let stand in warm place (85°F) until doubled, about 1 hour.

8. Punch down dough. Roll or pat dough on a large greased cookie sheet into a 9×7-inch oval. Brush with 1 tablespoon melted butter. Make a crease lengthwise with handle of wooden spoon just off the center. Fold lengthwise, bringing smaller section over the larger one. Brush top with egg white. Cover loosely with plastic wrap and let stand in warm place until almost doubled, about 45 minutes.

9. Heat oven to 350°F. Uncover bread and bake until evenly browned, 25 to 30 minutes. Remove immediately from cookie sheet and place on wire rack. Brush remaining 1 tablespoon melted butter over bread. Sift powdered sugar over bread. Cool.

Makes 1 loaf

Holiday Hint:

Stollen is the traditional Christmas bread of Germany. The rich, sweet yeast dough is studded with dried or candied fruit. This Dresden Stollen is made in the traditional shape.

Carrot-Raisin Bran Muffins

MAZOLA NO STICK® Cooking Spray
2 cups bran flake cereal with raisins
⅔ cup buttermilk
½ cup KARO® Dark Corn Syrup
1 cup flour
2 teaspoons baking soda
1 teaspoon cinnamon
¼ teaspoon salt
1 egg, slightly beaten
¼ cup sugar
¼ cup MAZOLA® Oil
1 cup shredded carrots

1. Preheat oven to 400°F. Spray 12 (2½-inch) muffin pan cups with cooking spray.

2. In large bowl, mix cereal, buttermilk and corn syrup; let stand 5 minutes. In medium bowl, combine flour, baking soda, cinnamon and salt; set aside. Add egg, sugar and oil to cereal mixture; mix until blended. Stir in flour mixture until well blended. Stir in carrots. Spoon into prepared muffin pan cups.

3. Bake 20 minutes or until lightly browned and firm to touch. Cool in pan on wire rack 5 minutes.

Makes 12 muffins

Prep Time: 20 minutes
Bake Time: 20 minutes, plus cooling

Cinnamon Honey Buns

¼ cup butter or margarine, softened and divided

½ cup honey, divided

¼ cup chopped toasted nuts

2 teaspoons ground cinnamon

1 loaf (1 pound) frozen bread dough, thawed according to package directions

⅔ cup raisins

Grease 12 muffin cups with 1 tablespoon butter. To prepare honey-nut topping, mix together 1 tablespoon butter, ¼ cup honey and chopped nuts. Place 1 teaspoon topping in each muffin cup. To prepare filling, mix together remaining 2 tablespoons butter, remaining ¼ cup honey and cinnamon. Roll out bread dough onto floured surface into 18×8-inch rectangle. Spread filling evenly over dough. Sprinkle with raisins. Starting with long side, roll dough into log. Cut log into 12 (1½-inch) slices. Place 1 slice, cut-side up, into each prepared muffin cup. Set muffin pan in warm place; let dough rise 30 minutes. Place muffin pan on foil-lined baking sheet. Bake at 375°F 20 minutes or until buns are golden brown. Remove from oven; cool in pan 5 minutes. Invert muffin pan to remove buns.   *Makes 12 buns*

Favorite recipe from **National Honey Board**

Southern Biscuit Muffins

2½ cups all-purpose flour

¼ cup sugar

1½ tablespoons baking powder

¾ cup cold butter

1 cup cold milk

Preheat oven to 400°F. Grease 12 (2½-inch) muffin cups. (These muffins brown better on the sides and bottom when baked without paper liners.)

Combine flour, sugar and baking powder in large bowl. Cut in butter with pastry blender until mixture resembles coarse crumbs. Stir in milk just until flour mixture is moistened. Spoon evenly into prepared muffin cups.

Bake 20 minutes or until golden. Remove from pan. Cool on wire rack.   *Makes 12 muffins*

Tip: These muffins taste like baking powder biscuits and are very quick and easy to make. Serve them with jelly, jam or honey.

Cinnamon Honey Buns

Raisin-Streusel Coffee Cake

1½ cups all-purpose flour

  2 teaspoons baking powder

¼ teaspoon baking soda

¼ teaspoon salt

¾ cup granulated sugar

  2 tablespoons margarine, softened

¾ cup nonfat sour cream

  1 egg

  1 teaspoon vanilla extract

½ cup MOTT'S® Chunky Apple Sauce

⅓ cup firmly packed light brown sugar

¼ cup raisins

  2 tablespoons crunchy nut-like cereal
     nuggets

1. Preheat oven to 350°F. Spray 9-inch round cake pan with nonstick cooking spray.

2. In small bowl, combine flour, baking powder, baking soda and salt.

3. In large bowl, beat granulated sugar and margarine with electric mixer at medium speed until blended. Whisk in sour cream, egg and vanilla. Gently mix in apple sauce.

4. Add flour mixture to apple sauce mixture; stir until well blended. Pour batter into prepared pan.

5. In small bowl, combine brown sugar, raisins and cereal. Sprinkle over batter.

6. Bake 50 minutes or until toothpick inserted in center comes out clean. Cool 15 minutes on wire rack. Serve warm or cool completely. Cut into 14 wedges. *Makes 14 servings*

Holiday Hint:

This lower-fat coffee cake is an ideal alternative to the traditional rich breakfast coffee cakes popular duing the holidays. Cover with colorful plastic wrap, add a bow and give as a gift.

Blueberry Coffee Cake

2⅓ cups all-purpose flour

1⅓ cups plus 2 tablespoons granulated sugar, divided

½ teaspoon salt

¾ CRISCO® Stick or ¾ cup CRISCO® all-vegetable shortening

¾ cup milk

3 eggs

2 teaspoons baking powder

1 teaspoon vanilla

1 cup ricotta cheese

1 tablespoon finely grated fresh lemon peel

1 cup fresh or frozen blueberries

½ cup chopped walnuts

⅓ cup packed brown sugar

1 teaspoon cinnamon

Confectioners' Sugar Icing (recipe follows)

1. Heat oven to 350°F. Grease 13×9×2-inch baking pan. Place cooling rack on countertop.

2. Combine flour, 1⅓ cups granulated sugar and salt in a bowl. Cut in shortening with pastry blender or 2 knives until crumbly. Reserve 1 cup mixture for topping. Add milk, 2 eggs, baking powder and vanilla to remaining mixture. Beat at medium speed 2 minutes, scraping bowl. Spread in prepared pan.

3. Combine remaining 2 tablespoons sugar, remaining egg, ricotta cheese and lemon peel in bowl. Mix well. Sprinkle blueberries over batter in the pan. Spoon cheese mixture over berries. Spread cheese mixture gently and evenly.

4. Mix reserved crumb mixture, nuts, brown sugar and cinnamon. Sprinkle over cake. Bake at 350°F 45 minutes or until toothpick inserted in center comes out clean. *Do not overbake.* Remove to cooling rack. Cool slightly. Drizzle with Confectioners' Sugar Icing. *Makes 12 servings*

Confectioners' Sugar Icing: Combine 1 cup confectioners' sugar, 1 tablespoon milk, orange juice or liqueur and ¼ teaspoon vanilla in small bowl. Stir in additional milk, 1 teaspoon at a time, until icing is of desired drizzling consistency. Makes about ½ cup.

Festive Cakes & Pies

Chocolate Bundt Cake with White Chocolate Glaze

1 package (18.25 ounces) chocolate cake mix

3 whole eggs *or* ¾ cup cholesterol-free egg substitute

3 jars (2½ ounces each) puréed baby food prunes

¾ cup warm water

2 to 3 teaspoons instant coffee granules

2 tablespoons canola oil

½ cup white chocolate chips

1 tablespoon milk

1. Preheat oven to 350°F. Lightly grease and flour Bundt pan; set aside.

2. Beat all ingredients except white chocolate chips and milk in large bowl with electric mixer at high speed 2 minutes. Pour into prepared pan. Bake 40 minutes or until toothpick inserted in center comes out clean; cool 10 minutes. Invert cake onto serving plate; cool completely.

3. To prepare glaze, combine white chocolate chips and milk in small microwavable bowl. Microwave at MEDIUM (50% power) 50 seconds; stir. Microwave at MEDIUM at additional 30-second intervals until chips are completely melted; stir well after each 30 second interval.

4. Pour warm glaze over cooled cake. Let stand about 30 minutes. Garnish as desired; serve.

Makes 16 servings

Tip: To grease and flour cake pans, use a paper towel, waxed paper or your fingers to apply a thin, even layer of shortening. Sprinkle flour into the greased pan; shake or tilt the pan to coat evenly with flour, then tap lightly to remove any excess.

Prep Time: 10 minutes
Bake Time: 40 minutes

Chocolate Bundt Cake with White Chocolate Glaze

Golden Holiday Fruitcake

1½ cups butter, softened

1½ cups sugar

6 eggs

2 teaspoons grated lemon peel

2 tablespoons fresh lemon juice

3 cups all-purpose flour

2 teaspoons baking powder

½ teaspoon baking soda

¼ teaspoon salt

1½ cups golden raisins

1½ cups pecan halves

1½ cups red and green candied pineapple
    chunks

1 cup dried apricot halves, cut in half

1 cup halved red candied cherries

1 cup halved green candied cherries

Light corn syrup

Candied and dried fruit for garnish

Preheat oven to 325°F. Grease and flour 10-inch tube pan. Beat butter in large bowl with electric mixer at medium speed until creamy. Add sugar; beat until light and fluffy. Add eggs, 1 at a time, beating well after each addition. Stir in lemon peel and juice. Combine flour, baking powder, baking soda and salt in large bowl. Reserve ½ cup flour mixture. Gradually blend remaining flour mixture into butter mixture on low speed. Combine raisins, pecans, pineapple, apricots and cherries in large bowl. Toss fruit mixture with reserved ½ cup flour mixture. Stir fruit mixture into butter mixture. Spoon evenly into prepared pan.

Bake 1 hour 20 minutes to 1 hour 30 minutes until wooden pick inserted in center comes out clean. Cool in pan 15 minutes. Remove from pan to wire rack; cool completely. Store up to 1 month tightly covered at room temperature. (If desired, cake may be stored wrapped in a wine- or brandy-soaked cloth in airtight container. Cake may be frozen up to 2 months.)

Before serving, lightly brush surface of cake with corn syrup. Arrange candied and dried fruit decoratively on top. Brush fruit with corn syrup.

Makes one 10-inch round fruitcake

Holiday Hint:

If you find a fruitcake difficult to cut, try chilling it in the refrigerator before cutting. Slice fruitcake using a thin, sharp knife, but do not use a serrated bread knife.

Fluted Chocolate-Maraschino Cake

²⁄₃ cup butter or margarine, softened

1¾ cups sugar

2 eggs

1¼ teaspoons almond extract

1 teaspoon vanilla extract

1¾ cups all-purpose flour

¾ cup HERSHEY'S Dutch Processed Cocoa

1½ teaspoons baking soda

1½ cups dairy sour cream

Powdered sugar

Cherry Whipped Cream (recipe follows)

Maraschino cherries (optional)

1. Heat oven to 350°F. Grease and flour 12-cup fluted tube pan.

2. Beat butter and sugar in large bowl until creamy. Add eggs, almond and vanilla extracts; beat well. Combine flour, cocoa and baking soda; add to butter mixture alternately with sour cream, beating well. Pour into pan.

3. Bake 45 to 50 minutes or until wooden pick inserted into center comes out clean. Cool 15 minutes; remove from pan to wire rack. Cool completely. Sift with powdered sugar. Garnish with Cherry Whipped Cream and maraschino cherries, if desired. *Makes 12 servings*

Cherry Whipped Cream: Beat 1 cup whipping cream, 3 tablespoons powdered sugar, ½ teaspoon almond extract and ¼ teaspoon vanilla extract in medium bowl until stiff. Stir in ½ cup chopped maraschino cherries. Makes about 1 cup.

Holiday Hint:

To whip cream, use a bowl that is deep enough to allow cream to double in volume. Cream whips more quickly if it is very cold. It also is helpful to chill the bowl and beaters, especially if your kitchen is warm.

Pineapple Upside-Down Cake

1 (8-ounce) can crushed pineapple in juice, undrained
2 tablespoons margarine, melted, divided
½ cup firmly packed light brown sugar
6 whole maraschino cherries
1½ cups all-purpose flour
2 tablespoons baking powder
¼ teaspoon salt
1 cup granulated sugar
½ cup MOTT'S® Natural Apple Sauce
1 whole egg
3 egg whites, beaten until stiff

1. Preheat oven to 375°F. Drain pineapple; reserve juice. Spray sides of 8-inch square baking pan with nonstick cooking spray.

2. Spread 1 tablespoon melted margarine evenly in bottom of prepared pan. Sprinkle with brown sugar; top with pineapple. Slice cherries in half. Arrange cherries, cut side up, so that when cake is cut, each piece will have cherry half in center.

3. In small bowl, combine flour, baking powder and salt.

4. In large bowl, combine granulated sugar, apple sauce, whole egg, remaining 1 tablespoon melted margarine and reserved pineapple juice.

5. Add flour mixture to apple sauce mixture; stir until well blended. Fold in egg whites. Gently pour batter over fruit, spreading evenly.

6. Bake 35 to 40 minutes or until lightly browned. Cool on wire rack 10 minutes. Invert cake onto serving plate. Serve warm or cool completely. Cut into 12 pieces. *Makes 12 servings*

Holiday Hint:

For best results when beating egg whites, allow them to stand at room temperature for 30 minutes before beating. Egg whites must be completely free of egg yolk or they will not reach maximum volume.

Pineapple Upside-Down Cake

Golden Apple Mincemeat Cake

3 cups flour

4 teaspoons baking powder

1 teaspoon ground allspice

1 teaspoon ground cinnamon

½ teaspoon salt

1½ cups vegetable oil

1½ cups packed brown sugar

2 cups grated Washington Golden Delicious apples

1 cup prepared mincemeat

½ cup chopped pecans

1½ teaspoons vanilla

3 eggs

1 to 2 tablespoons powdered sugar

Hard Sauce (recipe follows)

Preheat oven to 350°F. Combine flour, baking powder, allspice, cinnamon and salt in large bowl; set aside. In large bowl of electric mixer, combine oil and brown sugar; beat well. Add half the flour mixture; mix well. Blend in grated apples, mincemeat, pecans and vanilla. Add remaining flour mixture. Add eggs, 1 at a time; beat well after each addition. Turn into greased 10-inch Bundt pan. Bake 1 hour or until wooden toothpick inserted near center comes out clean. Cool in pan 15 minutes; turn out onto wire rack. When cool, sprinkle with powdered sugar. If desired, cake can be served slightly warm with Hard Sauce.

Makes 16 servings

Hard Sauce: Beat ½ cup margarine and ⅛ teaspoon salt until light and fluffy. Gradually beat in 1 cup powdered sugar. Stir in 1 tablespoon brandy. Refrigerate 1 hour.

Favorite recipe from **Washington Apple Commission**

Lemon Semolina Syrup Cake

2 cups farina or semolina flour

1 cup sugar

1½ teaspoons baking powder

¼ teaspoon salt

2 cups plain low-fat yogurt

2 tablespoons FILIPPO BERIO® Extra Light Tasting Olive Oil

Finely grated peel of 1 lemon

12 to 15 walnut halves

1 cup light corn syrup

2 tablespoons lemon juice

Fresh strawberries (optional)

Preheat oven to 350°F. Grease 9-inch springform pan with olive oil.

In large bowl, combine farina, sugar, baking powder and salt. With wooden spoon or spatula, mix in yogurt, olive oil and lemon peel until well blended. *Do not use electric mixer.* Pour batter into prepared pan. Score top of batter with tip of sharp knife, making 12 to 15 squares or diamond shapes,

continued on page 268

about ½ inch deep. (Marks will not remain completely visible before baking, but will show slightly when baked.) Place walnut half in center of each square or diamond shape.

Bake 45 minutes or until golden brown and toothpick inserted in center comes out clean. Meanwhile, in small saucepan, combine corn syrup and lemon juice. Heat over medium heat, stirring frequently, until mixture is hot.

When cake tests done, remove from oven. Make ½-inch-deep cuts through scored portions, cleaning knife after each cut. Immediately pour hot syrup over cake in pan. Let stand 1 to 2 hours or until syrup is absorbed and cake is cool. Remove side of pan; serve with strawberries, if desired. Refrigerate any remaining cake.   *Makes 10 to 12 servings*

Holiday Poke Cake

2 baked 8- or 9-inch round white cake layers, cooled completely

2 cups boiling water

1 package (4-serving size) JELL-O® Brand Gelatin Dessert, any red flavor

1 package (4-serving size) JELL-O® Brand Lime Flavor Gelatin Dessert

1 tub (8 or 12 ounces) COOL WHIP® Whipped Topping, thawed

PLACE cake layers, top sides up, in 2 clean 8- or 9-inch round cake pans. Pierce cake with large fork at ½-inch intervals.

STIR 1 cup of the boiling water into each flavor of gelatin in separate bowls at least 2 minutes until completely dissolved. Carefully pour red gelatin over 1 cake layer and lime gelatin over second cake layer. Refrigerate 3 hours.

DIP 1 cake pan in warm water 10 seconds; unmold onto serving plate. Spread with about 1 cup of the whipped topping. Unmold second cake layer; carefully place on first cake layer. Frost top and side of cake with remaining whipped topping.

REFRIGERATE at least 1 hour or until ready to serve. Decorate as desired.   *Makes 12 servings*

Preparation Time: 30 minutes
Refrigerating Time: 4 hours

Saucy Apple Cake

CAKE

> 1 Butter Flavor CRISCO® Stick or 1 cup Butter Flavor CRISCO® all-vegetable shortening plus additional for greasing
>
> 1 cup granulated sugar
>
> 1 cup firmly packed light brown sugar
>
> 4 eggs
>
> 2 teaspoons pure almond extract
>
> 1 teaspoon ground cinnamon
>
> ½ teaspoon ground nutmeg
>
> 3 cups sifted all-purpose flour
>
> 1½ teaspoons salt
>
> 1 teaspoon baking powder
>
> 1 teaspoon baking soda
>
> 1 jar (16 ounces) applesauce, divided
>
> ½ cup apple juice, apple cider, brandy or water
>
> 1 cup chopped black walnuts
>
> 1 cup coarsely grated, peeled Golden Delicious apple (about ½ pound or 1 large apple)
>
> Confectioners' sugar (optional)

TOPPING

> Reserved ½ cup applesauce
>
> ¼ teaspoon ground cinnamon
>
> 1 container (8 ounces) frozen whipped topping, thawed

1. Heat oven to 350°F. Grease 10-inch (12-cup) Bundt® or tube pan with shortening. Flour lightly.

2. For cake, combine 1 cup shortening, granulated sugar, brown sugar, eggs, almond extract, 1 teaspoon cinnamon and nutmeg in large bowl. Beat at low speed of electric mixer until blended. Beat at high speed 3 to 4 minutes or until light and fluffy.

3. Combine flour, salt, baking powder and baking soda in medium bowl. Reserve ½ cup applesauce for topping. Add remaining applesauce and apple juice to creamed mixture alternately with flour mixture, beating at low speed after each addition until well blended. Stir in nuts and apple with spoon. Spoon into pan.

4. Bake at 350°F for 50 to 60 minutes or until toothpick inserted in center comes out clean. *Do not overbake.* Cool 5 minutes before removing from pan. Place cake, fluted side up, on wire rack. Cool completely. Dust with confectioners' sugar, if desired.

5. For topping, fold reserved ½ cup applesauce and ¼ teaspoon cinnamon into whipped topping. Place spoonful on each serving.

Makes 1 (10-inch) bundt cake
(12 to 16 Servings)

Black Forest Cake

1 package (2-layer size) chocolate cake mix
  plus ingredients to prepare mix
2 cans (20 ounces each) tart pitted cherries,
  undrained
1 cup granulated sugar
¼ cup cornstarch
1½ teaspoons vanilla
  Frosting (recipe follows)

1. Preheat oven to 350°F. Grease and flour two (9-inch) round cake pans; set aside.

2. Prepare cake mix according to package directions. Divide batter between prepared pans.

3. Bake 30 to 35 minutes or until wooden toothpick inserted into centers comes out clean. Cool in pans on wire racks 10 minutes. Remove from pans; cool completely on racks.

4. Meanwhile, drain cherries, reserving ½ cup juice. Combine reserved juice, cherries, sugar and cornstarch in 2-quart saucepan. Cook over low heat until thickened, stirring constantly. Stir in vanilla. Prepare Frosting.

5. With long serrated knife, split each cooled cake layer horizontally in half. Crumble one split layer; set aside.

6. Reserve 1½ cups Frosting for decorating cake; set aside. Place one cake layer on cake plate. Spread with 1 cup Frosting; top with ¾ cup cherry topping. Top with second cake layer; repeat layers of Frosting and cherry topping. Top with third cake layer.

7. Frost side of cake with remaining Frosting. Pat reserved crumbs onto frosting on side of cake. Spoon reserved frosting into pastry bag fitted with star decorator tip. Pipe around top and bottom edges of cake. Spoon remaining Cherry Topping onto top of cake.   *Makes one 3-layer cake*

Frosting: Beat together 3 cups cold whipping cream and ⅓ cup powdered sugar in chilled deep medium bowl with electric mixer at high speed until stiff peaks form.

Holiday Hint:

To fill a pastry bag, insert the decorating tip with a coupler. Fold the top of the bag down before filling. Fill, then unfold the top of the bag. To prevent the frosting from squeezing out of the top of the bag, twist the top tightly against the frosting.

Black Forest Cake

Pineapple-Coconut Party Cake

CAKE

2 cups granulated sugar

1 Butter Flavor CRISCO® Stick or 1 cup Butter Flavor CRISCO® all-vegetable shortening plus additional for greasing

3 eggs

1 teaspoon vanilla

1 teaspoon coconut extract

3 cups sifted all-purpose flour

1 tablespoon baking powder

1 cup milk

TOPPING

1 can (20 ounces) crushed pineapple or pineapple tidbits in unsweetened juice

1 tablespoon cornstarch

1 cup firmly packed light brown sugar

1 cup shredded coconut

1 cup chopped pecans

½ teaspoon rum extract *or* ¼ cup rum

¼ teaspoon vanilla

12 to 16 maraschino cherries, drained

1. Heat oven to 350°F. Grease 13×9×2-inch pan with shortening. Flour lightly.

2. For cake, combine granulated sugar and 1 cup shortening in large bowl. Beat at medium speed of electric mixer until light and fluffy. Add eggs, 1 at a time, beating well after each addition. Beat in 1 teaspoon vanilla and coconut extract until blended.

3. Combine flour and baking powder in medium bowl. Add to creamed mixture alternately with milk, beating at low speed after each addition until well blended. Beat at medium speed 2 minutes. Pour into pan. Spread evenly. (Batter will be very thick.)

4. Bake at 350°F for 35 to 45 minutes or until toothpick inserted in center comes out clean. *Do not overbake.* (Cake will rise above top of pan and then fall slightly. Cake may be slightly lower in center.) Cool completely in pan on wire rack.

5. For topping, drain 2 tablespoons juice from pineapple. Combine juice and cornstarch in small bowl. Stir to dissolve.

6. Combine pineapple, remaining juice and brown sugar in medium saucepan. Bring to a boil. Stir in cornstarch mixture. Boil and stir 1 minute or until mixture is thickened and clear. Remove from heat. Stir in coconut, nuts, rum extract and ¼ teaspoon vanilla.

7. Use large fork or skewer to poke holes in top of cake. Pour topping over cake, spreading to edges. Arrange cherries on top of cake so that when cake is cut, each slice will have cherry in center. Refrigerate at least 30 minutes before serving.

Makes 1 (13×9×2-inch) cake (12 to 16 servings)

Note: Prepare cake and topping the day before serving, if desired.

Pineapple-Coconut Party Cake

Apricot Cream Cake

FILLING

 2 cups chopped dried apricots (¼- to ½-inch pieces)
 ⅔ cup sugar
 ⅓ cup chopped pecans

TOPPING

 ⅓ cup flake coconut
 ¼ cup sugar
 ¼ cup chopped pecans
 1 tablespoon Butter Flavor CRISCO® Stick or 1 tablespoon Butter Flavor CRISCO® all-vegetable shortening, melted

CAKE

 1 package (8 ounces) light (Neufchâtel) cream cheese, softened
 ½ Butter Flavor CRISCO® Stick or ½ cup Butter Flavor CRISCO® all-vegetable shortening
 1¼ cups sugar
 2 eggs
 1 teaspoon vanilla
 2 cups sifted all-purpose flour
 1 teaspoon baking powder
 ½ teaspoon baking soda
 ¼ teaspoon salt
 ⅓ cup milk

DECORATIONS

 10 pecan halves
 Caramel sundae topping
 10 dried apricot halves

1. For filling, place chopped apricots in medium saucepan. Add water to cover (about 1 cup). Bring to a boil. Reduce heat. Cover. Simmer until tender. Stir in ⅔ cup sugar. Cool completely. Stir in ⅓ cup nuts.

2. For topping, combine coconut, ¼ cup sugar, ¼ cup nuts and melted shortening in small bowl. Stir to mix.

3. Heat oven to 350°F. Grease 10-inch springform pan. Flour lightly.

4. For cake, combine cream cheese and ½ cup shortening in large bowl. Beat at high speed of electric mixer until fluffy. Add 1¼ cups sugar gradually, beating until light and fluffy. Add eggs and vanilla. Beat 2 minutes.

5. Combine flour, baking powder, baking soda and salt in small bowl. Add to creamed mixture alternately with milk, beating at medium speed 1 minute after each addition. Spread half of batter (about 2¼ cups) into pan. Spoon filling over batter to within ½ inch of edge. Cover with remaining batter. Sprinkle with topping.

6. Bake at 350°F for 45 to 50 minutes or until cake begins to pull away from side of pan and toothpick inserted in center comes out clean. *Do not overbake.* Cool 30 minutes. Loosen cake from side of pan with knife or metal spatula. Remove side of pan. Invert cake on wire rack. Remove bottom of pan using thin metal spatula or pancake turner. Cool 30 minutes. Place cake, top side up, on serving plate. Cool completely.

7. For decorations, brush nut halves lightly with caramel sundae topping. Place 1 nut half in center of each apricot half. Press apricot half around nut. Place filled apricots around edge of cake.

Makes 1 (10-inch) round cake (12 servings)

Orange Carrot Cake

1 cup margarine or butter, softened

1 cup GRANDMA'S® Molasses Unsulphured

4 eggs

½ cup orange juice

1 cup all-purpose flour

1 cup whole wheat flour

2 teaspoons baking soda

1 teaspoon ground cinnamon

½ teaspoon salt

2 cups shredded carrots

½ cup chopped walnuts

FROSTING

1 package (3 ounces) cream cheese, softened

2 tablespoons margarine or butter, softened

1½ cups powdered sugar

1 teaspoon grated orange peel

Heat oven to 350°F. Grease two 8- or 9-inch round cake pans.

In large bowl, combine margarine, molasses, eggs and orange juice; mix well. Stir in flours, baking soda, cinnamon and salt; mix well. Stir in carrots and walnuts. Pour into prepared pans. Bake at 350°F 30 to 35 minutes or until toothpick inserted in centers comes out clean. Cool 15 minutes; remove from pans. Cool completely.

In small bowl, combine all frosting ingredients; beat until smooth. Place one cake layer on serving plate; spread top with frosting. Top with second layer; spread top with frosting. If desired, garnish with additional orange peel and walnuts.

Makes 12 servings

Holiday Hint:

Molasses is the by-product of the process that produces sugar. When cane or beet juice is boiled to produce sugar crystals, the remaining liquid is molasses.

Sour Cream Coffee Cake with Chocolate and Walnuts

¾ cup butter, softened

1½ cups packed light brown sugar

3 eggs

2 teaspoons vanilla

3 cups all-purpose flour

2 teaspoons baking powder

2 teaspoons ground cinnamon

1½ teaspoons baking soda

½ teaspoon ground nutmeg

¼ teaspoon salt

1½ cups sour cream

½ cup semisweet chocolate chips

½ cup chopped walnuts

Powdered sugar

Preheat oven to 350°F. Grease and flour 12-cup Bundt pan or 10-inch tube pan. Beat butter in large bowl with electric mixer on medium speed until creamy. Add brown sugar; beat until fluffy. Beat in eggs and vanilla until blended. Combine flour, baking powder, cinnamon, baking soda, nutmeg and salt; add to butter mixture on low speed alternately with sour cream, beginning and ending with flour mixture until well blended. Stir in chocolate and walnuts. Spoon into prepared pan.

Bake 45 to 50 minutes until wooden pick inserted near center comes out clean. Cool in pan 15 minutes. Remove from pan to wire rack; cool completely. Store tightly covered at room temperature. Sprinkle with powdered sugar before serving. *Makes one 10-inch coffee cake*

Orange Glow Bundt Cake

1 (18.25-ounce) package moist yellow cake mix

1 tablespoon grated orange peel

1 cup orange juice

¼ cup sugar

1 tablespoon TABASCO® brand Pepper Sauce

1¾ cups confectioners' sugar

Preheat oven to 375°F. Grease 12-cup Bundt pan. Prepare cake mix according to package directions, adding orange peel to batter. Bake 35 to 40 minutes or until toothpick inserted in center of cake comes out clean.

Meanwhile, heat orange juice, sugar and TABASCO® Sauce to boiling in 1-quart saucepan. Reduce heat to low; simmer, uncovered, 5 minutes. Remove from heat. Reserve ¼ cup orange juice mixture for glaze.

Remove cake from oven. With wooden skewer, poke holes in cake (in pan) in several places. Spoon remaining orange juice mixture over cake. Cool cake in pan 10 minutes. Carefully invert cake onto wire rack to cool completely.

Combine reserved ¼ cup orange juice mixture and confectioners' sugar in small bowl until smooth. Place cake on platter; spoon glaze over cake. Garnish with clusters of dried cranberries, mint leaves and grated orange peel.

Makes 12 servings

Sour Cream Coffee Cake with Chocolate and Walnuts

Fun & Fruity Upside-Down Cake

1¼ cups sifted cake flour
2 teaspoons baking powder
¼ teaspoon salt
½ cup (1 stick) butter, softened and divided
1¼ cup packed brown sugar, divided
1 egg
½ cup milk
½ teaspoon vanilla
½ teaspoon lemon extract
1 (20-ounce) can crushed pineapple, well drained
1 (16-ounce) can sour pie cherries, drained
Fresh mint leaves for garnish (optional)

1. Preheat oven to 350°F.

2. Combine flour, baking powder and salt in medium bowl; set aside.

3. Beat together ¼ cup butter and ¾ cup brown sugar in large bowl until light and fluffy.

4. Blend in egg. Add flour mixture alternately with milk, beating well after each addition. Blend in vanilla.

5. Melt remaining ¼ cup butter in 9-inch ovenproof skillet or 9-inch cake pan. Stir in remaining brown sugar. If necessary, tilt skillet to evenly cover bottom with brown sugar mixture.

6. Top brown sugar mixture with pineapple.

7. Reserve a few cherries for garnish, if desired. Spoon remaining cherries over pineapple; top with batter.

8. Bake 50 minutes or until wooden pick inserted in center comes out clean.

9. Cool cake in pan on wire rack 10 minutes. Loosen edges and turn upside down onto cake plate. Garnish with reserved cherries and mint leaves, if desired. *Makes one 9-inch cake*

Holiday Hint:

Upside-down cakes, once known as skillet cakes, were created by early American settlers who didn't have baking ovens. Upside-down cakes are now just as often baked as prepared on top of the range.

Fun & Fruity Upside-Down Cake

Jeweled Brownie Cheesecake

¾ cup (1½ sticks) butter or margarine

4 squares (1 ounce each) unsweetened baking chocolate

1½ cups sugar

4 large eggs

1 cup all-purpose flour

1¾ cups "M&M's"® Chocolate Mini Baking Bits, divided

½ cup chopped walnuts, optional

1 (8-ounce) package cream cheese, softened

1 teaspoon vanilla extract

Preheat oven to 350°F. Lightly grease 9-inch springform pan; set aside. Place butter and chocolate in large microwave-safe bowl. Microwave at HIGH 1 minute; stir. Microwave at HIGH an additional 30 seconds; stir until chocolate is completely melted. Add sugar and 3 eggs, one at a time, beating well after each addition; blend in flour. Stir in 1¼ cups "M&M's"® Chocolate Mini Baking Bits and nuts, if desired; set aside. In large bowl, beat cream cheese, remaining 1 egg and vanilla. Spread half of the chocolate mixture in prepared pan. Carefully spread cream cheese mixture evenly over chocolate mixture, leaving 1-inch border. Spread remaining chocolate mixture evenly over top, all the way to the edges. Sprinkle with remaining ½ cup "M&M's"® Chocolate Mini Baking Bits. Bake 40 to 45 minutes or until firm to the touch. Cool completely. Store in refrigerator in tightly covered container. *Makes 12 slices*

Eggnog Cheesecake

CRUST

2 cups vanilla wafer crumbs

6 tablespoons butter or margarine, melted

½ teaspoon ground nutmeg

FILLING

4 packages (8 ounces each) PHILADELPHIA® Cream Cheese, softened

1 cup sugar

3 tablespoons all-purpose flour

3 tablespoons rum

1 teaspoon vanilla

2 eggs

1 cup whipping cream

4 egg yolks

HEAT oven to 325°F.

CRUST

MIX crumbs, butter and nutmeg; press onto bottom and 1½-inches up sides of 9-inch springform pan. Bake 10 minutes.

FILLING

BEAT cream cheese, sugar, flour, rum and vanilla at medium speed with electric mixer until well blended. Add eggs, 1 at a time, mixing at low speed after each addition, just until blended.

continued on page 282

Jeweled Brownie Cheesecake

BLEND in cream and egg yolks; pour into crust.

BAKE 1 hour and 10 minutes to 1 hour and 15 minutes or until center is almost set. Run knife or metal spatula around rim of pan to loosen cake; cool before removing rim of pan. Refrigerate 4 hours or overnight. Garnish with COOL WHIP® Whipped Topping and ground nutmeg.

Makes 12 servings

Prep Time: 25 minutes
Bake Time: 1 hour 15 minutes

Chocolate Swirl Cheesecake

> 1 package (11.1 ounces) JELL-O® No Bake Real Cheesecake
> 2 tablespoons sugar
> 1/3 cup butter or margarine, melted
> 2 squares BAKER'S® Semi-Sweet Baking Chocolate
> 1½ cups cold milk, divided

STIR Crust Mix, sugar and melted butter thoroughly with fork in 8- or 9-inch pie plate until crumbs are well moistened. First press firmly against side of pie plate first, using finger or large spoon to shape edge. Press remaining crumbs firmly onto bottom of pie plate using measuring cup.

MICROWAVE chocolate and 2 tablespoons of the milk in microwavable bowl on HIGH 1½ minutes or until chocolate is almost melted. Stir until chocolate is completely melted.

POUR cold milk into medium bowl. Add Filling Mix. Beat with electric mixer on lowest speed until blended. Beat on medium speed 3 minutes. (Filling will be thick.) Stir ¼ cup of the filling into melted chocolate until well blended. Spoon remaining filling into crust. Place spoonfuls of chocolate mixture over filling in crust. Cut through cheesecake filling with knife several times to marbleize.

REFRIGERATE at least 1 hour. Garnish as desired. Store leftover cheesecake in refrigerator.

Makes 8 servings

How To Serve: For ease in serving, dip bottom of pie plate in hot water for 10 to 15 seconds prior to slicing.

Special Extras: Garnish cheesecake with additional melted BAKER'S Semi-Sweet Baking Chocolate drizzled on top. To melt chocolate, place 1 square chocolate in heavy-duty zipper-style plastic sandwich bag. Seal bag tightly. Microwave on HIGH about 1 minute or until chocolate is melted. Fold down top of bag and snip a tiny (about ⅛-inch) piece off 1 corner. Hold top of bag firmly, drizzle chocolate over cheesecake.

Preparation Time: 15 minutes
Refrigerating Time: 1 hour

Kahlúa® Marbled Pumpkin Cheesecake

¾ cup gingersnap crumbs
¾ cup graham cracker crumbs
¼ cup powdered sugar
¼ cup (4 tablespoons) melted unsalted butter
2 (8-ounce) packages cream cheese, softened
1 cup granulated sugar
4 eggs
1 (1-pound) can pumpkin
½ teaspoon ground cinnamon
¼ teaspoon ground ginger
¼ teaspoon ground nutmeg
½ cup KAHLÚA®

Heat oven to 350°F. In bowl, combine gingersnap and graham cracker crumbs with powdered sugar and butter. Toss to combine. Press evenly onto bottom of 8-inch springform pan. Bake 5 minutes. Cool.

In mixer bowl, beat cream cheese until smooth. Gradually add granulated sugar and beat until light. Add eggs, one at a time, beating well after each addition. Transfer 1 cup mixture to separate bowl and blend in pumpkin, cinnamon, ginger, nutmeg and Kahlúa®. Pour half of pumpkin mixture into prepared crust. Top with half of cream cheese mixture. Repeat layers using remaining pumpkin and cream cheese mixtures. Using table knife, cut through layers with uplifting motion in four to five places to create marbled effect. Place on baking sheet and bake at 350°F for 45 minutes. Without opening oven door, let cake stand in turned-off oven 1 hour. Remove from oven and cool, then chill. Remove from pan.

Makes about 12 servings

Philadelphia® 3-Step® Crème Brûlée Cheesecake

2 packages (8 ounces each) PHILADELPHIA® Cream Cheese, softened
½ cup granulated sugar
1 teaspoon vanilla
2 eggs
1 egg yolk
1 ready-to-use graham cracker crust (6 ounces or 9-inch)
½ cup packed brown sugar
1 teaspoon water

1. MIX cream cheese, granulated sugar and vanilla at medium speed with electric mixer until well blended. Add eggs and egg yolk; mix until blended.

2. POUR into crust.

3. BAKE at 350°F, 40 minutes or until center is almost set. Cool. Refrigerate 3 hours or overnight. Just before serving, heat broiler. Mix brown sugar and water; spread over cheesecake. Place on cookie sheet. Broil 4 to 6 inches from heat 1 to 1½ minutes or until topping is bubbly.

Makes 8 servings

Prep Time: 10 minutes
Bake Time: 40 minutes

Decadent Turtle Cheesecake

2½ cups crushed chocolate cookies

¼ cup (½ stick) butter, melted

2 packages (8 ounces each) cream cheese, softened

1 cup sugar

1½ tablespoons all-purpose flour

¼ teaspoon salt

1½ teaspoons vanilla

3 eggs

2 tablespoons whipping cream

Caramel Topping (recipe follows)

Chocolate Topping (recipe follows)

1 cup chopped toasted pecans

1. Preheat oven to 450°F. Combine cookie crumbs and butter in medium bowl; press onto bottom of 9-inch springform pan.

2. Beat cream cheese in large bowl until creamy. Add sugar, flour, salt and vanilla; mix well. Add eggs, one at a time, beating well after each addition. Blend in cream. Pour over crust. Bake 10 minutes.

3. *Reduce oven temperature to 200°F.* Bake 35 to 40 minutes more or until set. Loosen cake from rim of pan; cool. Removing rim of pan.

4. Prepare Caramel Topping and Chocolate Topping. Drizzle over cheesecake. Refrigerate cheesecake. Sprinkle with pecans just before serving. *Makes one 9-inch cheesecake*

Caramel Topping: Combine 7 ounces (½ bag) caramels and ⅓ cup whipping cream in small saucepan; stir over low heat until smooth.

Chocolate Topping: Combine 4 squares (1 ounce each) semisweet chocolate, 1 teaspoon butter and 3 tablespoons whipping cream in small saucepan; stir over low heat until smooth.

Philadelphia® 3-Step® Fruit Topped Cheesecake

2 packages (8 ounces each) PHILADELPHIA® Cream Cheese, softened

½ cup sugar

½ teaspoon vanilla

2 eggs

1 ready-to-use graham cracker pie crust (6 ounces or 9 inch)

2 cups sliced fresh fruit slices

2 tablespoons strawberry or apple jelly, heated (optional)

1. MIX cream cheese, sugar and vanilla with electric mixer on medium speed until well blended. Add eggs; mix until blended.

2. POUR into crust.

3. BAKE at 350°F for 40 minutes or until center is almost set. Cool. Refrigerate 3 hours or overnight. Top with fruit; drizzle with jelly, if desired.

Makes 8 servings

Prep Time: 10 minutes
Bake Time: 40 minutes

Decadent Turtle Cheesecake

Black Bottom Cheesecake Cups

CHEESECAKE FILLING

1 container (8 ounces) fat-free cream cheese

¼ cup sugar

1 egg

CHOCOLATE BATTER

1½ cups all-purpose flour

¾ cup sugar

⅓ cup unsweetened cocoa powder

1 teaspoon baking soda

½ teaspoon salt

1 cup water

⅓ cup Dried Plum Purée (recipe follows) or prepared dried plum butter *or* 1 jar (2½ ounces) first-stage baby food dried plums

1 tablespoon instant espresso coffee powder *or* 2 tablespoons instant coffee granules

1 tablespoon white vinegar

2 teaspoons vanilla

½ cup semisweet chocolate chips

ALMOND TOPPING

¼ cup finely chopped blanched almonds

2 tablespoons sugar

Preheat oven to 350°F. Line eighteen 2¾-inch (⅓-cup capacity) muffin cups with cupcake liners. Coat liners lightly with vegetable cooking spray. To make filling, in small mixer bowl, beat filling ingredients at medium speed until smooth; set aside.

To make chocolate batter, in large bowl, combine first five batter ingredients. In medium bowl, beat water, dried plum purée, espresso powder, vinegar and vanilla until blended. Mix into flour mixture. Spoon into muffin cups, dividing equally. Top each with heaping teaspoonful of filling mixture. Sprinkle with chocolate chips.

To make topping, mix almonds and sugar; sprinkle over chocolate chips. Bake in center of oven about 25 minutes or until pick inserted into chocolate portion comes out clean. Cool in pans 5 minutes; remove from pans to wire racks to cool completely.

Makes 18 cupcakes

Plum Purée: Combine 1⅓ cups (8 ounces) pitted dried plums and 6 tablespoons hot water in container of food processor or blender. Pulse on and off until dried plums are finely chopped and smooth. Store leftovers in covered container in refrigerator for up to two months. Makes 1 cup.

*Favorite recipe from **California Dried Plum Board***

Black Bottom Cheesecake Cups

Easy Rich No-Bake Chocolate Cheesecake

Almond Crumb Crust (recipe follows)
1 package (8 ounces) HERSHEY'S Semi-Sweet Baking Chocolate, broken into pieces
3 packages (3 ounces each) cream cheese, softened
¼ cup sugar
¼ cup (½ stick) butter or margarine, softened
1 teaspoon vanilla extract
1 cup (½ pint) cold whipping cream

1. Prepare Almond Crumb Crust; set aside.

2. Place chocolate in small microwave-safe bowl. Microwave at HIGH (100%) 1 to 1½ minutes or until chocolate is melted when stirred. Set aside; cool slightly. Beat cream cheese, sugar, butter and vanilla in large bowl until smooth. Add melted chocolate; beat on low speed of mixer.

3. Beat whipping cream in small bowl until stiff; fold into chocolate mixture. Pour mixture into prepared crust. Cover; refrigerate until firm.

Makes about 8 servings

Almond Crumb Crust: Heat oven to 350°F. Stir together 1 cup finely chopped slivered almonds, ¾ cup vanilla wafer crumbs and ¼ cup powdered sugar in medium bowl. Pour ¼ cup (½ stick) melted butter or margarine over crumb mixture; blend well. Press mixture onto bottom and ½ inch up side of 9-inch springform pan. Bake 8 to 10 minutes or until lightly browned. Cool completely.

Prep Time: 25 minutes
Bake Time: 8 minutes
Chill Time: 4 hours

Perfect Pumpkin Pie

1 (15-ounce) can pumpkin (2 cups)
1 (14-ounce) can EAGLE® BRAND Sweetened Condensed Milk (NOT evaporated milk)
2 eggs
1 teaspoon ground cinnamon
½ teaspoon ground ginger
½ teaspoon ground nutmeg
½ teaspoon salt
1 (9-inch) unbaked pie crust
Favorite Topping (recipes follow, optional)

1. Preheat oven to 425°F. In large bowl, combine all ingredients except crust and toppings; mix well.

2. Pour into prepared pie crust. Bake 15 minutes.

3. Reduce oven heat to 350°F. Continue baking 35 to 40 minutes, or as directed with one Favorite Topping or, until knife inserted 1 inch from edge comes out clean. Cool. Garnish as desired. Store covered in refrigerator. *Makes 1 (9-inch) pie*

Sour Cream Topping: In medium bowl, combine 1½ cups sour cream, 2 tablespoons sugar and 1 teaspoon vanilla extract. After pie has baked 30 minutes at 350°F, spread evenly over top; bake 10 minutes.

Streusel Topping: In medium bowl, combine ½ cup packed brown sugar and ½ cup all-purpose flour; cut in ¼ cup (½ stick) cold butter or margarine until crumbly. Stir in ¼ cup chopped nuts. After pie has baked 30 minutes at 350°F, sprinkle evenly over top; bake 10 minutes.

Chocolate Glaze: In small saucepan over low heat, melt ½ cup semi-sweet chocolate chips and 1 teaspoon solid shortening. Drizzle or spread over top of baked and cooled pie.

Prep Time: 20 minutes
Bake Time: 50 to 55 minutes

Chocolate Peppermint Pie

1 cup crushed chocolate-covered mint-flavored cookies

3 tablespoons hot water

1 prepared graham cracker crumb crust (6 ounces)

½ package (4 ounces) PHILADELPHIA® Cream Cheese, softened

⅓ cup sugar

2 tablespoons milk

¼ teaspoon peppermint extract

1 tub (8 ounces) COOL WHIP® Whipped Topping, thawed

6 to 10 drops green food coloring

Additional thawed COOL WHIP® Whipped Topping

Green gumdrop spearmint leaves (optional)

Red cinnamon candies (optional)

MIX cookies and hot water in small bowl. Spread evenly on bottom of crust.

BEAT cream cheese in large bowl with electric mixer on medium speed until smooth. Gradually beat in sugar, milk and peppermint extract until well blended. Gently stir in whipped topping. Divide mixture in half; stir food coloring into ½ of the whipped topping mixture until evenly colored. Spoon green and white whipped topping mixtures alternately into crust. Smooth top with spatula.

REFRIGERATE 3 hours or until set. Garnish with additional whipped topping before serving. Decorate with spearmint leaves and cinnamon candies to make holly leaves and berries. Store leftover pie in refrigerator. *Makes 8 servings*

Cranberry Apple Nut Pie

Rich Pie Pastry (recipe follows)

1 cup sugar

3 tablespoons all-purpose flour

¼ teaspoon salt

4 cups sliced peeled tart apples

2 cups fresh cranberries

½ cup golden raisins

½ cup coarsely chopped pecans

1 tablespoon grated lemon peel

2 tablespoons butter

1 egg, beaten

Preheat oven to 425°F. Divide pie pastry in half. Roll one half on lightly floured surface to form 13-inch circle. Fit into 9-inch pie plate; trim edges. Reroll scraps and cut into decorative shapes, such as holly leaves and berries, for garnish; set aside.

Combine sugar, flour and salt in large bowl. Stir in apples, cranberries, raisins, pecans and lemon peel; toss well. Spoon fruit mixture into unbaked pie crust. Dot with butter. Roll remaining half of pie pastry on lightly floured surface to form 11-inch circle. Place over filling. Trim and seal edges; flute. Cut 3 slits in center of top crust. Moisten pastry cutouts and use to decorate top crust as desired. Lightly brush top crust with egg.

Bake 35 to 40 minutes or until apples are tender when pierced with fork and pastry is golden brown. Cool in pan on wire rack. Serve warm or cool completely. *Makes 1 (9-inch) pie*

Rich Pie Pastry

2 cups all-purpose flour

¼ teaspoon salt

6 tablespoons butter

6 tablespoons lard

6 to 8 tablespoons cold water

Combine flour and salt in medium bowl. Cut in butter and lard with pastry blender or 2 knives until mixture resembles coarse crumbs. Sprinkle water, 1 tablespoon at a time, over flour mixture, mixing until flour is moistened. Shape dough into ball. Roll, fill and bake as recipe directs. *Makes pastry for 1 (9-inch) double pie crust*

Holiday Hint:

Lard makes very tender and flaky pie crusts, because it is high in fat. If you prefer, you may substitute vegetable shortening for the lard in this pie crust recipe.

Santa's Cookies

Chocolate Cherry Bars

1 cup (2 sticks) butter or margarine

¾ cup HERSHEY'S Cocoa or HERSHEY'S Dutch Processed Cocoa

2 cups sugar

4 eggs

1½ cups plus ⅓ cup all-purpose flour, divided

⅓ cup chopped almonds

1 can (14 ounces) sweetened condensed milk (not evaporated milk)

½ teaspoon almond extract

1 cup HERSHEY'S MINI KISSES™ Semi-Sweet or Milk Chocolate Baking Pieces

1 cup chopped maraschino cherries, drained

1. Heat oven to 350°F. Generously grease 13×9×2-inch baking pan.

2. Melt butter in large saucepan over low heat; stir in cocoa until smooth. Remove from heat. Add sugar, 3 eggs, 1½ cups flour and almonds; mix well. Pour into prepared pan. Bake 20 minutes.

3. Meanwhile, whisk together remaining 1 egg, remaining ⅓ cup flour, sweetened condensed milk and almond extract. Pour over baked layer; sprinkle Mini Kisses™ and cherries over top. Return to oven.

4. Bake additional 20 to 25 minutes or until set and edges are golden brown. Cool completely in pan on wire rack. Refrigerate until cold, 6 hours or overnight. Cut into bars. Cover; refrigerate leftover bars. *Makes about 48 bars*

Chocolate Cherry Bars

Ice Skates

½ cup (1 stick) butter, softened
1¼ cups honey
1 cup packed brown sugar
1 egg, separated
5½ cups self-rising flour
1 teaspoon ground ginger
1 teaspoon ground cinnamon
½ cup milk
    Assorted colored icings, candies and small
    candy canes

1. Beat butter, honey, brown sugar and egg yolk in large bowl at medium speed of electric mixer until light and fluffy.

2. Combine flour, ginger and cinnamon in small bowl. Add alternately with milk to butter mixture; beat just until combined. Cover; refrigerate 30 minutes.

3. Preheat oven to 350°F. Grease cookie sheets.

4. Roll dough on lightly floured surface to ¼-inch thickness. Cut out dough using 3½-inch boot-shaped cookie cutter. Place cutouts 2 inches apart on prepared cookie sheets.

5. Bake 8 to 10 minutes or until lightly browned. Cool 2 minutes on cookie sheets. Remove to wire racks; cool completely.

6. Decorate cookies with colored icings and candies to look like ice skates, attaching candy canes as skate blades.   *Makes about 4 dozen cookies*

Scottish Shortbread

5 cups all-purpose flour
1 cup rice flour
2 cups butter, softened
1 cup sugar
    Candied fruit (optional)

Preheat oven to 325°F. Sift together flours. Beat butter and sugar in large bowl with electric mixer until creamy. Blend in ¾ of flour until mixture resembles fine crumbs. Stir in remaining flour by hand. Press dough firmly into ungreased 15½×10½×1-inch jelly-roll pan or two 9-inch fluted tart pans; crimp and flute edges of dough in jelly-roll pan, if desired. Bake 40 to 45 minutes or until light brown. Place pan on wire rack. Cut into bars or wedges while warm. Decorate with candied fruit, if desired. Cool completely. Store in airtight containers.

Makes about 4 dozen bars or 24 wedges

Ice Skates

Caramel Fudge Brownies

1 jar (12 ounces) hot caramel ice cream
    topping
1¼ cups all-purpose flour, divided
¼ teaspoon baking powder
    Dash salt
4 squares (1 ounce each) unsweetened
    chocolate, coarsely chopped
¾ cup butter
2 cups sugar
3 eggs
2 teaspoons vanilla
¾ cup semisweet chocolate chips
¾ cup chopped pecans

1. Preheat oven to 350°F. Lightly grease 13×9-inch baking pan.

2. Combine caramel topping and ¼ cup flour in small bowl; set aside. Combine remaining 1 cup flour, baking powder and salt in small bowl; mix well.

3. Place unsweetened chocolate and butter in medium microwavable bowl. Microwave at HIGH 2 minutes or until butter is melted; stir until chocolate is completely melted.

4. Stir sugar into melted chocolate. Add eggs and vanilla; stir until combined. Add flour mixture, stirring until well blended. Spread chocolate mixture evenly in prepared pan.

5. Bake 25 minutes. Immediately after removing brownies from oven, spread caramel mixture over brownies. Sprinkle top evenly with chocolate chips and pecans.

6. Return pan to oven; bake 20 to 25 minutes or until topping is golden brown and bubbling. *Do not overbake.* Cool brownies completely in pan on wire rack. Cut into 2×1½-inch bars.

7. Store tightly covered at room temperature or freeze up to 3 months.   *Makes 3 dozen brownies*

Holiday Hint:

Be sure to watch these brownies carefully during the last 20 to 25 minutes of baking (step 6). Overbaking will harden the caramel around the edges of the pan. Remove brownies from the oven while the caramel is soft.

Caramel Fudge Brownies

Nutty Lemon Crescents

1 package (18 ounces) refrigerated sugar cookie dough
1 cup chopped pecans, toasted*
1 tablespoon grated lemon peel
1½ cups powdered sugar, divided

*To toast pecans, spread in single layer on baking sheet. Bake in preheated 350°F oven 8 to 10 minutes or until golden brown, stirring frequently.

1. Preheat oven to 375°F. Remove dough from wrapper according to package directions.

2. Combine dough, pecans and lemon peel in large bowl. Stir until thoroughly blended. Shape level tablespoonfuls of dough into crescent shapes. Place 2 inches apart on ungreased cookie sheets. Bake 8 to 9 minutes or until set and very lightly browned. Cool 2 minutes on cookie sheets. Remove to wire racks.

3. Place 1 cup powdered sugar in shallow bowl. Roll warm cookies in powdered sugar. Cool completely. Sift remaining ½ cup powdered sugar over cookies just before serving.

Makes about 4 dozen cookies

Peanut Maple Triangles

1¼ cups powdered sugar, divided
½ cup creamy peanut butter
¼ cup plus 3 tablespoons maple-flavored syrup, divided
1 package (17½ ounces) frozen puff pastry dough, thawed
Nonstick cooking spray
1 to 2 tablespoons water

1. Preheat oven to 400°F. Combine ¼ cup powdered sugar, peanut butter and ¼ cup maple syrup in small bowl until well blended; set aside.

2. Cut pastry dough into 3-inch-wide strips. Place rounded teaspoon peanut butter mixture about 1 inch from 1 end of each strip.

3. Starting at end of each strip with filling, fold corner of pastry dough over filling so it lines up with other side of strip, forming a triangle. Continue folding like a flag in triangular shape, using entire strip. Repeat process with remaining pastry dough and filling.

4. Place triangles about 2 inches apart on ungreased baking sheets, seam-side down; spray with cooking spray. Bake 6 to 8 minutes or until golden brown. Remove from baking sheets to wire rack to cool.

5. Combine remaining 1 cup sugar, 3 tablespoons syrup and 1 tablespoon water in small bowl. Add additional water, if needed, for desired consistency. Glaze cookies just before serving.

Makes 28 cookies

Nutty Lemon Crescents

Chocolate Cheesecake Bars

CRUST

- 1 cup graham cracker crumbs
- ¼ cup firmly packed brown sugar
- ⅓ Butter Flavor CRISCO® Stick or ⅓ cup Butter Flavor CRISCO® all-vegetable shortening, melted

FILLING

- 1 package (8 ounces) cream cheese, softened
- ½ cup granulated sugar
- 3 tablespoons cocoa
- 2 eggs
- 1 tablespoon all-purpose flour
- ½ teaspoon vanilla

TOPPING

- 2 tablespoons Butter Flavor CRISCO® Stick or 2 tablespoons Butter Flavor CRISCO® all-vegetable shortening
- 1 package (3 ounces) cream cheese, softened
- 1 cup powdered sugar
- ½ teaspoon vanilla

1. Heat oven to 350°F. Place cooling rack on countertop.

2. For crust, combine graham cracker crumbs and brown sugar. Stir in melted shortening. Press into ungreased 8-inch square baking pan.

3. Bake at 350°F for 10 minutes. *Do not overbake.*

4. For filling, beat 8-ounce package cream cheese in small bowl at medium speed of electric mixer until smooth. Add, one at a time, granulated sugar, cocoa, eggs, flour and vanilla. Mix well after each addition. Pour over baked crust.

5. Bake for 30 minutes. *Do not overbake.* Cool to room temperature on cooling rack.

6. For topping, combine 2 tablespoons shortening and 3-ounce package cream cheese in small bowl. Beat at medium speed until well blended. Add powdered sugar and vanilla. Beat until smooth. Spread over filling. Cut into bars about 2×1½ inches. Refrigerate.   *Makes 20 bars*

Holiday Hint:

Did you forget to soften the cream cheese? Don't worry. Let your microwave come to the rescue. Place an 8-ounce unwrapped block of cream cheese on a microwavable plate. Heat it at MEDIUM (50% power) 15 to 20 seconds or just until softened.

Angel Pillows

½ Butter Flavor CRISCO® Stick or ½ cup Butter Flavor CRISCO® all-vegetable shortening plus additional for greasing

1 package (3 ounces) cream cheese, softened

1 tablespoon milk

¼ cup firmly packed brown sugar

½ cup apricot preserves

1¼ cups all-purpose flour

1½ teaspoons baking powder

1½ teaspoons ground cinnamon

¼ teaspoon salt

½ cup coarsely chopped pecans or flake coconut

FROSTING

1 cup confectioners' sugar

¼ cup apricot preserves

1 tablespoon Butter Flavor CRISCO® Stick or 1 tablespoon Butter Flavor CRISCO® all-vegetable shortening

Flake coconut or finely chopped pecans (optional)

Heat oven to 350°F. Grease baking sheets. Place sheets of foil on countertop for cooling cookies. Cream ½ cup shortening, cream cheese and milk at medium speed of electric mixer until well blended. Beat in brown sugar. Beat in preserves. Combine flour, baking powder, cinnamon and salt. Mix into creamed mixture. Stir in nuts. Drop 2 level measuring tablespoons of dough into a mound to form each cookie. Place 2 inches apart on prepared baking sheets.

Bake one baking sheet at a time at 350°F for 14 minutes. *Do not overbake.* Cool on baking sheet one minute. Remove cookies to foil to cool completely.

For frosting, combine confectioners' sugar, preserves and shortening in small mixing bowl. Beat with electric mixer until well blended. Frost cooled cookies. Sprinkle coconut over frosting, if desired. *Makes 1½ dozen cookies*

TIP: Try peach or pineapple preserves in place of apricot.

Prep Time: 25 minutes
Bake Time: 14 minutes

Holiday Hint:

Try substituting other flavors of preserves for the apricot preserves in these great-tasting holiday cookies. Peach and pineapple preserves are good choices.

Viennese Hazelnut Butter Thins

1 cup hazelnuts
1¼ cups all-purpose flour
¼ teaspoon salt
1¼ cups powdered sugar
1 cup butter, softened
1 egg
1 teaspoon vanilla
1 cup semisweet chocolate chips

1. Preheat oven to 350°F. To remove skins from hazelnuts, spread in single layer on baking sheet. Bake 10 to 12 minutes or until toasted and skins begin to flake off; let cool slightly. Wrap hazelnuts in heavy kitchen towel; rub against towel to remove as much of the skins as possible.

2. Place hazelnuts in food processor. Process using on/off pulsing action until hazelnuts are ground but not pasty.

3. Combine flour and salt in small bowl. Beat powdered sugar and butter in medium bowl with electric mixer at medium speed until light and fluffy. Beat in egg and vanilla. Gradually add flour mixture. Beat in ground hazelnuts at low speed until well blended.

4. Place dough on sheet of waxed paper. Using waxed paper to hold dough, roll back and forth to form log 12 inches long and 2½ inches wide. Wrap log in plastic wrap; refrigerate until firm, at least 2 hours or up to 48 hours.

5. Preheat oven to 350°F. Cut dough into ¼-inch-thick slices; place on ungreased cookie sheets.

6. Bake 10 to 12 minutes or until edges are very lightly browned. Let cookies stand on cookie sheets 1 minute. Remove cookies to wire racks; cool completely.

7. Place chocolate chips in 2-cup glass measure. Microwave at HIGH 1 to 1½ minutes or until melted, stirring after 1 minute and at 30-second intervals after first minute.

8. Dip cookies into chocolate, coating about ½ of each cookie. Let excess drip back into cup. Or, spread chocolate on cookies with a narrow spatula. Transfer cookies to waxed paper; let stand at room temperature 1 hour or until set.

Makes about 3 dozen cookies

Note: To store cookies, place in airtight container between layers of waxed paper. Cookies can be frozen for up to 3 months.

Viennese Hazelnut Butter Thins

Ornament Brownies

6 squares (1 ounce each) semisweet
    chocolate, coarsely chopped
1 tablespoon freeze dried coffee granules
1 tablespoon boiling water
¾ cup all-purpose flour
¾ teaspoon ground cinnamon
½ teaspoon baking powder
¼ teaspoon salt
½ cup sugar
¼ cup butter, softened
2 eggs
    Prepared vanilla frosting or icing
    Assorted food colors
    Small candy canes, assorted candies and
    sprinkles for decoration

1. Preheat oven to 350°F. Grease 8-inch square baking pan; set aside. Melt chocolate in small heavy saucepan over low heat, stirring constantly; set aside. Dissolve coffee granules in boiling water in small cup; set aside.

2. Place flour, cinnamon, baking powder and salt in small bowl; stir to combine.

3. Beat sugar and butter in large bowl with electric mixer at medium speed until light and fluffy. Beat in eggs, 1 at a time. Beat in melted chocolate and coffee until well combined. Add flour mixture. Beat at low speed until well blended. Spread batter evenly in prepared pan.

4. Bake 30 to 35 minutes or until center is set. Remove to wire rack; cool completely. Cut into holiday shapes using 2-inch cookie cutters.

5. Tint frosting with food colors to desired color. Spread over each brownie shape. Break off top of small candy cane to create loop. Insert in top of brownie. Decorate with assorted candies and sprinkles as desired. *Makes about 8 brownies*

Holiday Hint:

To melt the chocolate in a microwave oven, place six squares in a small microwavable bowl. Microwave at HIGH for 2 minutes; stir. Microwave, stirring every 30 seconds until the chocolate is melted.

Ornament Brownies

Holiday Thumbprint Cookies

1 package (8 ounces) sugar-free low-fat
    yellow cake mix
3 tablespoons orange juice
2 teaspoons grated orange peel
½ teaspoon vanilla
4 teaspoons strawberry all-fruit spread
2 tablespoons pecans, chopped

Preheat oven to 350°F. Spray baking sheets with nonstick cooking spray.

Beat cake mix, orange juice, orange peel and vanilla in medium bowl with electric mixer at medium speed for 2 minutes until mixture looks crumbly. Increase speed to medium and beat 2 minutes or until smooth dough forms. *Dough will be very sticky.*

Coat hands with nonstick cooking spray. Roll dough into 1-inch balls. Place balls 2½ inches apart on prepared baking sheets. Press center of each ball with thumb. Fill each thumbprint with ¼ teaspoon fruit spread. Sprinkle with nuts.

Bake 8 to 9 minutes or until cookies are light golden brown and lose their shininess. *Do not overbake.* Remove to wire racks; cool completely.

Makes 20 cookies

Spicy Pumpkin Cookies

2 CRISCO® Sticks or 2 cups CRISCO®
    All-Vegetable Shortening
2 cups sugar
1 can (16 ounces) solid pack pumpkin
2 eggs
2 teaspoons vanilla
4 cups all-purpose flour
2 teaspoons baking powder
2 teaspoons ground cinnamon
1 teaspoon salt
1 teaspoon baking soda
1 teaspoon ground nutmeg
½ teaspoon ground allspice
2 cups raisins
1 cup chopped nuts

1. Heat oven to 350°F.

2. Combine shortening, sugar, pumpkin, eggs and vanilla in large bowl; beat well.

3. Combine flour, baking powder, cinnamon, salt, baking soda, nutmeg and allspice in medium bowl. Add to pumpkin mixture; mix well. Stir in raisins and nuts. Drop rounded teaspoonfuls of dough, 2 inches apart, onto greased cookie sheet.

4. Bake at 350°F for 12 to 15 minutes. Cool on wire rack. If desired, frost with vanilla frosting.

Makes about 7 dozen cookies

Holiday Thumbprint Cookies

Chocolate-Dipped Walnut Biscotti

1¼ cups granulated sugar
1 Butter Flavor CRISCO® Stick or 1 cup
   Butter Flavor CRISCO® all-vegetable
   shortening
2 eggs
¼ cup light corn syrup or regular pancake
   syrup
1 tablespoon vanilla
3 cups all-purpose flour
¾ teaspoon baking powder
½ teaspoon baking soda
½ teaspoon salt
1 cup walnuts, coarsely chopped
1 package (8 ounces) white chocolate,
   coarsely chopped
   Red and green food color

1. Heat oven to 350°F. Place sheets of foil on countertop for cooling cookies.

2. Combine sugar and shortening in large bowl. Beat at medium speed of electric mixer until well blended. Add eggs, syrup and vanilla. Beat until well blended and fluffy.

3. Combine flour, baking powder, baking soda and salt. Add gradually to creamed mixture at low speed. Mix until well blended. Stir in walnuts.

4. Divide dough in half. Shape each half of dough into a log 2½ inches wide, 1-inch high and 9-inches long. Place on ungreased baking sheet.

5. Bake one log at a time at 350°F for 17 minutes. Remove log from oven. Cool 10 minutes on baking sheet. Cut diagonally into 1-inch wide cookies. Place cookies on their sides on baking sheet. Bake for an additional 8 to 10 minutes. DO NOT OVERBAKE. Cool 2 minutes on baking sheet. Remove cookies to foil to cool completely.

6. Place chocolate pieces in a microwave-safe bowl. Microwave at 100% (HIGH) 30 seconds. Stir. Repeat at 30 second intervals until melted. Divide melted chocolate into two bowls. Add food coloring, red in one bowl, green in the other, drop by drop, until desired shade is reached. Dip one end of half of cookies into red chocolate and the other half into green chocolate. Allow to set completely. *Makes about 2 dozen cookies*

Maple Pecan Sandwich Cookies

COOKIES

1¼ cups firmly packed light brown sugar

1 Butter Flavor CRISCO® Stick or 1 cup Butter Flavor CRISCO® all-vegetable shortening

2 eggs

¼ cup maple syrup or maple flavored pancake syrup

1 teaspoon maple extract

½ teaspoon vanilla

2½ cups all-purpose flour (plus 4 tablespoons), divided

1½ cups finely ground pecans

¾ teaspoon baking powder

½ teaspoon baking soda

½ teaspoon salt

20 to 30 pecan halves (optional)

FILLING

1¼ cups confectioners' sugar

3 tablespoons Butter Flavor CRISCO® Stick or 3 tablespoons Butter Flavor CRISCO® all-vegetable shortening

1 teaspoon maple extract

Dash salt

2½ teaspoons milk

1. For cookies, place brown sugar and shortening in large bowl. Beat at medium speed of electric mixer until well blended. Add eggs, syrup, maple extract and vanilla; beat until well blended and fluffy.

2. Combine 2½ cups flour, ground pecans, baking powder, baking soda and salt. Add gradually to shortening mixture, beating at low speed until well blended. Divide dough into 4 equal pieces; shape each into disk. Wrap with plastic wrap. Refrigerate 1 hour or until firm.

3. Heat oven to 375°F. Place sheets of foil on countertop for cooling cookies.

4. Sprinkle about 1 tablespoon flour on large sheet of waxed paper. Place disk of dough on floured paper; flatten slightly with hands. Turn dough over; cover with another large sheet of waxed paper. Roll dough to ¼-inch thickness. Cut out with floured 3-inch scalloped round cookie cutter. Place 2 inches apart on ungreased baking sheet. Roll out remaining dough. Place pecans in center of half of cookies, if desired.

5. Bake one baking sheet at a time at 375°F for 5 to 7 minutes or until lightly browned around edges. *Do not overbake.* Cool 2 minutes on baking sheet. Remove cookies to foil to cool completely.

6. For filling, place confectioners' sugar, shortening, maple extract and salt in medium bowl. Beat at low speed until smooth. Add milk; beat until mixture is smooth. Spread filling on flat side of 1 plain cookie. Cover with flat side of second cookie with pecan. Repeat with remaining cookies and filling. Garnish as desired.

Makes about 2 dozen sandwich cookies

Gooey Caramel Chocolate Bars

2 cups all-purpose flour

1 cup granulated sugar

¼ teaspoon salt

2 cups (4 sticks) butter, divided

1 cup packed light brown sugar

⅓ cup light corn syrup

1 cup (6 ounces) semisweet chocolate chips

Preheat oven to 350°F. Line 13×9-inch baking pan with foil. Combine flour, granulated sugar and salt in medium bowl; stir until blended. Cut in 14 tablespoons (1¾ sticks) butter until mixture resembles coarse crumbs. Press onto bottom of prepared pan. Bake 18 to 20 minutes or until lightly browned around edges. Remove pan to wire rack; cool completely.

Combine 1 cup (2 sticks) butter, brown sugar and corn syrup in heavy medium saucepan. Cook over medium heat 5 to 8 minutes or until mixture boils, stirring frequently. Boil gently 2 minutes, without stirring. Immediately pour over cooled base; spread evenly to edges of pan with metal spatula. Cool completely.

Melt chocolate in double boiler over hot (not boiling) water. Stir in remaining 2 tablespoons butter. Pour over cooled caramel layer and spread evenly to edges of pan with metal spatula. Refrigerate 10 to 15 minutes until chocolate begins to set. Remove; cool completely. Cut into bars.

Makes 3 dozen bars

Tony's Tiger Bites™

1 package (10 ounces) regular-size marshmallows (about 40)

¼ cup margarine

⅓ cup peanut butter

7½ cups KELLOGG'S FROSTED FLAKES® cereal

MICROWAVE DIRECTIONS

1. In 4-quart microwave-safe bowl, melt marshmallows and margarine at HIGH 3 minutes or until melted, stirring after 1½ minutes.

2. Stir in peanut butter until mixture is smooth. Add KELLOGG'S FROSTED FLAKES® cereal, stirring until well coated.

3. Using buttered spatula or waxed paper, press mixture into 13×9×2 inch pan coated with cooking spray. Cut into 1½×2-inch bars when cool. *Makes 32 bars*

Note: Use fresh marshmallows for best results.

Range-Top Directions: Melt margarine in large saucepan over low heat. Add marshmallows, stirring until completely melted. Remove from heat. Follow steps 2 and 3 above.

Left to right: Gooey Caramel Chocolate Bars and Oat-Y Nut Bars (page 316)

Fireside Cookie

1 package (18 ounces) refrigerated cookie
    dough, any flavor
All-purpose flour (optional)
Icings, red licorice bites, black string
    licorice, gum drops and assorted candies

1. Preheat oven to 350°F. Line large cookie sheets with parchment paper.

2. Remove dough from wrapper. Using about ¼ of dough, roll into 12×3-inch strip. Trim to 11×2¼ inches; set aside. Roll remaining dough into 10×8-inch rectangle. Trim to 9×7¾ inches; place on prepared baking sheet. Place reserved dough strip at top of rectangle to make fireplace mantel. Roll remaining scraps and cut into stocking shapes. Place on prepared baking sheets.

3. Bake 10 minutes or until edges are lightly browned. Cool on baking sheets 5 minutes. Remove stocking cookies to wire rack. Slide large cookie and parchment paper onto wire rack; cool completely.

4. Decorate with icings and candies as shown, attaching stockings to fireplace cookie with icing.

Makes 1 large cookie

Coconut Macaroons

1 (14-ounce) can EAGLE® BRAND
    Sweetened Condensed Milk (NOT
    evaporated milk)
2 teaspoons vanilla extract
1 to 1½ teaspoons almond extract
2 (7-ounce) packages flaked coconut
    (5⅓ cups)

1. Preheat oven to 325°F. Line baking sheets with foil; grease and flour foil. Set aside.

2. In large bowl, combine Eagle Brand, vanilla and almond extract. Stir in coconut. Drop by rounded teaspoonfuls onto prepared sheets; with spoon, slightly flatten each mound.

3. Bake 15 to 17 minutes or until golden. Remove from baking sheets; cool on wire racks. Store loosely covered at room temperature.

Makes about 4 dozen cookies

Prep Time: 10 minutes
Bake Time: 15 to 17 minutes

Fireside Cookie

Frosted Butter Cookies

COOKIES

1½ cups butter, softened

¾ cup granulated sugar

3 egg yolks

3 cups all-purpose flour

1 teaspoon baking powder

2 tablespoons orange juice

1 teaspoon vanilla

FROSTING

4 cups powdered sugar

½ cup butter, softened

3 to 4 tablespoons milk

2 teaspoons vanilla

Food coloring (optional)

Colored sugars, flaked coconut and
cinnamon candies for decoration

For cookies, in large bowl, cream butter and granulated sugar. Add egg yolks; beat until light and fluffy. Add flour, baking powder, orange juice and vanilla; beat until well mixed. Cover; refrigerate 2 to 3 hours or until firm.

Preheat oven to 350°F. Roll out dough, half at a time, to ¼-inch thickness on well-floured surface. Cut out with holiday cookie cutters. Place 1 inch apart on ungreased cookie sheets. Bake 6 to 10 minutes or until edges are golden brown. Remove to wire racks to cool completely.

For frosting, beat powdered sugar, butter, milk and vanilla in bowl until fluffy. If desired, divide frosting into small bowls and tint with food coloring. Frost cookies; decorate as desired.

Makes about 3 dozen cookies

Kahlúa® Kisses

¾ teaspoon instant coffee powder

⅓ cup water

1 cup plus 2 tablespoons sugar

¼ cup KAHLÚA® Liqueur

3 egg whites, room temperature

¼ teaspoon cream of tartar

Dash salt

In heavy 2-quart saucepan, dissolve coffee powder in water. Add 1 cup sugar; stir over low heat until sugar dissolves. Do not allow to boil. Stir in Kahlúa®. Brush down sides of pan frequently with pastry brush dipped in cold water. Bring mixture to a boil over medium heat. *Do not stir*. Boil until candy thermometer registers 240° to 242°F, about 15 minutes, adjusting heat if necessary to prevent boiling over. Mixture will be very thick. Remove from heat (temperature will continue to rise).

Immediately beat egg whites with cream of tartar and salt until soft peaks form. Add remaining 2 tablespoons sugar; continue beating until stiff peaks form. Gradually beat hot Kahlúa® syrup into egg whites, beating after each addition to thoroughly mix. Continue beating 4 to 5 minutes or until meringue is very thick, firm and cooled to lukewarm.

Line baking sheet with foil, shiny side down. Using pastry bag fitted with large star tip, pipe meringue into kisses about 1½ inches wide at base and 1½ inches high onto baking sheet. Bake on center rack of 200°F oven for 4 hours. Without opening door, turn off oven. Let kisses dry in oven 2 hours or until crisp. Remove from oven; cool completely on baking sheet. Store in airtight container up to 1 week.   *Makes 2½ dozen cookies*

White Chocolate Coconut Macaroons

2⅔ cups (7 ounces) BAKER'S® ANGEL FLAKE® Brand Coconut

3 squares BAKER'S® Premium White Baking Chocolate, chopped

⅔ cup sugar

6 tablespoons flour

¼ teaspoon salt

4 egg whites

1 teaspoon almond extract

1 square BAKER'S® Semi-Sweet Baking Chocolate, melted

HEAT oven to 325°F.

MIX coconut, white chocolate, sugar, flour and salt in bowl. Stir in egg whites and almond extract until well blended. Drop by teaspoonfuls onto lightly greased and floured cookie sheets.

BAKE 20 minutes or until edges of cookies are golden brown. Immediately remove from cookie sheets. Cool on wire racks. Drizzle with melted chocolate.   *Makes about 3 dozen cookies*

Tip: To melt chocolate for drizzle, place 1 square BAKER'S® Semi-Sweet Baking Chocolate in zipper-style plastic sandwich bag. Close bag tightly. Microwave on HIGH about 1 minute or until chocolate is melted. Fold down top of bag tightly and snip a tiny piece off 1 corner (about ⅛ inch). Holding top of bag tightly, drizzle chocolate through opening over cookies.

White Chocolate Citrus Macaroons: Prepare White Chocolate Coconut Macaroons, stirring in 2 teaspoons grated lemon, lime or orange peel before baking.

Prep Time: 15 minutes
Baking Time: 20 minutes

Holiday Hint:

When shipping holiday cookies, choose soft, moist cookies. They will survive shipping better than fragile, crisp ones. Wrap each type of cookie separately to retain flavors and textures.

315

Chocolate Almond Cookies

1 cup (2 sticks) butter or margarine, softened
1 cup sugar
1 egg
½ teaspoon almond extract
½ teaspoon vanilla extract
2 cups all-purpose flour
½ cup HERSHEY'S Cocoa
¼ teaspoon baking powder
¼ teaspoon baking soda
⅛ teaspoon salt
1 cup HERSHEY'S MINI CHIPS™ Semi-
 Sweet Chocolate
 Additional sugar
 Slivered blanched almonds

1. Beat butter and 1 cup sugar in large bowl until fluffy. Add egg, almond and vanilla extracts; beat well. Combine flour, cocoa, baking powder, baking soda and salt; gradually add to butter mixture, beating to form smooth dough. Stir in small chocolate chips. If necessary, refrigerate dough about 1 hour or until firm enough to handle.

2. Heat oven to 350°F. Shape dough into 1⅛-inch balls; roll in sugar. Place about 2 inches apart on ungreased cookie sheet. Place three slivered almonds on top of each ball; press slightly.

3. Bake 9 to 10 minutes or until set. Cool slightly. Remove from cookie sheet to wire rack. Cool completely.   *Makes about 3½ dozen cookies*

Oat-Y Nut Bars

½ cup butter
½ cup honey
¼ cup packed brown sugar
¼ cup corn syrup
2¾ cups uncooked quick oats
⅔ cup raisins
½ cup salted peanuts

Preheat oven to 300°F. Grease 9-inch square baking pan. Melt butter with honey, brown sugar and corn syrup in medium saucepan over medium heat, stirring constantly. Bring to a boil; boil 8 minutes until mixture thickens slightly. Stir in oats, raisins and peanuts until well blended. Press evenly into prepared pan.

Bake 45 to 50 minutes or until golden brown. Place pan on wire rack; score top into 2-inch squares. Cool completely. Cut into bars.

Makes 16 bars

Chocolate Almond Cookies

Wild Rice Applesauce Bars

2 cups well-cooked wild rice, chopped
1 cup buttermilk or sour milk, divided
1 cup unsweetened applesauce
¼ cup vegetable oil
¾ cup shortening
1 cup firmly packed brown sugar
6 egg whites
2 teaspoons vanilla
2½ cups all-purpose flour
1 teaspoon baking soda
1 teaspoon salt
1 teaspoon cinnamon
1 cup chopped nuts
Powdered sugar

Preheat oven to 350°F. Grease bottom of 15×10×1-inch baking pan. In medium bowl, combine wild rice, ½ cup buttermilk, applesauce and oil; set aside. In large bowl, combine shortening, brown sugar, egg whites and vanilla; beat at high speed of electric mixer 5 minutes or until smooth and creamy. Add remaining ½ cup buttermilk; beat at low speed until well blended. Add flour, baking soda, salt and cinnamon; beat at low speed until well blended. Stir in wild rice mixture and nuts. Spread in prepared pan. Bake 20 to 25 minutes or until toothpick inserted in center comes out clean. Sprinkle with powdered sugar. Cool completely.   *Makes 48 bars*

Favorite recipe from **Minnesota Cultivated Wild Rice Council**

Chocolate Fudge-Peanut Butter Balls

2 cups (11½ ounces) milk chocolate chips
¼ cup half-and-half
⅓ cup creamy peanut butter
⅓ cup chopped peanuts

1. Melt chips with half-and-half in heavy, medium saucepan over low heat, stirring occasionally. Whisk in peanut butter until blended. Refrigerate until mixture is firm enough to shape into balls, but still soft, about 30 minutes, stirring occasionally.

2. Spread peanuts on waxed paper.

3. Shape scant 1 tablespoonful of the mixture into 1-inch balls. Roll balls in peanuts.

4. Store in refrigerator.   *Makes about 32 balls*

Wild Rice Applesauce Bars

Christmas Ornament Cookies

2¼ cups all-purpose flour
¼ teaspoon salt
1 cup sugar
¾ cup butter, softened
1 large egg
1 teaspoon vanilla
1 teaspoon almond extract
Icing (recipe follows)
Assorted candies and decors

Place flour and salt in medium bowl; stir to combine. Beat sugar and butter in large bowl with electric mixer at medium speed until light and fluffy. Beat in egg, vanilla and almond extract. Gradually add flour mixture. Beat at low speed until well blended. Divide dough in half; cover and refrigerate 30 minutes or until firm.

Preheat oven to 350°F. Working with 1 portion at a time, roll out dough on lightly floured surface to ¼-inch thickness. Cut dough into desired shapes with assorted floured cookie cutters. Reroll trimmings and cut out more cookies. Place cutouts on ungreased baking sheets. Using drinking straw or tip of sharp knife, cut hole near top of each cookie to allow for piece of ribbon or string to be inserted for hanger. Bake 10 to 12 minutes or until edges are golden brown. Let cookies stand on baking sheets 1 minute. Remove cookies to wire racks; cool completely.

Prepare Icing. Spoon Icing into small resealable plastic food storage bag. Cut off very tiny corner of bag; pipe Icing decoratively on cookies. Decorate with candies as desired. Let stand at room temperature 40 minutes or until set. Thread ribbon through each cookie hole to hang as Christmas tree ornaments. *Makes about 2 dozen cookies*

Icing

2 cups powdered sugar
2 tablespoons milk or lemon juice
Food coloring (optional)

Place powdered sugar and milk in small bowl; stir with spoon until smooth. (Icing will be very thick. If it is too thick, stir in 1 teaspoon additional milk.) Divide into small bowls and tint with food coloring, if desired.

Marbled Cheesecake Bars

2 cups finely crushed crème-filled chocolate sandwich cookies (about 24 cookies)
3 tablespoons butter or margarine, melted
3 (8-ounce) packages cream cheese, softened
1 (14-ounce) can EAGLE® BRAND Sweetened Condensed Milk (NOT evaporated milk)
3 eggs
2 teaspoons vanilla extract
2 (1-ounce) squares unsweetened chocolate, melted

1. Preheat oven to 300°F. Combine cookie crumbs and butter; press firmly on bottom of ungreased 13×9-inch baking pan.

2. In large bowl, beat cream cheese until fluffy. Gradually beat in Eagle Brand until smooth. Add eggs and vanilla; mix well. Pour half the batter evenly over prepared crust.

3. Stir melted chocolate into remaining batter; spoon over vanilla batter. With table knife or metal spatula, gently swirl through batter to marble.

4. Bake 45 to 50 minutes or until set. Cool. Chill. Cut into bars. Store covered in refrigerator.

Makes 24 to 36 bars

Helpful Hint: For best distribution of added ingredients (chocolate chips, nuts, etc.) or for even marbling, do not oversoften or overbeat the cream cheese.

Prep Time: 20 minutes
Bake Time: 45 to 50 minutes

Spritz Cookies

1¼ cups granulated sugar
  1 Butter Flavor CRISCO® Stick or 1 cup
    Butter Flavor CRISCO all-vegetable
    shortening
  2 eggs
¼ cup light corn syrup or regular pancake
    syrup
  1 tablespoon vanilla
  3 cups all-purpose flour
¾ teaspoon baking powder
½ teaspoon baking soda
½ teaspoon salt
    Colored sugar crystals (optional)
    Nonpareils (optional)
    Chocolate jimmies (optional)

1. Heat oven to 375°F. Place sheets of foil on countertop for cooling cookies.

2. Place sugar and 1 cup shortening in large bowl. Beat at medium speed of electric mixer until well blended. Add eggs, syrup and vanilla; beat until well blended and fluffy.

3. Combine flour, baking powder, baking soda and salt. Add gradually to shortening mixture; beat at low speed until well blended.

4. Fill cookie press with dough, following manufacturer's directions. Press dough about 1½ inches apart on ungreased baking sheet. Sprinkle with colored sugar, nonpareils or chocolate jimmies, if desired.

5. Bake one sheet at a time at 375°F for 7 to 9 minutes or until bottoms of cookies are golden. *Do not overbake.* Cool 2 minutes on baking sheet. Remove cookies to foil to cool completely.

Makes about 7½ dozen cookies

Banana Crescents

½ cup chopped almonds, toasted
6 tablespoons sugar, divided
½ cup margarine, cut into pieces
1½ cups plus 2 tablespoons all-purpose flour
⅛ teaspoon salt
1 extra-ripe, medium DOLE® Banana, peeled
2 to 3 ounces semisweet chocolate chips

• Pulverize almonds with 2 tablespoons sugar.

• Beat margarine, almonds, remaining 4 tablespoons sugar, flour and salt.

• Purée banana; add to almond mixture and mix until well blended.

• Roll tablespoonfuls of dough into logs, then shape into crescents. Place on ungreased cookie sheet. Bake in 375°F oven 25 minutes or until golden. Cool on wire rack.

• Melt chocolate in microwavable dish at MEDIUM (50% power) 1½ to 2 minutes, stirring once. Dip ends of cookies in chocolate. Refrigerate until chocolate is set.   *Makes 2 dozen cookies*

Chewy Toffee Almond Bars

1 cup (2 sticks) butter, softened
½ cup sugar
2 cups all-purpose flour
1¾ cups (10-ounce package) SKOR® English Toffee Bits or HEATH® BITS 'O BRICKLE™
¾ cup light corn syrup
1 cup sliced almonds, divided
¾ cup MOUNDS® Sweetened Coconut Flakes, divided

1. Heat oven to 350°F. Grease sides of 13×9×2-inch baking pan.

2. Beat butter and sugar until fluffy. Gradually add flour, beating until well blended. Press dough evenly into prepared pan.

3. Bake 15 to 20 minutes or until edges are lightly browned. Meanwhile, combine toffee bits and corn syrup in medium saucepan. Cook over medium heat, stirring constantly, until toffee is melted (10 to 12 minutes). Stir in ½ cup almonds and ½ cup coconut. Spread toffee mixture to within ¼-inch of edges of crust. Sprinkle remaining ½ cup almonds and remaining ¼ cup coconut over top.

4. Bake an additional 15 minutes or until bubbly. Cool completely in pan on wire rack. Cut into bars.
Makes about 36 bars

Banana Crescents

Golden Kolacky

½ cup butter, softened

4 ounces cream cheese, softened

1 cup all-purpose flour

Fruit preserves

Combine butter and cream cheese in large bowl; beat until smooth. Gradually add flour to butter mixture, blending until mixture forms soft dough. Divide dough in half; wrap each half in plastic wrap. Refrigerate until firm.

Preheat oven to 375°F. Roll out dough, half at a time, on floured surface to ⅛-inch thickness. Cut into 3-inch squares. Spoon 1 teaspoon preserves into center of each square. Bring up two opposite corners to center; pinch together tightly to seal. Fold sealed tip to one side; pinch to seal. Place 1 inch apart on ungreased cookie sheets. Bake 10 to 15 minutes or until lightly browned. Remove to wire racks; cool completely.

Makes about 2½ dozen cookies

Honey Nut Rugelach

1 cup butter or margarine, softened

3 ounces cream cheese, softened

½ cup honey, divided

2 cups flour

1 teaspoon lemon juice

1 teaspoon ground cinnamon, divided

1 cup finely chopped walnuts

½ cup dried cherries or cranberries

Cream butter and cream cheese until fluffy. Add 3 tablespoons honey and mix well. Mix in flour until dough holds together. Form into a ball, wrap and refrigerate 2 hours or longer. Divide dough into 4 equal portions. On floured surface, roll one portion of dough into 9-inch circle. Combine 2 tablespoons honey and lemon juice; mix well. Brush dough with ¼ of honey mixture; sprinkle with ¼ teaspoon cinnamon. Combine walnuts and cherries in small bowl; drizzle with remaining 3 tablespoons honey and mix well. Spread ¼ of walnut mixture onto circle of dough, stopping ½ inch from outer edge. Cut circle into 8 triangular pieces. Roll up dough starting at wide outer edge and rolling toward tip. Gently bend both ends to form a crescent. Place on oiled parchment paper-lined baking sheet and refrigerate 20 minutes or longer. Repeat with remaining dough and filling. Bake at 350°F 20 to 25 minutes or until golden brown. Cool on wire racks.

Makes 32 cookies

Freezing Tip: Unbaked cookies can be placed in freezer-safe containers or bags and frozen until ready to bake.

*Favorite recipe from **National Honey Board***

Golden Kolacky

Fudge-Filled Bars

1 (14-ounce) can EAGLE® BRAND Sweetened Condensed Milk (NOT evaporated milk)

1 (12-ounce) package semi-sweet chocolate chips

2 tablespoons butter or margarine

2 teaspoons vanilla extract

2 (18-ounce) packages refrigerated cookie dough (oatmeal-chocolate chip, chocolate chip, or sugar cookie dough)

1. Preheat oven to 350°F. In heavy saucepan over medium heat, combine Eagle Brand, chips and butter; heat until chips melt, stirring often. Remove from heat; stir in vanilla. Cool 15 minutes.

2. Using floured hands, press 1½ packages of cookie dough into ungreased 15×10×1-inch baking pan. Pour cooled chocolate mixture evenly over dough. Crumble remaining dough over filling.

3. Bake 25 to 30 minutes. Cool. Cut into bars. Store covered at room temperature.

Makes 48 bars

Helpful Hint: If you want to trim the fat in any Eagle Brand recipe, just use Eagle® Brand Fat Free or Low Fat Sweetened Condensed Milk instead of the original Eagle Brand.

Prep Time: 20 minutes
Bake Time: 25 to 30 minutes

Kringle's Cutouts

⅔ Butter Flavor CRISCO® Stick or ⅔ cup Butter Flavor CRISCO® all-vegetable shortening

¾ cup sugar

1 tablespoon plus 1 teaspoon milk

1 teaspoon vanilla

1 egg

2 cups all-purpose flour

1½ teaspoons baking powder

¼ teaspoon salt

1. Cream shortening, sugar, milk and vanilla in large bowl at medium speed of electric mixer until well blended. Beat in egg. Combine flour, baking powder and salt. Mix into creamed mixture. Cover; refrigerate several hours or overnight.

2. Heat oven to 375°F. Place sheets of foil on countertop for cooling cookies.

3. Roll dough, half at a time, to ⅛-inch thickness on floured surface. Cut into desired shapes. Place cookies 2 inches apart on ungreased cookie sheet. Sprinkle with colored sugar and decors, or leave plain to frost when cool.

4. Bake at 375°F for 7 to 9 minutes. *Do not overbake.* Cool 2 minutes on baking sheet. Remove cookies to foil to cool completely.

Makes about 3 dozen cookies

Hint: Floured pastry cloth and rolling pin cover make rolling out dough easier.

Fudge-Filled Bars

Divine Desserts

Caramel-Pecan Snowmen

48 pecan halves

20 vanilla-flavored caramels (about ½ of 14½-ounce package)

1 tablespoon water

6 ounces white almond bark

1 teaspoon shortening

3 chocolate-flavored caramels

Assorted candies

1. Spray baking sheet with nonstick cooking spray.

2. Arrange pecans on prepared baking sheet as shown in diagram, forming 6 snowmen.

3. Melt vanilla-flavored caramels with water in small saucepan over low heat, stirring frequently. Spoon caramel evenly over snowmen to join pecans together. Refrigerate 10 minutes or until set.

4. Melt almond bark with shortening, according to package directions. Spoon over snowmen as shown in photo.

5. With rolling pin, roll each chocolate caramel between 2 sheets of waxed paper to form 3-inch circle. Trim off edges of circle leaving a 2-inch square; reserve trimmings. Cut square in half to form two 1-inch-wide strips. Roll up 1-inch strips; place 1 on top of each snowman to form hat. Add ½-inch strip from trimmings at bottom of each hat to form brim. Repeat with remaining chocolate caramels and snowmen.

6. Decorate with candies as shown in photo.

Makes 6 snowmen

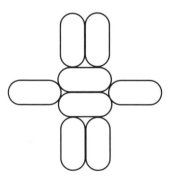

Caramel-Pecan Snowmen

Chocolate Peppermints

1 cup (6 ounces) semisweet chocolate chips
1 cup milk chocolate chips
¼ teaspoon peppermint extract
½ cup crushed peppermint candy

Line baking sheet with buttered waxed paper; set aside. Melt both kinds of chips in heavy, medium saucepan over low heat, stirring constantly. Stir in peppermint extract. Spread mixture in rectangle about ¼ inch thick on prepared baking sheet. Sprinkle with candy; press into chocolate. Refrigerate until almost firm. Cut into squares. Refrigerate until firm before removing from paper.

Makes about 100 mints

Holiday Hint:

Squares are easier to cut without breaking if chocolate is not completely firm. If you refrigerate the candy too long and it becomes brittle, let it stand at room temperature until soft enough to cut.

Blueberry Bread Pudding

1 package BOB EVANS® Frozen White
    Dinner Roll Dough, prepared according
    to package directions (day old)
5 eggs
1 cup whipping cream
¾ cup milk
½ cup granulated sugar
    Pinch salt
1 cup packed brown sugar
½ cup water
1 cup butter, melted
2 tablespoons vanilla extract
1 teaspoon ground cinnamon
1 cup fresh blueberries

Preheat oven to 350°F. Cut prepared dinner rolls into cubes; place in large bowl. Whisk together eggs, cream, milk, granulated sugar and salt; pour over bread cubes and toss to coat. Pour mixture into greased 11×7-inch baking dish; bake 1 hour.

To prepare sauce, stir brown sugar and water in medium saucepan until sugar is dissolved. Cook, uncovered, over medium heat until reduced by half. Remove from heat; stir in butter, vanilla and cinnamon until well blended. To serve, pour sauce over bread pudding and garnish with blueberries. Refrigerate leftovers.

Makes 9 servings

Chocolate Peppermints and
Chocolate-Nut Squares (page 344)

Baked Pear Dessert

2 tablespoons dried cranberries or raisins

1 tablespoon toasted sliced almonds

⅛ teaspoon cinnamon

⅓ cup unsweetened apple cider or apple juice, divided

1 medium unpeeled pear, cut in half lengthwise and cored

½ cup vanilla low-fat frozen ice cream or frozen yogurt

1. Preheat oven to 350°F. Combine cranberries, almonds, cinnamon and 1 teaspoon cider in small bowl.

2. Place pear halves, cut side up, in small baking dish. Mound almond mixture on top of pear halves. Pour remaining cider into dish. Cover with foil.

3. Bake pear halves 35 to 40 minutes or until pears are soft, spooning cider in dish over pears once or twice during baking. Serve warm and top with ice cream.

Makes 2 servings

Mocha Rum Balls

60 NILLA® Wafers, finely rolled (about 2½ cups crumbs)

1 cup powdered sugar

1 cup PLANTERS® Pecans, finely chopped

½ cup margarine or butter, melted

2 tablespoons light corn syrup

2 tablespoons unsweetened cocoa

¼ cup rum

1 teaspoon instant coffee granules

Powdered sugar, for coating

1. Mix crumbs, 1 cup powdered sugar, pecans, melted margarine or butter, corn syrup and cocoa in large bowl. Blend rum and instant coffee until coffee granules are dissolved; stir into crumb mixture. Let stand 15 minutes.

2. Shape mixture into 1-inch balls; roll in additional powdered sugar. Store in airtight container, separating layers with waxed paper. Flavor improves with standing.

Makes about 3 dozen

Preparation Time: 50 minutes
Total Time: 50 minutes

Baked Pear Dessert

White Chocolate Bavarian Christmas Tree

INGREDIENTS

1 cup half-and-half

2 teaspoons vanilla

2 envelopes unflavored gelatin

6 eggs, separated*

12 ounces high-quality white or semisweet chocolate

1 teaspoon cream of tartar

1½ cups whipping cream, whipped

Decorations: Spearmint candy leaves, red cinnamon candies, red candy-coated licorice pieces, green miniature jaw breakers

SUPPLIES

8-cup tree mold or other decorative mold

*Use only grade A clean, uncracked eggs.

1. Combine half-and-half and vanilla in medium saucepan. Sprinkle gelatin over mixture; let stand 5 minutes. Stir over low heat until gelatin is completely dissolved.

2. Beat egg yolks in small bowl. Stir about ½ cup gelatin mixture into egg yolks; return egg yolk mixture to saucepan. Cook over low heat, stirring constantly, until thick enough to coat the back of a spoon.

3. Melt chocolate in top of double boiler over hot, not boiling, water, stirring constantly. Stir gelatin mixture into chocolate. Remove from heat; cool to room temperature.

4. Beat egg whites and cream of tartar until stiff peaks form. Gently fold cooled chocolate mixture into beaten egg whites. Fold in whipped cream.

5. Spoon mixture into 8-cup tree mold or other decorative mold. Refrigerate until set, 8 hours or overnight.

6. To unmold, pull chocolate mixture from edge of mold with moistened fingers. Or, run small metal spatula or pointed knife dipped in warm water around edge of mold. Dip bottom of mold briefly in warm water. Place serving plate on top of mold. Invert mold and plate and shake to loosen chocolate mixture. Gently remove mold. Decorate with candies. *Makes 12 to 14 servings*

Holiday Hint:

Unflavored gelatin must be softened in liquid before using. Sprinkle gelatin over water or other liquid used in the recipe. Let it stand for 5 minutes, then heat it over very low heat, stirring until gelatin granules are completely dissolved. Do not allow this mixture to boil or the gelatin will lose its thickening powers.

Rice Pudding Pear Tart

½ (15-ounce) package refrigerated pie crust

2 cups dry red wine

1 teaspoon ground cinnamon

2 large pears, peeled, halved and cored

2 cups cooked rice

2 cups half-and-half

½ cup plus 1 tablespoon sugar, divided

2 tablespoons butter or margarine

¼ teaspoon salt

2 eggs, beaten

1 teaspoon vanilla extract

Preheat oven to 450°F. Prepare pie crust according to package directions. Place in 10-inch tart pan. Bake 8 to 10 minutes or until lightly browned; set aside. Reduce oven temperature to 350°F.

Place wine and cinnamon in 10-inch skillet; bring to a boil. Add pears; reduce heat, cover and poach 10 minutes. Carefully turn pears in liquid; poach 5 to 10 minutes or until tender. Remove from wine; set aside.

Combine rice, half-and-half, ½ cup sugar, butter and salt in 3-quart saucepan. Cook over medium heat 12 to 15 minutes or until slightly thickened. Gradually stir ¼ of rice mixture into eggs; return mixture to saucepan, stirring constantly. Continue to cook 1 to 2 minutes. Stir in vanilla. Pour rice pudding mixture into prepared crust. Place pears, cut sides down, on cutting surface. Cut thin lengthwise slices into each pear one third of the way down from stem end. Fan pears over pudding mixture.

Bake 30 minutes or until pudding is set. Remove from oven; sprinkle with remaining 1 tablespoon sugar. Place tart in oven about 4 to 5 inches from heat; broil 1 to 2 minutes or until top is browned. Cool before serving. Garnish as desired. Tart can be made ahead, if desired.   *Makes 1 (10-inch) tart*

Favorite recipe from **USA Rice Federation**

Toffee Bits Desserts Sauce

1¾ cups (10-ounce package) SKOR® English Toffee Bits *or* 1¾ cups (10-ounce package) HEATH® BITS 'O BRICKLE™ Almond Toffee Bits

½ cup whipping cream

2 tablespoons light corn syrup

2 tablespoons butter

Vanilla ice cream

1. Stir together toffee bits, whipping cream and corn syrup in small saucepan.

2. Cook over medium heat, stirring constantly, until mixture comes to a boil. Remove from heat.

3. Add butter; stir until melted. Cool. Serve over ice cream.   *Makes about 1⅔ cups sauce*

Prep Time: 2 minutes
Cook Time: 10 minutes
Cool Time: 20 minutes

Tart Cherry and Almond Sugar Plums

1 cup (about 6½ ounces) dried tart cherries
1 cup slivered almonds
5 teaspoons kirsch (cherry liqueur)
⅔ cup coarse white or colored sugar

1. Line medium baking dish with waxed paper; set aside.

2. Place cherries, almonds and kirsch in food processor; process until mixture is finely chopped and comes together.

3. Place sugar in small bowl. Butter hands lightly. Form fruit mixture into 1-inch balls. Roll balls, one at a time, in sugar to coat evenly. Place 1 inch apart in prepared dish. Let stand 20 to 30 minutes or until firm. Cover tightly and refrigerate up to 3 days. *Makes about 20 balls*

White Chocolate-Dipped Apricots

3 ounces white chocolate, coarsely chopped
20 dried apricot halves

Line baking sheet with waxed paper; set aside. Melt white chocolate in bowl over hot (not boiling) water; stir constantly.

Dip half of each apricot piece in chocolate, coating both sides. Place on prepared baking sheet. Refrigerate until firm. Store in refrigerator in container between layers of waxed paper.
Makes 20 apricots

Divinity

½ cup corn syrup
½ cup water
2¼ cups sugar
2 egg whites
⅛ teaspoon cream of tartar
1 teaspoon vanilla
½ cup chopped almonds (optional)

1. Line 2 or 3 baking sheets with buttered waxed paper; set aside.

2. Combine corn syrup, water and sugar in heavy, medium saucepan. Cook over medium heat, stirring constantly, until sugar dissolves and mixture comes to a boil. Wash down side of pan frequently with pastry brush dipped in hot water to remove sugar crystals.

3. Add candy thermometer. Continue to cook until mixture reaches the hard-ball stage (255°F).

4. Meanwhile, beat egg whites and cream of tartar with electric mixer until stiff but not dry.

5. Slowly pour hot syrup in egg whites, beating constantly. Add vanilla; beat until candy forms soft peaks and starts to lose its gloss. Stir in almonds. Immediately drop tablespoonfuls of candy in mounds on prepared baking sheets.

6. Store in refrigerator in airtight container between layers of waxed paper or freeze up to 3 months. *Makes about 40 pieces*

Tart Cherry and Almond Sugar Plums and Apricot-Cranberry-Walnut Sugar Plums (page 338)

Grandma's® Gingerbread

½ cup shortening or butter

½ cup sugar

1 cup GRANDMA'S® Molasses

2 eggs

2½ cups all-purpose flour

1 teaspoon salt

2 teaspoons baking powder

½ teaspoons baking soda

1 teaspoon ginger

2 teaspoons cinnamon

½ teaspoon ground cloves

1 cup hot water

Heat oven to 350°F. In medium bowl, blend shortening with sugar, add molasses and eggs. Beat well. Sift dry ingredients, add alternately with water to molasses mixture. Bake in greased 9-inch square pan, about 50 minutes. *Makes 8 servings*

Holiday Hint:

To add a special touch to this spicy gingerbread, serve it with a light sprinkling of confectioners' sugar. If desired, garnish it with your choice of fresh fruit.

Apricot-Cranberry-Walnut Sugar Plums

½ cup (about 3 ounces) dried apricots

½ cup (about 3 ounces) dried cranberries

½ cup walnut pieces

¼ teaspoon ground nutmeg

2 tablespoons plus 2 teaspoons orange liqueur

⅔ cup coarse white or colored sugar

1. Line medium baking dish with waxed paper; set aside.

2. Place apricots, cranberries, walnuts, nutmeg and orange liqueur in food processor; process until mixture is finely chopped and comes together.

3. Place sugar in small bowl. Butter hands lightly. Form fruit mixture into 1-inch balls. Roll in sugar to coat evenly. Place in prepared pan. Let stand 20 to 30 minutes or until firm. Cover tightly and refrigerate up to 3 days. *Makes about 20 balls*

Grandma's® Gingerbread

Cran-Raspberry Hazelnut Trifle

2 cups hazelnut-flavored liquid dairy creamer

1 package (3.4 ounces) instant vanilla pudding and pie filling mix

1 package (about 11 ounces) frozen pound cake, thawed

1 can (21 ounces) raspberry pie filling

1 can (16 ounces) whole berry cranberry sauce

1. Combine dairy creamer and pudding in medium bowl; beat with wire whisk 1 to 2 minutes or until thickened.

2. Cut pound cake into ¾-inch cubes. Combine pie filling and cranberry sauce in medium bowl; blend well.

3. Layer ⅓ of cake cubes, ¼ of fruit sauce and ⅓ of pudding mixture in 1½- to 2-quart straight-sided glass serving bowl. Repeat layers twice; top with remaining fruit sauce. Cover; refrigerate until serving time.   *Makes 8 servings*

Serving Suggestion: Garnish trifle with whipped topping and fresh mint sprigs.

Prep Time: 20 minutes

Pecan Brittle

½ cup corn syrup

1 cup sugar

1 cup pecan halves

1 tablespoon butter or margarine, cut into pieces

1 teaspoon vanilla

1½ teaspoons baking soda

1. Butter large baking sheet; set aside.

2. Combine corn syrup and sugar in 2-quart microwave-safe bowl. Stir in pecans. Microwave at HIGH 5 to 5½ minutes until syrup is golden brown.

3. Stir in butter and vanilla. Microwave at HIGH 1½ minutes.

4. Stir in baking soda (mixture will foam up) and immediately pour onto prepared baking sheet; do not scrape side of bowl. Stretch as thin as possible, using 2 forks.

5. Cool, then break in pieces. Store tightly covered.
Makes about ¾ pound

Hint: If kitchen is cold, warm baking sheet before pouring out brittle. It will spread more easily and will be thinner.

Cran-Raspberry Hazelnut Trifle

Cookies 'n' Crème Fudge

3 (6-ounce) packages white chocolate baking
    squares
1 (14-ounce) can EAGLE® BRAND
    Sweetened Condensed Milk (NOT
    evaporated milk)
$\frac{1}{8}$ teaspoon salt
2 cups coarsely crushed chocolate crème-
    filled sandwich cookies (about
    20 cookies)

1. Line 8-inch square baking pan with foil. In
heavy saucepan over low heat, melt chocolate with
Eagle Brand and salt. Remove from heat. Stir in
crushed cookies. Spread evenly in prepared pan.
Chill 2 hours or until firm.

2. Turn fudge onto cutting board. Peel off foil; cut
into squares. Store tightly covered at room
temperature.   *Makes about 2½ pounds*

Prep Time: 10 minutes
Chill Time: 2 hours

Caramel-Marshmallow Apples

1 package (14 ounces) caramels
1 cup miniature marshmallows
1 tablespoon water
5 or 6 small apples

1. Line baking sheet with buttered waxed paper; set
aside.

2. Combine caramels, marshmallows and water in
medium saucepan. Cook over medium heat,
stirring constantly, until caramels melt. Cool
slightly while preparing apples.

3. Rinse and thoroughly dry apples. Insert flat
sticks in stem ends of apples.

4. Dip each apple in caramel mixture, coating
apples. Remove excess caramel mixture by scraping
apple bottoms across rim of saucepan. Place on
prepared baking sheet. Refrigerate until firm.
          Makes 5 or 6 apples

Caramel-Nut Apples: Roll coated apples in
chopped nuts before refrigerating.

Caramel-Chocolate Apples: Drizzle melted milk
chocolate over coated apples before refrigerating.

Festive Cranberry Mold

½ cup water
1 package (6 ounces) raspberry-flavored
    gelatin
1 can (8 ounces) cranberry sauce
1⅔ cups cranberry juice cocktail
1 cup sliced bananas (optional)
½ cup walnuts, toasted (optional)

In medium saucepan over medium-high heat, bring water to a boil. Add gelatin and stir until dissolved. Fold in cranberry sauce. Reduce heat to medium and cook until sauce is melted. Stir in cranberry juice cocktail.

Refrigerate mixture until slightly thickened. Fold in banana slices and walnuts, if desired. Pour mixture into 4-cup mold; cover and refrigerate until gelatin is set. *Makes 8 servings*

Chocolate-Nut Squares

1 cup (6 ounces) semisweet chocolate chips
1 cup milk chocolate chips
1 tablespoon shortening
1 package (14 ounces) caramels
2 tablespoons butter or margarine
3 tablespoons milk
2 cups coarsely chopped pecans

Line 8-inch square pan with buttered foil; set aside. Melt both kinds of chips with shortening in heavy, small saucepan over very low heat, stirring constantly. Spoon half the chocolate mixture into prepared pan, spreading evenly over bottom and ¼ inch up sides of pan. Refrigerate until firm.

Meanwhile, combine caramels, butter and milk in heavy, medium saucepan. Cook over medium heat, stirring constantly. When mixture is smooth, stir in pecans. Cool to lukewarm. Spread caramel mixture evenly over chocolate in pan. Melt remaining chocolate mixture again over very low heat, stirring constantly; spread over caramel layer. Refrigerate until almost firm. Cut into squares. Store in refrigerator. *Makes about 2 pounds*

Tip: Squares are easier to cut without breaking if chocolate is not completely firm.

Festive Cranberry Mold

Oats 'n' Apple Tart

1½ cups quick-cooking oats

½ cup brown sugar, divided

1 tablespoon plus ¼ teaspoon ground
    cinnamon, divided

5 tablespoons butter or margarine, melted

2 medium sweet apples, such as Golden
    Delicious, unpeeled, cored and thinly
    sliced

1 teaspoon lemon juice

¼ cup water

1 envelope unsweetened gelatin

½ cup apple juice concentrate

1 package (8 ounces) reduced-fat cream
    cheese, softened

⅛ teaspoon ground nutmeg

Preheat oven to 350°F. Combine oats, ¼ cup brown sugar and 1 tablespoon cinnamon in medium bowl; stir. Add butter and stir until combined. Press into bottom and up sides of 9-inch pie plate. Bake 7 minutes or until set. Cool on wire rack.

Toss apple slices with lemon juice in small bowl; set aside. Place water in small saucepan. Sprinkle gelatin over water; let stand 3 to 5 minutes. Stir in apple juice concentrate. Cook and stir over medium heat until gelatin is dissolved. *Do not boil.* Remove from heat and set aside.

Beat cream cheese on medium speed of electric mixer in medium bowl until fluffy and smooth. Add remaining ¼ cup brown sugar, ¼ teaspoon cinnamon and nutmeg. Mix until smooth. Slowly beat in gelatin mixture on low speed until blended and creamy, about 1 minute. *Do not overbeat.*

Arrange apple slices in crust. Pour cream cheese mixture evenly over top. Refrigerate 2 hours or until set.   *Makes 8 servings*

Cherries in the Snow

1 package (8 ounces) PHILADELPHIA®
    Cream Cheese, softened

½ cup sugar

2 cups thawed COOL WHIP® Whipped
    Topping

1 can (20 ounces) cherry pie filling, divided

MIX cream cheese and sugar in large bowl until smooth. Gently stir in whipped topping.

LAYER ¼ cup cream cheese mixture and 2 tablespoons pie filling in each of 4 stemmed glasses or bowls. Repeat layers.

Makes 4 servings

Prep Time: 10 minutes

Holiday Nog Mold

1½ cups boiling water
1 package (8-serving size) *or* 2 packages (4-serving size each) JELL-O® Brand Lemon Flavor Gelatin
½ cup cold water
1½ cups cold milk
1 package (4-serving size) JELL-O® Vanilla Flavor Instant Pudding & Pie Filling
2 teaspoons rum extract
⅛ teaspoon ground nutmeg
2 cups thawed COOL WHIP® Whipped Topping

STIR boiling water into gelatin in large bowl at least 2 minutes until completely dissolved. Stir in cold water. Cool 30 minutes at room temperature.

POUR milk into medium bowl. Add pudding mix. Beat with wire whisk 30 seconds. Immediately stir into cooled gelatin until smooth. Stir in rum extract and nutmeg. Refrigerate about 15 minutes or until slightly thickened (consistency of unbeaten egg whites). Gently stir in whipped topping with wire whisk until smooth. Pour into 6-cup mold which has been sprayed with no stick cooking spray.

REFRIGERATE 4 hours or until firm. Unmold.

Makes 10 servings

How To Unmold: Dip mold in warm water for about 15 seconds. Gently pull gelatin from around edges with moist fingers. Place moistened serving plate on top of mold. Invert mold and plate; holding mold and plate together, shake slightly to loosen. Gently remove mold and center gelatin on plate.

Special Extra: Garnish with sugar-frosted cranberries or grapes and additional COOL WHIP Whipped Topping, if desired.

Prep Time: 25 minutes plus refrigerating

Double Dipped Apples

MAZOLA NO STICK® Cooking Spray
5 medium apples
5 wooden sticks
1 package (14 ounces) caramel candies,
   unwrapped
¼ cup KARO® Light or Dark Corn Syrup
¾ cup chopped walnuts
1 cup (6 ounces) semisweet chocolate chips
1 teaspoon MAZOLA® Oil

1. Spray cookie sheet with cooking spray; set aside. Wash and dry apples; insert stick into stem end.

2. In small, deep microwavable bowl microwave caramels and corn syrup at HIGH 3 to 4 minutes or until caramels are melted and smooth, stirring after each minute.

3. Dip apples in hot caramel mixture, turning to coat well. Allow caramel to drip from apples for a few seconds, then scrape excess from bottom of apples. Roll bottom half in walnuts. Place on prepared cookie sheet. Refrigerate at least 15 minutes.

4. In small microwavable bowl, microwave chocolate and oil at HIGH 1 to 2 minutes; stir until melted.

5. Drizzle apples with chocolate. Refrigerate 10 minutes or until chocolate is firm. Wrap apples individually; store in refrigerator.

Makes 5 apples

Prep Time: 20 minutes, plus cooling

Holiday Snack Parfaits

2 cups boiling water, divided
1 package (4-serving size) JELL-O® Brand
   Flavor Gelatin, any red flavor
1 package (4-serving size) JELL-O® Brand
   Lime Flavor Gelatin
2 cups cold water, divided
1 tub (8 ounces) COOL WHIP® Whipped
   Topping, thawed
Holiday sprinkles (optional)

STIR 1 cup boiling water into both red and lime gelatin in separate bowls at least 2 minutes until completely dissolved. Stir 1 cup cold water into each bowl. Pour into separate 9-inch square pans.

REFRIGERATE 4 hours or until firm. Cut each pan into ½-inch cubes. Layer alternating flavors and whipped topping into 8 dessert glasses. Garnish with additional whipped topping and sprinkles. *Makes 8 servings*

Variation: Substitute any flavor JELL-O Brand Gelatin to make this recipe seasonal!

Prep Time: 10 minutes plus refrigerating

Cranberry Apple Crisp

⅓ to ½ cup granulated sugar

3 tablespoons ARGO® or KINGSFORD'S® Corn Starch

1 teaspoon ground cinnamon

½ teaspoon ground nutmeg

5 to 6 cups cubed peeled tart apples

1 cup fresh or frozen cranberries

½ cup KARO® Light Corn Syrup

1 teaspoon grated orange peel

TOPPING

½ cup chopped walnuts or uncooked oats

⅓ cup packed brown sugar

¼ cup all-purpose flour

¼ cup (½ stick) margarine or butter

1. Preheat oven to 350°F.

2. In large bowl combine granulated sugar, corn starch, cinnamon and nutmeg. Add apples, cranberries, corn syrup and orange peel; toss to mix well. Spoon into shallow 2-quart baking dish.

3. For Topping, combine nuts, brown sugar and flour. With pastry blender or 2 knives, cut in margarine until mixture resembles very coarse crumbs. Sprinkle over cranberry mixture.

4. Bake 50 minutes or until apples are tender and juices that bubble up in center are shiny and clear. Cool slightly; serve warm.

Makes 6 to 8 servings

Prep Time: 15 minutes
Bake Time: 50 minutes

Mint Truffles

1 package (10 ounces) mint chocolate chips

⅓ cup whipping cream

¼ cup butter or margarine

1 container (3½ ounces) chocolate sprinkles

Line baking sheet with waxed paper; set aside. Melt chips with whipping cream and butter in heavy, medium saucepan over low heat, stirring occasionally. Pour into pie pan. Refrigerate until mixture is fudgy, but soft, about 2 hours.

Shape about 1 tablespoonful mixture into 1¼-inch ball. To shape, roll mixture between palms. Repeat procedure with remaining mixture. Place balls on waxed paper.

Place sprinkles in shallow bowl; roll balls in sprinkles. Place truffles in petit four or candy cups. (If sprinkles won't stick because truffle has set, roll truffle between palms until outside is soft.) Truffles may be refrigerated 2 to 3 days or frozen several weeks.

Makes about 24 truffles

Tip: Truffles can also be coated with unsweetened cocoa, powdered sugar, chopped nuts, sprinkles or cookie crumbs to add flavor and prevent the truffle from melting in your fingers.

Cranberry Apple Crisp

Amaretto Cheesecake Tart

CRUST

¾ cup amaretti cookie crumbs

¾ cup zwieback crumbs

1 tablespoon sugar

¼ cup Dried Plum Purée (recipe follows) or prepared dried plum butter

FILLING

1 carton (16 ounces) nonfat cottage cheese

4 ounces fat-free cream cheese, softened

2 eggs

2 tablespoons almond-flavored liqueur

TOPPING & GLAZE

2 oranges, peeled and sliced into rounds

1 kiwifruit, peeled and sliced into rounds

2 tablespoons apple jelly, melted

Fresh raspberries, orange peel and mint leaves for garnish

Preheat oven to 325°F. To prepare crust, in medium bowl, combine crumbs and sugar. Cut in dried plum purée with pastry blender until mixture resembles coarse crumbs. Press onto bottom and up side of 9-inch tart pan with removable bottom. To prepare filling, process cottage cheese and cream cheese in food processor 3 to 5 minutes or until smooth. Add eggs and liqueur; process until blended. Pour into prepared crust. Bake in center of oven 30 minutes or until filling is set. Cool on wire rack; refrigerate until completely chilled. Arrange fruit on top of filling. Brush fruit with jelly. Garnish with raspberries, orange peel and mint. Cut into wedges. *Makes 10 servings*

Plum Purée: Combine 1⅓ cups (8 ounces) pitted dried plums and 6 tablespoons hot water in container of food processor or blender. Pulse on and off until dried plums are finely chopped and smooth. Store leftovers in covered container in refrigerator for up to two months. Makes 1 cup.

Favorite recipe from **California Dried Plum Board**

Holiday Hint:

Amaretti cookies are very crisp, light Italian macaroons. They are flavored with almond. Look for them in the Italian section of your supermarket or at a speciality grocer.

Amaretto Cheesecake Tart

Reindeer Cupcakes

1 package (2-layer size) chocolate cake mix
    plus ingredients to prepare mix
$\frac{1}{4}$ cup ($\frac{1}{2}$ stick) butter, softened
4 cups powdered sugar
5 to 6 tablespoons brewed espresso, divided
$\frac{1}{2}$ cup (3 ounces) semisweet chocolate chips,
    melted
1 teaspoon vanilla
    Dash salt
24 pretzel twists, broken in half
    Assorted candies for decoration

1. Preheat oven to 350°F. Line 24 (2½-inch) muffin pan cups with paper muffin cup liners.

2. Prepare cake mix according to package directions. Spoon batter into prepared muffin pans. Bake 15 to 20 minutes or until toothpick inserted into centers comes out clean. Cool in pans on wire racks 10 minutes. Remove to racks; cool completely.

3. Beat butter in large bowl with electric mixer at medium speed until creamy. Gradually add powdered sugar and 4 tablespoons espresso; beat until smooth. Beat in melted chocolate, vanilla and salt. Add remaining espresso, 1 tablespoon at a time, until frosting is of desired spreading consistency.

4. Frost cooled cupcakes with frosting. Decorate with broken pretzel pieces for antlers and assorted candies for reindeer faces. *Makes 24 cupcakes*

Fresh Persimmons with Apricot Dessert Topping

8 medium persimmons
2 mangoes or 4 peaches, peeled and pitted
1 teaspoon lemon juice
$\frac{1}{3}$ cup reduced calorie soft cream cheese
2 tablespoons apricot preserves
1 tablespoon skim milk
$\frac{1}{2}$ teaspoon lime juice
$\frac{1}{4}$ teaspoon grated lime peel
$\frac{1}{3}$ cup thawed frozen whipped topping

Slice persimmons and mangos into medium bowl. Toss with lemon juice; set aside.

Combine cream cheese and preserves in small bowl with wire whisk until smooth. Stir in milk, lime juice and lime peel. Fold in whipped topping.

Arrange persimmon and mango slices on platter. Serve with apricot topping. *Makes 4 servings*

Holiday Hint:

Persimmons are glossy orange fruits with green caps. Although a variety of persimmons is native to the United States, Asian varieties are commonly found in supermarkets in the autumn. Ripe persimmons should be soft to the touch.

Reindeer Cupcakes

Brown Sugar Fudge

1⅓ cups granulated sugar
1⅓ cups whipping cream
⅔ cup packed brown sugar
1 tablespoon light corn syrup
¼ cup butter
½ cup white chocolate chips
½ cup chopped walnuts

Butter 8-inch square pan; set aside. Lightly butter side of heavy, large saucepan.

Combine granulated sugar, whipping cream, brown sugar and corn syrup in prepared saucepan. Cook over medium heat, stirring constantly, until sugar dissolves and mixture comes to a boil. Add candy thermometer. Stir mixture occasionally. Continue to cook until mixture reaches the soft-ball stage (238°F).

Remove from heat. Slice butter into thin slices and place on top of cooling mixture. Let stand about 10 minutes. Add white chocolate chip and nuts. Stir until butter and vanilla milk chips are completely melted. Spread into prepared pan. Refrigerate until firm. Cut into squares. Store in refrigerator. *Makes about 1 pound*

Merry Berry Desserts

½ cup sliced strawberries and/or banana
1 package (4-serving size) JELL-O® Brand Strawberry Flavor Gelatin
1 cup boiling water
1 cup cold water
1 ripe banana, cut up
1 tub (8 ounces) COOL WHIP® Whipped Topping, thawed

ARRANGE strawberry and/or banana slices in bottoms of 6 muffin cups. Dissolve gelatin completely in boiling water in medium bowl. Stir in cold water. Spoon 3 tablespoons of the gelatin into each muffin cup. Refrigerate until set but not firm.

PLACE remaining gelatin and banana in blender container; cover. Blend on high speed 1 minute. Add 1½ cups of the whipped topping; cover. Blend until well mixed. Spoon over clear gelatin.

REFRIGERATE 4 hours or until firm. To unmold, run small metal spatula around edge of each muffin cup. Dip pan into warm water, just to rim, for about 10 seconds. Place moistened tray on top of pan. Invert; holding pan and tray together, shake slightly to loosen. Gently remove pan. Place desserts on individual serving plates. Garnish with remaining whipped topping. *Makes 6 servings*

Brown Sugar Fudge

Cranberry Orange Dessert

1½ cups boiling water

  1 package (8-serving size) *or* 2 packages
      (4-serving size each) JELL-O® Brand
      Cranberry Flavor Gelatin

  1 can (16 ounces) whole berry cranberry
      sauce

1½ cups cold water

  1 can (15.5 ounces) DOLE® Mandarin
      Oranges, drained

1½ cups HONEY MAID® Graham Crumbs

  ½ cup sugar, divided

  ½ cup (1 stick) butter or margarine, melted

  1 package (8 ounces) PHILADELPHIA®
      Cream Cheese, softened

  2 tablespoons milk

  2 tubs (8 ounces each) COOL WHIP®
      Whipped Topping, thawed, divided

STIR boiling water into gelatin in large bowl at least 2 minutes until completely dissolved. Stir in cranberry sauce until melted. Stir in cold water. Refrigerate about 1¼ hours or until slightly thickened (consistency of unbeaten egg whites). Gently stir in mandarin oranges.

MEANWHILE, stir crumbs, ¼ cup of the sugar and butter in 13×9-inch baking dish. Firmly press mixture onto bottom of baking dish. Refrigerate until ready to fill.

BEAT cream cheese, remaining ¼ cup sugar and milk in large bowl with wire whisk until smooth.

Gently stir in 1 tub whipped topping. Spread evenly over crust. Spoon gelatin mixture over cream cheese layer.

REFRIGERATE 3 hours or until firm. Just before serving, spread or dollop with remaining whipped topping. *Makes 16 servings*

Helpful Hint: Soften cream cheese in microwave on HIGH 15 to 20 seconds.

Prep Time: 25 minutes plus refrigerating

Merry Cherry Holiday Dessert

1½ cups boiling water

  1 package (8-serving size) *or* 2 packages (4-serving size) JELL-O® Brand Cherry Flavor Gelatin Dessert, or any red flavor

1½ cups cold water

  1 can (21 ounces) cherry pie filling

  4 cups angel food cake cubes

  3 cups cold milk

  2 packages (4-serving size) JELL-O® Vanilla Flavor Instant Pudding & Pie Filling

  1 tub (8 ounces) COOL WHIP® Whipped Topping, thawed

STIR boiling water into gelatin in large bowl at least 2 minutes until completely dissolved. Stir in cold water and cherry pie filling. Refrigerate about 1 hour or until slightly thickened (consistency of unbeaten egg whites). Place cake cubes in 3-quart serving bowl. Spoon gelatin mixture over cake. Refrigerate about 45 minutes or until set but not firm (gelatin should stick to finger when touched and should mound).

POUR milk into large bowl. Add pudding mixes. Beat with wire whisk 1 minute. Gently stir in 2 cups of the whipped topping. Spoon over gelatin mixture in bowl.

REFRIGERATE 2 hours or until set. Top with remaining whipped topping and garnish as desired.

Makes 16 servings

Preparation Time: 20 minutes
Refrigerating Time: 3¾ hours

Chocolate "Ornaments"

1 package (8 squares) BAKER'S® Semi-Sweet Chocolate

½ packages (4 ounces) PHILADELPHIA® Cream Cheese, cubed, softened

1 tub (8 ounces) COOL WHIP® Whipped Topping, thawed

  Assorted coatings, such as: powdered sugar, finely chopped nuts, toasted BAKER'S® ANGEL FLAKE Coconut, grated BAKER'S® Semi-Sweet Chocolate, cookie crumbs or multicolored sprinkles

MICROWAVE chocolate in large microwavable bowl on HIGH 2 minutes or until chocolate is almost melted, stirring halfway through heating time. Stir until chocolate is completely melted. Add cream cheese; stir with wire whisk until smooth. Cool 20 minutes or until room temperature. Gently stir in whipped topping with wire whisk until blended.

FREEZE 1 hour; scoop into 1-inch balls. If necessary, freeze balls 30 minutes longer or until firm enough to roll. Roll in assorted coatings as desired. Refrigerate or freeze until ready to serve.

Makes 2½ to 3 dozen

Tip: When freezing these "ornaments" or delicate cookies, freeze first in a single layer on baking sheet, then pack in plastic boxes with wax paper between layers and store in the freezer.

Decadent Truffle Tree

INGREDIENTS

1⅓ cups whipping cream

¼ cup packed brown sugar

¼ teaspoon salt

¼ cup light rum

2 teaspoons vanilla

16 ounces semisweet chocolate, chopped

16 ounces milk chocolate, chopped

Finely chopped nuts and assorted sprinkles

SUPPLIES

1 (9-inch tall) foam cone

About 70 wooden toothpicks

1. Heat cream, sugar, salt, rum and vanilla in medium saucepan over medium heat until sugar is dissolved and mixture is hot. Remove from heat; add chocolates, stirring until melted, (return pan to low heat if necessary). Pour into shallow dish. Cover and refrigerate until just firm, about 1 hour.

2. Shape about half the mixture into 1¼-inch balls. Shape remaining mixture into ¾-inch balls. Roll balls in nuts and sprinkles. Refrigerate truffles until firm, about 1 hour.

3. Cover cone with foil. Starting at bottom of cone, attach larger truffles with wooden toothpicks. Use smaller truffles toward the top of the cone. Refrigerate until serving time.

Makes 1 tree (6 dozen truffles)

Note: If kitchen is very warm, keep portion of truffle mixture chilled as you shape and roll balls.

Praline Pecans & Cranberries

3½ cups pecan halves

¼ cup light corn syrup

¼ cup packed light brown sugar

2 tablespoons butter or margarine

1 teaspoon vanilla

¼ teaspoon baking soda

1½ cups dried cranberries or cherries

1. Preheat oven to 250°F. Grease 13×9-inch baking pan. Set aside. Cover large baking sheet with heavy-duty foil. Set aside.

2. Spread pecans in single layer on prepared baking sheet.

3. Combine corn syrup, sugar and butter in small microwavable bowl. Microwave at HIGH 1 minute. Stir. Microwave 30 seconds to 1 minute or until boiling rapidly. Stir in vanilla and baking soda until well blended. Drizzle evenly over pecans; stir with wooden spoon until evenly coated.

4. Bake 1 hour, stirring every 20 minutes with wooden spoon. Immediately transfer mixture to prepared baking sheet, spreading pecans evenly over foil with lightly greased spatula.

5. Cool completely. Break pecans apart with wooden spoon. Combine pecans and cranberries in large bowl.

6. Store in airtight container at room temperature up to 2 weeks. *Makes about 5 cups*

Decadent Truffle Tree

Almond-Pear Strudel

¾ cup slivered almonds, divided

5 to 6 cups thinly sliced crisp pears (4 to 5 medium pears)

1 tablespoon grated lemon peel

1 tablespoon lemon juice

⅓ cup plus 1 teaspoon sugar, divided

2 teaspoons ground cinnamon

1 teaspoon ground nutmeg

4 tablespoons melted butter or margarine, divided

6 sheets (¼ pound) phyllo dough

½ teaspoon almond extract

1. Preheat oven to 300°F. Spread almonds in shallow baking pan. Bake 10 to 12 minutes or until lightly browned, stirring frequently; cool and cover. Set aside.

2. Place sliced pears in large microwavable container. Stir in lemon peel and lemon juice. Microwave at HIGH 6 minutes or until tender; cool. Cover pears and refrigerate overnight. Combine ⅓ cup sugar, cinnamon and nutmeg in small bowl; cover and set aside.

3. Place butter in microwavable container. Microwave at HIGH 20 seconds or until melted. Lay 2 sheets plastic wrap on work surface to make 20-inch square. Place 1 phyllo sheet in middle of plastic wrap. (Cover remaining phyllo dough with damp kitchen towel to prevent dough from drying out.) Brush 1 teaspoon melted butter onto phyllo sheet. Place second phyllo sheet over first; brush with 1 teaspoon butter. Repeat layering with remaining sheets of phyllo. Cover with plastic wrap. Cover remaining butter. Refrigerate phyllo dough and butter overnight or up to 1 day.

4. Preheat oven to 400°F. Drain reserved pears in colander. Toss pears with reserved sugar mixture and almond extract. Melt reserved butter.

5. Uncover phyllo dough and spread pear mixture evenly over phyllo, leaving 3-inch strip on far long side. Sprinkle pear mixture with ½ cup toasted almonds. Brush strip with 2 teaspoons melted butter. Beginning at long side of phyllo opposite 3-inch strip, carefully roll up jelly-roll style, using plastic wrap to gently lift, forming strudel. Place strudel, seam side down, onto buttered baking sheet. Brush top with 1 teaspoon butter.

6. Bake 20 minutes or until deep golden. Brush again with 1 teaspoon butter. Combine remaining ¼ cup toasted almonds with remaining butter; sprinkle on top of strudel. Sprinkle with remaining 1 teaspoon sugar. Bake an additional 5 minutes. Cool 10 minutes; sprinkle with powdered sugar, if desired. *Makes 8 servings*

Almond-Pear Strudel

Christmas Mouse Ice Creams

2 cups fat-free vanilla ice cream

1 package (4 ounces) single-serving graham cracker crusts

6 chocolate sandwich cookies, separated and cream filling removed

12 black jelly beans

6 red jelly beans

36 chocolate sprinkles (approximately ¼ teaspoon)

1. Place 1 rounded scoop (about ⅓ cup) ice cream into each crust. Freeze 10 minutes.

2. Press 1 cookie half into each side of ice cream scoops for ears. Decorate with black jelly beans for eyes, red jelly beans for noses and chocolate sprinkles for whiskers. Freeze 10 minutes. Serve.

Makes 6 servings

Cranberry Mousse Mold

1½ cups boiling water

1 package (8-serving size) *or* 2 packages (4-serving size each) JELL-O® Brand Cranberry Flavor Gelatin Dessert

1 cup cold water

1 can (16 ounces) whole berry cranberry sauce

1 tub (8 ounces) COOL WHIP® Whipped Topping, thawed

STIR boiling water into gelatin in large bowl 2 minutes or until completely dissolved. Stir in cold water and cranberry sauce. Spoon 2 cups gelatin mixture into 6-cup mold. Refrigerate about 30 minutes or until set but not firm (should stick to finger and mound).

MEANWHILE, refrigerate remaining gelatin mixture about 30 minutes or until slightly thickened (consistency of unbeaten egg whites).

STIR in 2 cups whipped topping with wire whisk until smooth. Pour over gelatin layer in mold.

REFRIGERATE 4 hours or until firm. Unmold. Garnish with remaining whipped topping.

Makes 12 servings

Unmolding: Dip mold in warm water for about 15 seconds. Gently pull gelatin from around edges with moist fingers. Place moistened serving plate on top of mold. Invert mold and plate; holding mold and plate together, shake slightly to loosen. Gently remove mold and center gelatin on plate.

Prep Time: 30 minutes

Christmas Mouse Ice Cream

Acknowledgments

The publisher would like to thank the companies and organizations listed below for the use of their recipes and photographs in this publication.

A.1.® Steak Sauce

Barilla America, Inc.

Bays English Muffin Corporation

BelGioioso® Cheese, Inc.

Birds Eye®

Blue Diamond Growers®

Bob Evans®

Butterball® Turkey Company

California Dried Plum Board

California Poultry Federation

California Wild Rice Advisory Board

Cherry Marketing Institute

Colorado Potato Administrative Committee

ConAgra Grocery Products Company

Delmarva Poultry Industry, Inc.

Del Monte Corporation

Dole Food Company, Inc.

Eagle® Brand

Egg Beaters®

Filippo Berio® Olive Oil

Fleischmann's® Original Spread

Florida Department of Agriculture and Consumer Services, Bureau of Seafood and Aquaculture

Grandma's® is a registered trademark of Mott's, Inc.

Grey Poupon® Dijon Mustard

Guiltless Gourmet®

Harveys® Bristol Cream®

Hebrew National®

Heinz U.S.A.

Hershey Foods Corporation

Holland House® is a registered trademark of Mott's, Inc.

Hormel Foods, LLC

The HV Company

Kahlúa® Liqueur

Kellogg Company

Kikkoman International Inc.

Acknowledgments

The publisher would like to thank the companies and organizations listed below for the use of their recipes and photographs in this publication.

The Kingsford Products Company

Kraft Foods Holdings

Lawry's® Foods, Inc.

© Mars, Incorporated 2002

McIlhenny Company (TABASCO® brand Pepper Sauce)

Minnesota Cultivated Wild Rice Council

Mott's® is a registered trademark of Mott's, Inc.

National Chicken Council

National Fisheries Institute

National Honey Board

National Onion Association

National Turkey Federation

Nestlé USA

NILLA® Wafers

North Dakota Beef Commission

Perdue Farms Incorporated

PLANTERS® Nuts

The Procter & Gamble Company

Reckitt Benckiser

Riviana Foods Inc.

Sargento® Foods Inc.

The J.M. Smucker Company

StarKist® Seafood Company

Tyson Foods, Inc.

Uncle Ben's Inc.

Unilever Bestfoods North America

USA Dry Pea & Lentil Council

USA Rice Federation

Veg-All®

Washington Apple Commission

Wisconsin Milk Marketing Board

Index

Index

Index

Index

371

Index

Index

Index

Index

Index

Index

Index

Index

Index

Index

Notes

Notes

METRIC CONVERSION CHART

VOLUME MEASUREMENTS (dry)

⅛ teaspoon = 0.5 mL
¼ teaspoon = 1 mL
½ teaspoon = 2 mL
¾ teaspoon = 4 mL
1 teaspoon = 5 mL
1 tablespoon = 15 mL
2 tablespoons = 30 mL
¼ cup = 60 mL
⅓ cup = 75 mL
½ cup = 125 mL
⅔ cup = 150 mL
¾ cup = 175 mL
1 cup = 250 mL
2 cups = 1 pint = 500 mL
3 cups = 750 mL
4 cups = 1 quart = 1 L

VOLUME MEASUREMENTS (fluid)

1 fluid ounce (2 tablespoons) = 30 mL
4 fluid ounces (½ cup) = 125 mL
8 fluid ounces (1 cup) = 250 mL
12 fluid ounces (1½ cups) = 375 mL
16 fluid ounces (2 cups) = 500 mL

WEIGHTS (mass)

½ ounce = 15 g
1 ounce = 30 g
3 ounces = 90 g
4 ounces = 120 g
8 ounces = 225 g
10 ounces = 285 g
12 ounces = 360 g
16 ounces = 1 pound = 450 g

DIMENSIONS

1/16 inch = 2 mm
⅛ inch = 3 mm
¼ inch = 6 mm
½ inch = 1.5 cm
¾ inch = 2 cm
1 inch = 2.5 cm

OVEN TEMPERATURES

250°F = 120°C
275°F = 140°C
300°F = 150°C
325°F = 160°C
350°F = 180°C
375°F = 190°C
400°F = 200°C
425°F = 220°C
450°F = 230°C

BAKING PAN SIZES

Utensil	Size in Inches/Quarts	Metric Volume	Size in Centimeters
Baking or Cake Pan (square or rectangular)	8 × 8 × 2	2 L	20 × 20 × 5
	9 × 9 × 2	2.5 L	23 × 23 × 5
	12 × 8 × 2	3 L	30 × 20 × 5
	13 × 9 × 2	3.5 L	33 × 23 × 5
Loaf Pan	8 × 4 × 3	1.5 L	20 × 10 × 7
	9 × 5 × 3	2 L	23 × 13 × 7
Round Layer Cake Pan	8 × 1½	1.2 L	20 × 4
	9 × 1½	1.5 L	23 × 4
Pie Plate	8 × 1¼	750 mL	20 × 3
	9 × 1¼	1 L	23 × 3
Baking Dish or Casserole	1 quart	1 L	—
	1½ quart	1.5 L	—
	2 quart	2 L	—